MINORITY POLITICS IN A MULTINATIONAL STATE

The German Social Democrats in Czechoslovakia, 1918–1938

NANCY MERRIWETHER WINGFIELD

EAST EUROPEAN MONOGRAPHS, BOULDER
DISTRIBUTED BY COLUMBIA UNIVERSITY PRESS, NEW YORK

1989

EAST EUROPEAN MONOGRAPHS, NO. CCLIX

TABLE OF CONTENTS

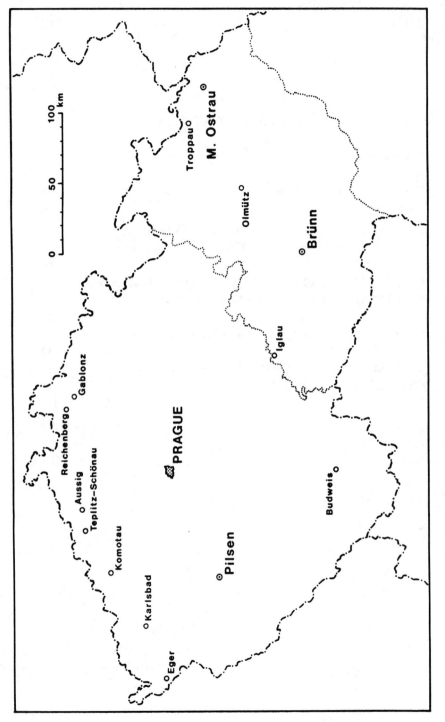

BOHEMIA AND MORAVIA–SILESIA

ACKNOWLEDGMENTS

My topic required research in five European countries: the Federal Republic of Germany, Czechoslovakia, Austria, the Netherlands and England. Grants from the American Council of Learned Societies, the Friedrich Ebert Stiftung, the Fulbright-Hays Program and the International Research and Exchanges Board (IREX) enabled me to complete my research at numerous institutions abroad.

The archivists, librarians and other staff members at the following institutions gave me their time and expertise: Archiv der sozialen Demokratie in Bonn; Bayerisches Hauptstaatsarchiv, Bayerische Staatsbibliothek, Collegium Carolinum and Sudetendeutsches Archiv in Munich; British Library and Public Record Office in London; Institut für Auslandsbeziehungen and Seliger-Archiv e. V. in Stuttgart; Renner-Institut in Vienna; Okresní archív Cheb; and Státní knihovna and Státní ústřední archív in Prague.

Of the numerous people who have aided in my research, several deserve special mention: Istvan Deak, my dissertation advisor at Columbia University; Robin Quinville, a history department colleague and friend; and Eva Schmidt-Hartmann, a research associate at the Collegium Carolinum; read and commented at great length on my manuscript in dissertation form. Martin Bachstein, Todd Huebner, Brian Ladd, Eva Segert, and T. Allan Smith have critiqued the revised manuscript. Their suggestions have helped me clarify my thinking and correct numerous errors. Otto Novák of Charles University, Prague, kindly helped me obtain permission to work in archives and libraries in Czechoslovakia. Heinrich Kuhn and the entire staff of the Sudetendeutsches Archiv put the archive and all its resources at my disposal whenever I was in Munich.

Conversations and correspondence with the following people, some of whom experienced firsthand the events about which I have written, provided me with greater insight into the period: the late Johann Wolfgang Brügel of London, Leopold Grünwald of Vienna, and Adolf Hassenöhrl, Rudolf Hesse, Franz Kunert, and Artur Strober of the Seliger-Archiv e. V. My thanks to all of them.

ABBREVIATIONS

The following acronymns and abbreviations are used in the text and footnotes. An asterisk denotes use in the footnotes only.

ADAP*	*Akten zur deutschen Auswärtigen Politik;* Documents on German Foreign Policy
ALÖS	*Auslandsbüro österreichischer Sozialisten;* exile organization of the Social Democratic Party of Austria
AdsD*	Archiv der sozialen Demokratie; Archive of Social Democracy, Bonn
ATUS	*Arbeiter- Turn- und Sportverband;* Workers' Gymnastic and Sports Association
BdL	*Bund der Landwirte;* German Agrarian Party
DAWG	*Deutsche Arbeits- und Wirtschaftsgemeinschaft;* German Labor and Economic Association
DNP	*Deutsche Nationalpartei;* German National Party
DNSAP	*Deutsche nationalsozialistische Arbeiterpartei;* German National Socialist Party
DSAP	*Deutsche sozialdemokratische Arbeiterpartei in der Tschechoslowakei;* German Social Democratic Workers' Party in Czechoslovakia
IFTU	International Federation of Trade Unions
IISH*	International Institute of Social History, Amsterdam
KSČ	*Komunistická strana Československá;* Communist Party of Czechoslovakia
NWJ*	Nachlass Wenzel Jaksch, Sudetendeutsches Archiv, Munich
OACh*	Okresní archív Cheb; Cheb District Archive

PRO-FO* Public Record Office, Foreign Office Records, London
ROI   *Rudá odborová internacionála;* Red International Trade Union
         Organization
SDAPÖ   *Sozialdemokratische Arbeiterpartei in Österreich;* Social
         Democratic Party of Austria
SdA*   Sudetendeutsches Archiv; Sudeten German Archive, Munich
SdP   *Sudetendeutsche Partei;* Sudeten German Party
SHF   *Sudetendeutsche Heimatfront;* Sudeten German Homefront
SNL*   Sammlung Norbert Linz; Norbert Linz Collection, Sudeten-
         deutsches Archiv, Munich
SOPADE   *Sozialdemokratische Partei Deutschlands;* exile organization of
         the Social Democratic Party of Germany
SPD   *Sozialdemokratische Partei Deutschlands;* Social Democratic
         Party of Germany
USPD   *Unabhängige Sozialdemokratische Partei Deutschlands;* Inde-
         pendent Social Democratic Party of Germany

GLOSSARY OF GEOGRAPHICAL NAMES

Except for the case of Prague, German designations, where they exist, will be used in place names in conformity with interwar German-language publications of the Czechoslovak government. If no German place name exists, the Czech designation will be used. German names are listed in the first column and the Czech equivalents in the second column followed by the Hungarian (H) or Polish (P) designation if applicable.

Asch	Aš
Aussig	Ústí nad Labem
Bergreichenstein	Kašperské Hory
Bodenbach	Podmokly
Böhmisch Budweis	České Budějovice
Böhmisch Krumau	Český Krumlov
Böhmisch Leipa	Česká Lípa
Brünn	Brno
Brüx	Most
Dux	Duchcov
Elbogen	Loket
Fischern	Rybáře
Friedek	Frýdek
Freistadt	Frýštát
Freudenthal	Bruntál
Gablonz	Jablonec
Graslitz	Kraslice
Iglau	Jihlava
Jägerndorf	Krnov
Kaaden	Kadaň

Karlsbad	Karlovy Vary
Katowitz	Katowice (P)
Komotau	Chomutov
Kratzau	Chrastava
Laun	Louny
Leitmeritz-Lobositz	Litoměřice-Lovosice
Mährisch Schönberg	Šumperk
Mährisch Trübau	Moravská Třebová
Marienbad	Mariánské Lázně
Neudek	Nejdek
Neustadt	Nové Město
Neu-Titschein	Nový Jičín
Ober-Leutensdorf	Horní Litvínov
Ober-Rosenthal	Horní Růžodol
Oderberg	Bohumín
Ostrau	Ostrava
Pilsen	Plzeň
Pressburg	Bratislava, Pozsony (H)
Pressnitz	Přísečnice
Prossnitz	Prostějovice
Reichenberg	Liberec
Rothau	Rotava
Römerstadt	Rýmařov
Rumburg	Rumburk
Saaz	Žatec
Schluckenau	Šluknov
Sternberg	Šternberk
Tannwald	Tanvald
Teplitz-Schönau	Teplice-Šánov
Teschen	Těšín, Cieszyn (P)
Tetschen	Děčín
Theresienstadt	Terezín
Trautenau	Trutnov
Troppau	Opava
Warnsdorf	Varnsdorf
Weipert	Vejprty
Weisskirchlitz	Nové Sedlice
Wigstadtl	Vítkov
Witkowitz	Vítkovice
Zwickau	Cvikov

FOREWORD

Czechoslovakia, although one of the most heterogeneous of the successor states, was constituted as an explicitly national state. The Czechs and the Slovaks, who were, it was argued, two branches of the same nation, comprised the national people, the "Czechoslovaks." The creation of an artificial Czechoslovak nationality was necessary to achieve a majority vis-à-vis the German, Hungarian, Polish and Ruthenian citizens of the nascent state, which in fact, contained more Germans than Slovaks. The Czechoslovak constituent national assembly had not been content to place the Czechs and the Slovaks on an equal level legally with the previously dominant Germans and Hungarians, but rather reduced both of the latter to a lesser position. While the Germans had indeed been dominant previously in Cisleithania, none of the diverse national groups living in the Austrian half of the Monarchy had been specifically obliged to regard itself as a minority. In the First Republic, the Germans, Hungarians, Poles, and Ruthenians, who made up one-third of the population, had legal minority status and were protected by minority treaties.

Although representatives of the national minorities had not participated in the Czechoslovak constituent national assembly, they did participate in all elections and after 1926, in government coalitions. The numerous political parties of the First Republic, no fewer than fourteen of which were represented in parliament at any given time, were sharply divided along national as well as social lines. Sometimes the Slovak political parties were part of a larger Czechoslovak organization, but as often they were independent. The Czech (or Czechoslovak) Agrarian, Clerical, Small Trader

xi

and Social Democratic parties all had their German and sometimes Hungarian counterparts, which during the period of German activism, were more or less allied with them. Only the Czechoslovak Communist Party was truly supranational.

The German Social Democratic Party of Czechoslovakia attempted to balance the often conflicting economic and national demands of its constituency during the interwar period. This balancing act brought the party under attack not only from the left but also from both the Czech and German nationalists. German nationalist politicians accused the Social Democrats of betraying the national interests of the Sudeten Germans through their internationalist politics. Both the Communists and the Czechoslovak Social Democrats accused the German Social Democrats of placing reactionary national interests ahead of class struggle while Czech nationalist politicians criticized both the economic and the national goals of the German Social Democrats. Despite this opposition, the German Social Democratic Party remained the most popular German political party in the country until after the advent of the Great Depression the effects of which were felt in Czechoslovakia beginning in 1930.

The purpose of this work is to examine the German Social Democratic Party as an institution. Although the economic dislocations wrought in Central Europe by the Depression and the attendant rise of radical right-wing politics were primarily responsible for the voter shift to the Sudeten German Party, both the lack of flexibility and the internal problems of the German Social Democratic Party were contributing factors. Analysis of party politics and leadership is necessary in order to explain how electoral support for the party dropped from almost fifty percent of the German vote in 1919 to less than ten percent within less than a generation. This was initially due to the party's inability to provide solutions to the national complaints of the Sudeten Germans, which had been exacerbated by economic dislocation during the Great Depression, as well as to the pressure of the Sudeten German Party and later to the influence of Nazi Germany. The advent of the worldwide economic downturn and the rise of the Sudeten German Party left the German Social Democrats in disarray. Their constituency was battered economically, while the relative lack of severity with which the Great Depression affected the ethnic Czech areas of Bohemia and Moravia as well as the contrast with economically ascendant Nazi Germany only made matters worse.

In the immediate postwar period, Czechoslovakia suffered economic problems. These were in part common to all of Europe and in part the result of the adjustment of economic, particularly industrial, output to the new borders of a small state. Primarily due to the timely application of conservative fiscal policies, Czechoslovakia did not, however, suffer to the same degree from economic convulsions as other Central European countries in the early 1920s.

From the mid-1920s, the Czechoslovak economy improved, and the period between 1926 and 1929 marked its interwar high point. During this time, the German activist political parties (those that accepted the existence of the Czechoslovak state) increased their share of the German electorate at the expense of the negativist parties (those that did not accept the Czechoslovak state). The activist parties also took part in the Czechoslovak government coalition for the first time. The German Social Democratic Party—which was not initially an activist party, although it participated in the political life of the republic—joined the coalition in 1929.

When the economic climate suddenly worsened during the 1930s, there was little the German activist parties could do to alleviate the situation. German voters began turning to the Sudeten German Party, whose antimodern *völkisch* rhetoric was becoming more and more attractive. With the exception of the Sudeten German Party, the German political parties did not attempt to appeal to the entire electorate, but rather to specific segments of the German population. By the mid-1930s, the Sudeten German Party had won the support of the majority of the German non-Marxist parties' former constituency and by 1938, more than 85 percent of the entire German vote. The German Social Democratic Party had little in its political arsenal to oppose the Sudeten German Party.

As long as the Sudeten German electorate believed that politics conciliatory to the Czechoslovak state offered them the most secure future, they tended to vote for the government parties, less because these parties cooperated with Prague, than because of the appeal that other aspects of these parties' programs held for them. Often political aims were more successfully realized by participation in coalitions than by nonparticipation.

During the interwar period, interpretations of nationality problems divided along the lines of both national and class interests. The Czechoslovak parties' support of the nation-state concept colored their perception of complaints in this area by the national minorities. Especially during the

1920s, the three Marxist parties—the Communists and the Czechoslovak and German Social Democrats—were often at odds with one another as well as with the non-Marxist parties over the significance of nationality problems in the First Republic.

Although the German Social Democrats consistently forcused on nationality differences, in the early postwar period both the Czechoslovak Communists and the Social Democrats tended to downplay, or to ignore altogether, the national aspects of social revolution in Czechoslovakia. Czechoslovak Communists writing in the 1930s recognized that national animosities had existed in 1918, but considered them merely an "instrument of the bourgeoisie," used to prevent socialist revolution. They explained the non-revolutionary situation in Czechoslovakia in the immediate postwar period as a bourgeois swindle: the proletariat had been led to believe that a socialist revolution would follow the nationalist revolution and the government of the newly formed state would be socialist. According to the Czechoslovak Communists, the revolutionary masses had been "stabbed in the back" by the bourgeoisie, with the help of the "social patriots" of the socialist right. They depicted the "revolutionary élan" of the proletariat as having frightened the bourgeoisie into seizing power from the authorities of the collapsing Habsburg Monarchy. Most Czechoslovak Communists also alleged that the opportunist, reformist Czechoslovak Social Democratic leadership had betrayed its working-class constituency to the Czechoslovak National Council.

It appears, in fact, that in 1918, the majority of the organized Czech working class, like most of the rest of the Czech population, supported the National Council and its limited goal of Czechoslovak independence. In contrast, the majority of the Germans, regardless of their politics and class background, wanted to remain part of Austria.

Some remarks about the term "Sudeten German" are necessary. Those Germans who had settled in the Bohemian Crownlands beginning in the fourteenth century, many coming to work in the mines of northwestern Bohemia at the invitation of the kings of Bohemia, were known for much of the duration of the Habsburg Monarchy as Bohemian Germans. The name "Sudeten," taken from a mountain range on the northern border of Bohemia-Moravia, to designate those Germans living in the historic crownlands, was coined at the beginning of the twentieth century. It came into general use only during the interwar period. Following the Second World

War, the term "Sudeten" was used in Anglo-American parlance to designate all Germans who had lived within the boundaries of the First Czechoslovak Republic and it is in this sense that "Sudeten" will be used here,
when needed to distinguish the Germans of Czechoslovakia from those
of the German Reich and Austria.

The use of this overarching term is not meant to imply a geographically
or historically unified German ethnic group in Czechoslovakia, for the
Germans of the First Republic did not comprise a cultural, geographic
or religious monolith. Most of the Germans in Czechoslovakia lived in
the border regions of Bohemia, Moravia and Silesia, which, from the
late nineteenth century, contained a growing Czech minority. Other
Germans lived in the Czech-dominated cities of the interior. The best
known are the Prague Germans, themselves a diverse group that included
a part of the old Habsburg hereditary nobility, only some of which identified with the German community there. Next, there were those Jews
who had assimilated to German culture. Although many of them lived
in the border regions, other German-speaking Jews lived in the larger,
predominantly Czech cities of the interior, for example, Brunn, Pilsen
and Prague. By the turn of the century, a number of Jews began claiming
their nationality as Czech. Particularly after the First World War, there
were Jews who demanded an ethnic identity that was neither Czech nor
German, but Jewish. Finally there were the Germans of Slovakia and
Ruthenia, some of whom lived in and around Pressburg on the Austro-
Slovak border where they comprised part of a larger German settlement
area. Others lived in linguistic enclaves or scattered throughout the interior
of the two provinces. Prior to 1918, these Germans, living in the Hungarian half of the Monarchy, had little contact with the Germans of the
Bohemian Crownlands.

Many proper names, especially place names, used in this work have at
least two designations, Czech and German. Because this topic concerns
a German-speaking organization, whose publications primarily used German names, these will be used here. German place names will be used, unless there is a standard English term, for example, "Prague," instead of the
Czech "Praha" or the German "Prag." The Czech-language equivalent for

the German place names will be found in the glossary of geographical terms.

The sources employed are primarily institutional, particularly the German Social Democratic Party periodicals and publications. Although party documents are incomplete, some can be found in the Institute of Social History in Amsterdam and in the Seliger-Archiv in Stuttgart. Czechoslovak and German government documents as well as publications of other political parties have been used where appropriate and available. Unfortunately, the party's two interwar chairmen, Ludwig Czech and Wenzel Jaksch, have left few papers. Czech's records were destroyed during the Second World War, while Jaksch's, housed in the Sudetendeutsches Archiv in Munich, consist primarily of materials from the Second World War and postwar period. Former party leaders' postwar memoirs and interviews tend to be both subjective and colored by hindsight, although these memoirs are useful for personal anecdotes and descriptions of the daily functioning of the party.

CHAPTER I

THE FORMATIVE YEARS
1918-1921

Introduction

The First World War precipitated the division of the European organized working-class movement, a development the ruling elites had never been able to achieve. Wartime disagreements crystallized at the end of 1918 into implacable opposition between the "reformers" of the socialist right, and the "revolutionaries" of the socialist left. On the example of the soviets of the Russian Revolution, workers' councils were formed in various areas of Central Europe, and in some places, the call was raised for revolution. At the war's end, socialist-dominated governments were formed in defeated Austria, Germany and Hungary. By 1920, however, left-wing socialists in these countries and elsewhere had repudiated their parties' cooperation with the bourgeoisie,[1] formed communist parties, accepted Lenin's 21 Points and joined the Third International.

Czechoslovakia experienced a democratic, national transformation as power passed peacefully during the closing days of the war from the Austrian government into the hands of the Czechoslovak National Council, in which the key positions were held by agrarian and liberal nationalist politicians. The Czech Social Democrats joined the non-working-class Czech and Slovak representatives to fashion the new state's constitution and government. There is evidence of only the faintest revolutionary activity in the Czech lands at this time. Contemporary reports suggest that the majority of the socialist leadership among both the Czechs and the Sudeten Germans neither expected nor desired a revolution on the example of Russia. The working class of Czechoslovakia formed a minority of the population in the face of a united bourgeois-agrarian coalition and these men realized that a revolution on the Russian agrarian model was not applicable to the more industrialized Czechoslovakia.[2]

German Social Democratic leaders (*Deutsche sozialdemokratische Arbeiterpartei in der Tschechoslowakischen Republik,* the DSAP) representing a "double minority" of both Germans and workers, recognized the degree to which the nationality factor affected prospects for a socialist revolution among their constituency. In the immediate postwar period, most German Social Democrats were more concerned with national self-determination—becoming part of German-Austria (Deutsch-Österreich)—than with revolution. The Czechoslovak Social Democrats (*Československá sociálně-demokraticka strana dělnická*),[3] members of the ruling all-national coalition until 1926, repudiated the national aspirations of the minorities in Czechoslovakia, asserting that all of their "legitimate" claims had been met by Czechoslovakia's compliance with the minority treaties signed by the Prague government at St. Germain on 10 September 1919 and at Trianon on 4 June 1921. The Czechoslovak Communist Party (*Komunistická strana Československa,* the KSČ)[4] officially recognized the need for a solution to the country's nationality problems at its first party congress in February 1923, when the creation of a nationality program was declared one of the party's most important tasks. The position of the KSČ on the nationality question—far-reaching rights for the nationalities, including broad self-administration—contradicted many of the principles adopted by the Second Congress of the Comintern, above all the call for reunification of splintered nations. Thus at its second congress in November 1924, the KSČ was obliged to reject as "overwhelmingly opportunistic" its original theses on the nationality question.

National rivalries help account for the lack of a united working class in Czechoslovakia during the immediate postwar period. These animosities were also partially responsible for the tardy formation of the KSČ; it was among the last European communist parties founded.

A Socio-Economic Description of the Sudeten Lands

The predominantly mountainous northern and western border regions of the Bohemian Crownlands, of little agricultural use outside the production of flax, oats, and potatoes, were, however, rich in natural resources, not least waterpower, that facilitated the early industrialization of the area. As in Western Europe, domestic industries had tended to develop first in less fertile areas, and income from spinning and weaving, for example, became more important than agricultural income in many households. Glass, textiles and luxury items predominated in the primarily light industry of the region which at the beginning of the nineteenth century was populated almost exclusively by Germans.

The increasing polarization of town and country dominant elsewhere in industrializing Europe was absent here. By the late nineteenth century, three-quarters of the German population in the region found its livelihood in industry and only one-quarter in agriculture, but some three-fourths of the population continued to live in rural areas, while only one-fourth lived in towns and cities. About three-fifths of the entire population resided in villages with fewer than 500 inhabitants.[5] In 1930, 51.5 percent of all residents of Bohemia still lived in communities of fewer than 2,000 residents, while in Moravia-Silesia, with its larger proportion of Czechs, the percentage was 49.6. Only 35.2 percent of the citizens of Weimar Germany, in contrast, lived in villages of fewer than 2,000 in 1925.[6] As late as 1936, no German city in Czechoslovakia had a population as large as 50,000, and only thirteen had more than 20,000 residents.[7] The largest cities in the Bohemian Crownlands—Brünn, Mährisch Ostrau, Pilsen, and Prague—were all outside the German settlement areas. Though all had German minorities, the German residents tended to be part of the middle and upper classes, rather than the working class.

Until the second half of the nineteenth century, the Czechs remained, for the most part, in their traditional homeland, the fertile agricultural heartlands of Bohemia-Moravia. The Czech regions, which began to industrialize in the 1880s, developed more along traditional European demographic lines.

In the German areas, groups of small villages grew up around industrial centers, supplanting the traditional German towns, whose populations began to drop. The denizens of these rural industrial villages did not concern themselves with the agriculture, but were involved instead with a specific aspect of production or with a particular branch of whatever industry was located in the area, usually glass or textiles. Sometimes, all those of working age were employed in a neighboring industrial center. Even in German industrial cities, workers tended to live outside the city limits.[8] In general, merchants, local church and government officials, as well as members of the free professions and other members of the middle classes, dominated the towns, while most of the working class lived on the outskirts, around the local factories.

The inherent weaknesses of the German industrial structure had become apparent before the turn of the century. Facilities were not modernized, nor were there sufficient population resources to support rapid expansion of labor intensive industry. Industries remained small to middle-sized—500 employees was considered large. Old-fashioned in structure and marginal in profit, many survived only because of the Habsburg Monarchy's high customs tariffs. By the 1890s, some parts of industrial Bohemia already suffered from chronic unemployment. Artisanal work done in the home (*Heimarbeit*) continued, even predominated, especially in southern and western Bohemia, where those employed as seasonal laborers during the summer months often worked at home during the winter.[9] After the First World War, some industries, particularly textiles, were thrown into competition with the larger, better rationalized textile industries of Saxony and never recovered.

In the Czech lands, heavy industry was centered in Prague, Pilsen, northern Moravia, and Silesia, but agricultural industry predominated. Because the Czech industries did not primarily produce luxury goods for export, they were less affected by international economic fluctuations than German industries. With the exception of glass and textiles, Czech industries were concentrated in the cities, insofar as they were not dependent on local raw materials. Industry in Czech villages tended to be agriculturally oriented: dairy products, distilleries, sugar refining.[10]

As the first Czechs began moving into previously German areas of the Bohemian Crownlands in search of work during the nineteenth century, many were Germanized. Those coming in the late nineteenth century, however, brought with them a growing sense of national awareness as well as a higher birthrate than that of their German counterparts. In general, when the Czechs and the Germans lived in the same areas, they still lived separately from each other. Sometimes, the division would run through the middle of a village or a town, each group leading its own cultural, economic and linguistic life.[11]

Migrating Czech workers primarily moved into unskilled occupations. They filled places left vacant by the more skilled German workers who had emigrated to other parts of the Monarchy or Wilhelmine Germany in search of a higher standard of living. As the need for highly skilled laborers decreased due to both changes in the methods of production and increased industrial concentration, younger, less-skilled Czech workers began replacing the master craftsmen who commanded larger salaries. Those Germans who remained in northwestern Bohemia felt very keenly the competition of the Czechs who, used to a lower standard of living, accepted lower wages.

In the Habsburg Monarchy

The forces of nationalism had haunted Czech and German Social Democrats since the early days of the organized working class movement in the Bohemian Crownlands. The renascence of Czech national consciousness paralleled the growth of the nascent socialist movement. Almost from the beginning, there was conflict between two goals: national revival and the unification of the working class without regard to nationality.[12] National rivalries had been inflamed beginning in mid-nineteenth century by the influx of Czech workers into predominantly German-speaking areas due to increased labor needs resulting from rapid industrial development. Much of the migration was to the industrial and mining areas of German-inhabited northern Bohemia, with Czechs also settling in the industrial areas of Lower Austria, especially Vienna, where they often became domestic servants, tailors, or small shopkeepers. Although Czech and German workers labored side by side in factories, management and ownership were almost exclusively German. At least initially, some Czechs formed a "floating element" in the labor force, moving on it a factory had difficulties and dismissed workers.

The social democrats of the Habsburg Monarchy had to contend with nationalist rhetoric as early as the 1870s. At its founding congress at Hainfeld in 1889, however, the Austrian Social Democratic Party (*Sozial-demokratische Arbeiterpartei in Österreich,* the SDAPÖ), simply accepted a Marxian formula recognizing national struggles as one of the means the ruling classes used to maintain their domination over the lower classes. The major points of the Hainfeld Program included the condemnation of private ownership of the means of production and the demand for the "dictatorship of the proletariat." Immediate goals were universal suffrage, the separation of Church and State, the abolition of the standing army and major social reforms.

The Austrian Social Democrats adopted a nationality program only at the Brünn Party Congress ten years later. It advocated the reorganization of Cisleithania as a federal state of nationalities, with autonomous territories delimited by nationality replacing the Crownlands. All territories would be allowed freedom of association, and were to be completely autonomous in cultural and national matters. The *Reichsrat* would enact a law to safeguard the rights of the national minorities. The nationality statutes adopted at Brünn remained part of the Austrian Social Democratic Party program for the duration of the Monarchy. Their tenets would be refined by party theoreticians Otto Bauer and Karl Renner, who developed sophisticated theories of nationality.[13]

The expansion of the Austrian franchise in 1897 and 1907, facilitated the growth of mass political parties during the last decades of the Monarchy as Austria moved toward limited democracy. Austrian political life was complicated by the tendency of most political parties to develop or divide along nationality lines. Political constellations varied, depending on the matter at hand. With the expansion of the franchise to include members of the working class, other political parties began making overtures to this group. These overtures were often nationalistic, as all parties other than the SDAPÖ were organized along national lines. Despite the flexibility Austrian Social Democratic leadership had shown since the foundation of the party, it was only partially successful in combating the nationalist appeals of other parties to its constituency. Seemingly insoluable problems existed.

First, Czech Social Democrats, perceived a threat to their interests from what they regarded as the centralizing and Germanizing tendencies of Vienna through the end of the nineteenth century. In addition, the Czechs objected to German domination of the upper echelons of the party. German Social Democrats, on the other hand, did not necessarily perceive bureaucratic centralization, which they tended to support, as a threat to the other groups in the Monarchy, nor were they prepared to yield their position in the party.

The Austrian Social Democratic Party was at this time a highly centralized organization, but it had not been able to absorb successfully the Czech organizations in Bohemia and Moravia. The contradictory demands of the Germans for centralization and the Czechs for autonomy within the party tested Austrian Social Democratic flexibility to the limit. The realistic attitudes expounded by party leaders, however, permitted them ultimately to accept the demands of the Czech Social Democrats for an autonomous faction in 1893, and then recognition as an independent party, *Československá sociálně-demokratická strana dělnická,* in 1896. Austrian Social Democratic leadership also moved to accommodate the Czechs by creating a more federalized party and trade union structure.

For the most part, social democrats in Austria worked together, despite the independence of the Czech Social Democrats, until 1911, when Czech trade union demands for autonomy caused a final division among the social democrats of Austria. Czech "centrists," who wanted to retain membership in the Vienna-based trade union center, were forced out of the party. The Czech Social Democratic deputies continued to vote as a class-based bloc with the rest of the Austrian Social Democrats, but broke ranks increasingly after 1911 to join with the other Czech political parties on nationality issues.

Thus Austrian Social Democracy never resolved the tensions between its two largest nationality groups, the Germans and the Czechs. A legacy of ill will manifested itself during the interwar period in the inability or, perhaps, the unwillingness of the Czech and German Social Democrats in Czechoslovakia to close ranks in the newly created state and provide supranational leadership for the working class.

Czech-German Social Democratic friction within the Habsburg Monarchy was, however, laid to rest, albeit temporarily, with the outbreak of the First World War. The majority of the Austrian Social Democrats, as social democrats elsewhere in Europe, supported their government. They were spared the necessity of taking a parliamentary position on the war question due to the suspension of the *Reichsrat* until 30 March 1917. The Czech Social Democrats followed the policy of *Burgfrieden* until that time. Most Austrian Social Democrats continued to support the Cisleithanian portion of the Monarchy's economic and political existence, if not the war, on ideological grounds until the winter of 1917-1918. Following his return from a Russian prisoner of war camp in late 1917,

Bauer and his adherents began moving toward the idea of complete self-determination of all peoples in the Monarchy and in January 1918, he announced a nationality program which recognized the right of non-Germans to self-determination and demanded the same right for the Germans of Austria.

Austrian Social Democratic leader Friedrich Adler, jailed following his assassination in November 1916 of Austrian Prime Minister Count Karl Stürgkh in protest against the war, influenced the pacifist left-wing that developed within the party. This group was weak, however, and lacked power, nor was it represented at the Social Democratic Conferences of Zimmerwald (1915) or Kienthal (1916). The Austrian Social Democratic left adopted the Zimmerwald Declaration, calling for the creation of a new international socialist commission to replace the paralyzed Second International, and for the resumption of the class struggle in order to force international peace.

Differences among the Czech Social Democrats had begun to manifest themselves during the last years of the war as well, when opponents of the party chairman, Bohumír Šmeral,[14] were elected to the party executive committee, prompting him to resign on 18 October 1917. The members of the newly-elected executive committee, who would later constitute the Czechoslovak Social Democratic right-wing leadership, placed more emphasis on Czech national-political aims than had Šmeral, who continued to support the existence of the Monarchy.

At the same time, Czech Social Democrats began negotiations with the Czech National Socialists (*Česká strana národních sociální*) to form a unified movement.[15] The Czech National Socialist Party was broadly-based, drawing much support at the time for the lower middle class, academics, civil servants and professionals, as well as workers. Founded in 1897 by former social democrats who had rejected the Marxist doctrine of class struggle, it was more nationalist than socialist in its orientation.[16] Many of the social democrats who opposed the proposed unification of the two parties were later to be found in the Czechoslovak Social Democratic left-wing.

As elsewhere in Europe, the Habsburg Monarchy had experienced unrest during the war, especially in its last years.[17] Major demonstrations, however took place only in 1917 and 1918 and were sparked more by shrinking food rations than by revolutionary fervor though the instransigent position of the Central Powers toward Russia at the Brest-Litovsk negotiations was also a contributing factor.[18] The 14 October 1918 one-day general strike organized by the Czech Social Democrats and Czech National Socialists under the banner of the Socialist Council (*Socialistická rada*), was directed primarily against the export of Bohemian foodstuffs and for national independence, rather than toward any particular socialist goals. During the interwar period, both the Czechoslovak Communists and Social Democrats played down the nationalistic aspect of the strike, anger because food was being taken "from the mouths of Czech children" to feed the Viennese. The Communists especially would focus on the socialist element of the Council, attributing a far greater class character to the strike than it actually had and stressing the role of the strike leaders, left-wing anarchist Luisa Landová-Štychová and Czech Social Democrat Šmeral, both later members of the Czechoslovak Communist Party.

The position of the Czech and German Social Democrats in Czechoslovakia at war's end could hardly have been more dissimilar. The Czech Social Democrats formed a major party in the newly-created state. The German members of the Austrian Social Democratic regional organizations in Bohemia, Moravia, and Silesia had become reluctant citizens of a country with borders based on the historic rights of the Bohemian Crownlands rather than on the spirit of self-determination laid out in Woodrow Wilson's Fourteen Points.

The War's End

Until the First World War, Czech national demands had been limited to a federalization of the Monarchy that would include substantial autonomy for the nationalities. This attitude was unanimous among all shades of the Czech political spectrum, though for varying reasons. Czech nationalists feared incorporation into the German Reich following a collapse of Austria-Hungary; many socialists supported Austria-Hungary's continued existence as an economic entity.[19]

These attitudes were changed, however, by the wartime efforts of Czech exile politicians Tomáš Masaryk and Edvard Beneš, whose negotiations resulted in allied recognition of an independent Czechoslovak state in September 1918.[20] When independence was declared on 18 October 1918 by Masaryk in Washington, D.C. and ten days later by Czech politicians in Prague, the anticipated boundaries of the nascent state went far beyond the ethnic claims of the Czechs to self-determination. In addition to the historic Bohemian Crownlands, Slovakia and Ruthenia, integral parts of the Kingdom of Hungary, were to become parts of Czechoslovakia. A professor of philosophy at Charles University in Prague before the First World War, Masaryk had been a leader of the intellectual-political "Realist" movement in the 1880s and 1890s; after 1900, he headed the small Czech People's Party (*Česká strana lidová*). His wartime efforts on behalf of national independence resulted in the intimate association of his name with the state, giving the philosopher-politician a moral and political stature that could not be approached by any other politician in interwar Czechoslovakia. Masaryk's conviction that the postwar Czechoslovak government should represent all shades of Czech and Slovak political opinion was instrumental in creating a coalition that included not only the agrarian and liberal national politicians, but also the Czechoslovak Social Democrats, the most successful political party in the 1919 and 1920 elections.

Differences of opinion among the Czech Social Democrats were temporarily eclipsed by the October 1918 creation of an independent Czechoslovak state. They quickly placed themselves on the side of the newly-created state, participating in the constituent National Assembly (consisting only of Czechs and Slovaks) that drafted the provisional constitution by which the country was governed until a definitive constitution was adopted on 29 May 1920.

As the Czech inhabitants of Bohemia, Moravia and Silesia celebrated the "liberation of the Czech people from the hated yoke [of the Habsburg Monarchy],"[22] the Germans in northern and western Bohemia demonstrated, protesting their involuntary inclusion into the Czechoslovak state. German Bohemia (Deutschböhmen) was constituted part of German-Austria on 29 October. It was followed by the Sudetenland, German Southern Bohemia (Deutschsüdböhmen or Böhmerwaldgau), and German Southern Moravia (Deutschsüdmähren). These provinces had but an ephemeral existence, for in early November, Czech Legionaries[23] began occupying German towns in Bohemia in order to unite the border regions with the rest of Czechoslovakia and strengthen Czech territorial claims at the Paris Peace Conference.[24]

The German Social Democrats in these regions took part in the short-lived provincial governments. In particular, Josef Seliger, later first chairman of the German Social Democratic Party, played a leading role in German Bohemia.[25] Both the Czechoslovak Communists and Social Democrats would later cite this participation as evidence of German nationalist attitudes taking precedence over socialist precepts within the DSAP, but this was not in fact the case.[26] This participation was in keeping both with national self-determination and with the Marxist conception that economically viable nations are a progressive step toward the creation of a socialist society, for it was assumed that German-Austria, and thus the German-speaking areas of Bohemia and Moravia, would join an economically viable Greater Germany.[27]

The Germans of western Bohemia had included some of the most radical pan-German nationalists of the Monarchy and the occasional strong-arm tactics of the Czech soldiers during the occupation of the border areas added to the ill will between the Czechs and the Germans there. The negative attitude of Czechs of all political persuasions toward Sudeten Germans in general, and their demands for self-determination in particular, did not improve matters.[28] Neither Finance Minister Alois Rašín's pointed comment to Seliger, "I don't negotiate with rebels," in November 1918,[29] nor Masaryk's allusion to Sudeten Germans shortly afterwards as "immigrants and colonists" improved the situation. This condescending attitude was not confined to one part of the Czech political spectrum. A February 1919 memorandum signed by leading members of the Czechoslovak Social Democratic Party at a meeting of the Socialist International in Bern, rejecting the International's support for the principle of national self-determination of peoples, referred to "originally Czech lands accepting visiting German immigrants who came there as colonists . . . ."[30]

Tension between Czechs and Germans erupted into violence on 4 March 1919 during demonstrations against the Prague government's refusal to allow Sudeten Germans to participate in German-Austrian elections. In many towns, they were broken up by soldiers and gendarmes and resulted in more than 1,000 injuries and 54 deaths, and provided Sudeten German nationalists with a rallying point against the Prague government which they would use throughout the interwar period.

Czech reaction was unsympathetic; even the Czechoslovak Social Democratic newspaper, *Právo lidu,* held the German Social Democrats responsible for the events of 4 March, although it criticized the use of the gendarmerie and the military to quash the demonstrations.[31] Because the Czechoslovak Social Democrats, like the social democrats of Austria and Germany, participated in their postwar government coalition, they were criticized by their own left wing for accepting non-socialist government policies. The continued participation of the Czechoslovak Social Democratic right in the coalition provided the impetus for the division in the party that developed between 1919 and 1921. The situation among the German Social Democrats in Czechoslovakia was different than that of the Czechs; the Germans did not participate in the government coalition and thus could not be accused of supporting its policies. The theoretical basis for the party division—revolution versus reform—was stronger with the German Social Democratic Party than the Czechoslovak Social Democratic Party.

The Development of the Socialist Left in Czechoslovakia

The German Social Democratic left in Czechoslovakia was centered in Reichenberg, one of the largest cities in German-speaking Bohemia, and an economic and political center for the Sudeten Germans. Reichenberg and the industrial villages surrounding it had long been both an important textile center and a center for the organized workers' movement. The Reichenberg German Social Democratic leadership also had a tradition of internationalism and opposition to the party leadership in Vienna.

As early as 1905, SDAPÖ member Josef Strasser, editor of the Reichenberg social democratic newspaper *Freigeist* (after 1911, *Vorwärts*), had opposed Renner's proposals for reform of the Monarchy on the basis of nationality. Strasser criticized Renner, writing that his projected general, equal franchise and "bourgeois democracy" for Cisleithania would not save the Monarchy, but hasten its downfall.[32] At the Innsbruck Party Congress in 1911, Strasser espoused Karl Kautsky's theories to oppose the federalizing tendencies within the SDAPÖ.[33] *Vorwärts*, edited after 1911 by Strasser's younger colleague, Karl Kreibich,[34] was the only SDAPÖ newspaper to oppose Austria-Hungary's ultimatum to Serbia in July 1914, and publication of the paper was therefore suspended on 27 July 1914 for the duration of the war.[35]

The *Quertreiber-Klub,* a left-oriented group within the wartime SDAPÖ, was also centered in Reichenberg. Composed of some two dozen persons, it included Kreibich and two younger associates, Otto Hahn and Alois Neurath, both of whom also wrote for the *Vorwärts* and were active in the local social democratic youth organization. The extent to which the *Quertreiber-Klub* members had actually opposed the war as well as the extent to which other SDAPÖ leaders had attempted to stymie this opposition was much debated between the DSAP and the KSČ during the interwar period.[36] It appears that by the time of the Armistice, a group of German Social Democrats from the Reichenberg area had begun to develop a world view that differed somewhat from that of the majority leadership of the SDAPÖ, and later of the DSAP.

Writing in the late 1950s, East German historian Othmar Feyl portrayed Kreibich and Strasser as leading the Reichenberg organization in a direction parallel to that of the left-wing of the Reich German Social Democratic Party (*Sozialdemokratische Partei Deutschlands,* the SPD). Feyl's attempt to trace a personal connection between the leaders of the social democratic left in Reichenberg and Rosa Luxemburg, Karl Liebknecht, and Franz Mehring in Germany, yields little except a common pacifism. His assertion that the Reichenberg left was influenced by the Weimar German Communist Party (*Kommunistische Partei Deutschlands,* the KPD) in the intial postwar period is, however, correct. The Reichenberg left received both theoretical material and information about the contemporary events in Soviet Russia illicitly via Berlin.[37]

The Czechoslovak Social Democratic Party was formed in December 1918, when the Slovak Social Democrats, formerly members of the Hungarian party, joined the Czech-Slavic Social Democratic Party. An intraparty left-wing quickly developed. The leadership of the Czechoslovak Social Democratic left-wing was not so ideologically unified as that of the German left. Moreover, some of the Czechs who had been part of the pacifist left during the war moved to the center and nationalist right-wing of their party at the war's end. The growing Czechoslovak Social Democratic left was united primarily by its opposition to the rest of the party, which advocated continued participation in the government coalition. It more resembled the Independent Social Democratic Party (*Unabhängige Sozialdemokratische Partei Deutschlands,* the USPD) of Weimar Germany, than the later KSČ, into which it would only slowly evolve.[38]

There were several geographic and ideological centers within the Czechoslovak left. The textile center of Brünn, the mining area of Kladno and the industrial suburbs of Prague provided it with most of its leadership and support. In addition to the intraparty left led by Šmeral and Josef Skalák, other groups, representing a variety of left political views, influenced the Czech left. They included various anarcho-communists associated with the magazines *Červen* (June) and *Kmen* (Trunk), the Czechoslovak Communist Party of Russia (*Československá komunistická strana na Rusi*) and the Czech Social Democratic Worker Party (*Česká sociálně demokratická strana dělnická*).

Czech prisoners of war who supported the goals of the Russian Revolution had founded the Czechoslovak Communist Party in the Soviet Union in May 1918. Led by Alois Muna of Kladno, they had been charged by Moscow with the organization of the Czechoslovak left into workers' councils. The Czech Social Democratic Worker Party, on the other hand, had been established by the Brünn centrists expelled from the Czech Social Democratic Party in 1911. Under the leadership of trade unionist Edmund Burian, this party joined the Czechoslovak Social Democratic Party in March 1919, adding to the pressure exerted on the party leadership by the left. Right-wing party executive committee members František Modráček, and Josef Hudec quit the party shortly thereafter in disgust with the growing strength of the left. They subsequently founded the Socialist Party of the Working People (*Socialistická strana československého lidu pracujícího*).

The communal (*Gemeinde*) elections of 15-16 June 1919 were the first test of the electoral strength of the social democratic parties of Czechoslovakia. The mutual antagonism of the Czechoslovak and German Social Democrats was reflected in a decision in April by the German Social Democrats of Bohemia to couple lists when necessary with other German political parties in ethnically mixed areas in order to pursue the Sudeten German struggle for self-determination.[39]

The local elections resulted in resounding victories for both the Czechoslovak and German Social Democrats, in fact, the greatest success enjoyed by either party during the interwar period. In Bohemia, Moravia, and Silesia, the Czechoslovak Social Democrats received 30.1 percent of the Czech vote, the German Social Democrats 42.1 percent of the German vote. Support for both parties was strongest in Bohemia, where the

Czechoslovak Social Democrats won one-third and the German Social Democrats, one-half, of the vote.[40] The social democrats of both nationalities took control of some municipal governments, although their victory was sapped both by the tendency of the other parties to form coalitions against them in the local administration and by their inexperience in communal politics. There is scant evidence of cooperation among the social democratic parties on the local level during this time.

The DSAP had been officially formed at the end of August 1919 from the provincial social democratic organizations of the Bohemian Crownlands. Teplitz textile worker-cum-journalist Seliger was elected party chairman. As a member of the *Reichsrat* from 1907 to 1918 and head of the SDAPÖ Bohemian provincial organization, Seliger was an important figure in the SDAPÖ and seemed the logical choice for party chairman. He faced little or no opposition. The DSAP supported the republic and rejected government by workers' councils, thus maintaining the reformist tradition of the old Austrian Social Democratic Party. The constituency of the working class parties of Czechoslovakia, including the Czech National Socialists, did not form a majority of the electorate and the German Social Democrats rejected the concept of minority dictatorship.

Czech politicians considered Seliger's call for extensive autonomy for Czechoslovakia's national minorities to be the most controversial part of the German Social Democratic party program.[41] He envisioned the creation of a corporate body through which each nationality would govern itself by means of a national council and a government. These governing bodies would be responsible for legal regulation of the nationalities, administration of the educational system, maintenance of ethnic culture, and conclusion of agreements with other nationalities concerning the minorities. The program was based on the nationality statutes adopted by the 1899 Party Congress in Brünn. It was a continuation of the "territorial" principle of nationality which the Czech Social Democrats had already rejected in 1899, believing that nationality did not necessarily correspond to geopolitical entities.[42]

Although the 1919 congress itself was a fairly quiet affair, with little hint of the disagreements that would shake the party in the next year, there was already some indication of future internal problems. Emil Strauss, Seliger's son-in-law and an influential party journalist of relatively reformist views, criticized Kreibich for using his position as editor of *Vorwärts* to comment on what Strauss regarded as the internal affairs of other socialist parties. Kreibich supported the USPD against Gustav Noske, the controversial SPD Defense Minister in Weimar Germany, and made no secret of his sympathy for the fledgling Soviet government.[43] Although some delegates, including many from Reichenberg, stood politically to the left of the others and made scattered calls for workers' councils and revolution, their motions appear to have received no serious consideration from the majority of delegates. The influence of the USPD, still ascendant in neighboring Germany, rather than the influence of distant Moscow, where the Bolsheviks were still struggling for survival, best explains the radicalism of some of the delegates.

Both *Právo lidu* and *Sociální demokrat,* representing the Czechoslovak Social Democratic Party right leadership and the left-wing respectively, accepted the theoretical foundations of the German Social Democratic Party's program, but were highly critical of its nationalist orientation. *Sociální demokrat,* founded by Šmeral in February 1919, condemned Seliger's call for the creation of an autonomous German region as a concept that the German national, liberal newspaper *Bohemia,* would happily endorse.[44] Comments in *Právo lidu* were particularly critical of the DSAP's call for national autonomy arguing that Seliger's idea of a "new Switzerland" would, in reality, "atomize" Czechoslovakia.[45] Further, the first concern of social democrats should be preparation for class struggle. Václav Vacek, a left-wing social democrat pointed out in a *Právo lidu* editorial that the German Social Democrats were now demanding the same autonomy in Czechoslovakia that they had denied the Czech Social Democrats in the Habsburg Monarchy. Their demands, he wrote, would be judged accordingly.[46]

As West German historian Klaus Zessner has noted, the importance of the August 1919 party program was that in some ten months, the German Social Democrats had moved from a negative attitude toward the Czechoslovak state, demanding separation from it, to recognition of the state and demands for autonomy within it.[47] The party's name, the "German Social Democratic Workers' Party in Czechoslovakia," underscores this point. The change did not receive the recognition it deserved from either contemporary Czechoslovak politicians or later Czechoslovak historians.

If the Czechoslovak Social Democrats were united in opposition to German demands for national autonomy, this was all that united them. Complaints from the Czechoslovak Social Democratic left began almost as soon as party leader Vlastimil Tusar formed the second Czechoslovak government on 8 July 1919.[48] The complaints were voiced principally in the *Sociální demokrat* and the Kladno *Svoboda*, whose position within the party was similar to that of the *Vorwärts* within the DSAP. The right and center of the Czechoslovak Social Democratic Party were attacked by their own left and by the German Social Democrats both for their willingness to govern in coalition with the agrarians and for their foreign policy.[49] The party leadership was reproached for supporting the anti-Bolshevism of the Entente, its hostility toward Béla Kun's Hungarian Soviet Republic and its toppling of the short-lived Slovak Soviet Republic, headed by the Czech, communist Antonín Janoušek. These attacks, both public and private, prompted *Právo lidu* to print a series of articles defending the Tusar government not only from the other parties, but also from within its own party. Pains were taken to differentiate the goals of the Czechoslovak Social Democrats from those of the government coalition, the implication being that the party had to compromise some of its socialist demands in order to preserve the coalition.[50] The Tusar government could legitimately claim that participation in the coalition had enabled it to achieve goals long desired by social democrats: laws concerning land reform, child labor and unemployment insurance were enacted.

Disgruntled members of the Czechoslovak Social Democratic left had begun meeting in October 1919 and two months later constituted themselves into a separate group within the party, the Marxist Left.[51] Their manifesto opposed continued participation in the coalition government and demanded the recall of all social democratic government ministers, the development of joint policies with Czechoslovakia's minority social democratic parties, the dictatorship of the proletariat, and the party's membership in the Third International.

Reaction from the German Social Democratic leadership was initially positive. They welcomed the manifesto as a step toward building a supranational social democratic working-class party in Czechoslovakia.[52] Soon the Germans became more cautious; some DSAP politicians felt that nationalist feeling among the Czechoslovak Social Democrats was so

strong that the "International" within the republic sought by the Czechoslovak Marxist Left could not be realized in the foreseeable future.[53] An
additional reason for caution was the possible effect these demands could
have on an already restive German Social Democratic left. The Reichenberg leadership, indeed, greeted the Marxist Left's manifesto enthusiastically as a basis for cooperation between the Czech and German working
class, although the manifesto did not, as Kreibich noted, directly address
the nationality question, which was of paramount interest to all factions
within the DSAP.[54]

The publication of the Marxist Left's manifesto prompted a storm of
disagreement over continued Czechoslovak Social Democratic participation in the coalition. There was conflict between orthodox opposition
to participation in bourgeois governments and the temptation to form a
social democratic pressure group within the government. Most members
of the Marxist Left believed that the decision made at the December
1918 party congress to participate in the government was limited to the
duration of the constituent National Assembly. This period passed with
the advent of the first national elections in April 1920.[55] The Czechoslovak Social Democratic right, over the protests of the Marxist Left, chose
to participate in Czechoslovakia's first representative government, with
Tusar as prime minister.

Although with 11.1 percent of the total vote in Czechoslovakia, the
German Social Democrats were the largest German political party, and
the third largest party in the republic, neither the Czechoslovak nor the
German Social Democrats gave any real thought to the possibility of
DSAP participation in the government. Nationalist feelings still ran too
high on both sides for the Germans to be offered a share in governing
"naše republika" ("our republic"), nor was the DSAP prepared to play
second fiddle to the Czechoslovak Social Democrats in government politics. Meetings between leaders of the two social democratic parties on 5
and 25 May appear to have been limited to the discussion of common
interests.[56]

The thirty-one German Social Democratic deputies were primarily
trade union officials and journalists. Seven of the deputies were also members of the party executive committee and one deputy, Dominik Leibl,
headed the Small Farmers' Union (*Kleinbauernverband*). The majority of
the sixteen senators were also trade union and party officials. Six of the

deputies and three of the senators had served in the Austrian *Reichsrat,* giving the DSAP the greatest representational continuity with the prewar period among the German political parties.

Soon after the April elections, the German Social Democratic left made its political demands known with the publication of the so-called *Reichenberger Richtlinien.* Its demands were similar to those of the Marxist Left, with class issues taking precedence over nationality issues. They included the creation of a workers' council system, supranational action by the proletariat of Czechoslovakia, an immediate treaty with Soviet Russia and participation in the Third International.[57] The German Social Democratic Party leadership opposed the demands of the *Richtlinien* with the same arguments it had used against calls for immediate creation of a proletarian state and workers' council system in 1919: the kind of revolution that had occurred in agrarian Russia during wartime was not possible in industrialized Czechoslovakia during peacetime.[58] The official reaction of the Czechoslovak Social Democrats to the *Richtlinien* was negligible. *Sociální demokrat* published it in full without comment.[59] The Czechoslovak Social Democratic right paid even less attention to it, concentrating on the continuing battle between left and right within the party.

On 29 May 1920, shortly after the formation of the Tusar government, twenty-four Czechoslovak Social Democratic deputies publicly announced their opposition to their party's participation in the government. They asserted that the national or bourgeois "revolution" in Czechoslovakia must develop into a socialist or proletarian revolution. Such a revolution would not come through cooperation with bourgeois deputies.[60]

In the spring of 1920, politics were taken into the streets of Central Europe. Violence in Bavaria in the wake of the Kapp Putsch and the growing strength of the counter-revolution in Hungary are but two examples. In Czechoslovakia, there was the spectacle of the Tusar government trying Marxist Left leader Muna and some of his associates for high treason. After a highly publicized trial, the defendants were convicted in late May and pardoned in June, in the general political amnesty that followed Masaryk's election as the country's first president.

Spring and summer 1920 were a time of worker unrest: there were strikes for higher wages and over food shortages (in the Sudeten lands) and continued, scattered demands for the formation of workers' councils. The 590 strikes and 24 lockouts, affecting more than 660,000 workers, which took place in 1920, were a high for Czechoslovakia in the first half of the interwar period. Social democratic trade unions, following the example set by their Weimar counterparts, began a blockade of Allied shipments of armaments from Austria to Poland during the Polish-Soviet war.[61] Like Berlin, Prague remained studiously neutral in the war.[62] The government was attacked for its position by the social democratic left for its failure to support a "workers" state against a "bourgeois" state, and, to a lesser degree, by some of the parties of the Czech right which opposed Polish claims to the Teschen district. The Entente powers also expressed considerable dissatisfaction with Prague's position, but from the other direction. The Tusar government was caught between the social democratic left and the Polonophobe right which felt the government was not friendly enough to Soviet Russia and a part of the Czechoslovak right, but especially the Entente powers which wanted the trade union blockade of Entente arms to Poland to be broken.[63]

During the summer, it became apparent to the adherents of the Marxist Left that it was an ideological contradiction both to admire the tenets of the Bolshevik Revolution and to support the Tusar government, which practiced anti-Bolshevik policies. The problem of continued government participation exacerbated the internal problems of the Czechoslovak Social Democrats, hastening the division of the party, although not the formation of a Czechoslovak Communist Party. It also became clear during the summer that the Marxist Left was gaining strength and would command approximately two-thirds of the delegates at the party congress planned for late September. These delegates were committed to joining the Third International.

In mid-September 1920, three decisive, related events occurred: the Czechoslovak Social Democratic Party congress was postponed, the Tusar government fell, and the Marxist Left occupied the party headquarters, Lidový dům (House of the People) in Prague. The party executive and representatives decided on 14 September to delay the congress planned for the following week until December (it would actually be held in November). They believed that the Marxist Left, influenced by Moscow, was secretly trying to build a communist organization within the Czechoslovak Social Democratic Party and disrupt its activities.[64] On 15 September, the Tusar government fell, due both to the difficult international situation and to the Czechoslovak Social Democratic Party's internal problems. It was replaced by a "nonpolitical" government of officials headed by the civil servant Jan Černý.

The Slovak Social Democrats, although part of the Czechoslovak Social Democratic Party as of December 1919, initially retained their separate organization under the leadership of Ivan Dérer, a lawyer. An attempt by part of the Slovak Social Democratic leadership to postpone the Slovak Social Democratic congress, also scheduled for September 1920, was decisively defeated in a 117 to 11 vote of the party executive. Delegates to the congress, which met as scheduled, overwhelmingly supported the Marxist Left.[65]

Understandably angered by the preemptive actions of the party executive, the Marxist Left refused to postpone the congress and held its own congress on the originally scheduled date under the auspices of the Czechoslovak Social Democratic Party, attracting 338 of the original 527 delegates. The Marxist Left declared itself the true representative of the Czechoslovak Social Democratic Party and claimed possession of the party headquarters, press and treasury. The ensuing occupation of the *Právo lidu* offices by a workers' council—comprising the majority of the staff—led to the publication for a brief period of the two opposing party papers, both entitled *Právo lidu,* one by the Marxist Left and one by the party leaders.

Both *Právo lidu* and the party headquarters were legally owned by party members Jaroslav Astor, František Hummelhans, and Antonín Němec, because according to Czechoslovak law, political parties could not own property. The three, all part of the Czechoslovak Social Democratic Party right leadership, went to court to prevent further publication of *Právo lidu* by the Marxist Left and to force the return of the party headquarters to them as the legal custodians of the party property.[66] The courts acted quickly to prevent further publication of the paper *(Staré) právo lidu* by the Marxist Left.[67] On 21 September, the Marxist Left therefore began to publish *Rudé právo.*

After the Marxist Left's occupation of party headquarters, the Czechoslovak Social Democratic Right leadership began referring to the Marxist Left as "communist." Following a series of independent conferences by the Marxist Left, the Czechoslovak Social Democratic Right leadership began to prepare for the growing possibility of a party split and moved to salvage what it could of the party. On 1 October, it announced the expulsion of fifteen party members for organization of and participation in

"Communist" conferences, for giving unauthorized speeches, and for the forcible occupation of party property. Among those expelled were Marxist Left leaders Muna, Skalák and Šmeral. From this point, if not before, there was no possibility of the two groups coming to terms with one another. The right-wing party leadership considered the appropriation of party property by the Marxist Left a serious breach of party discipline. The Marxist Left considered the attempted postponement of the party congress and the recourse to legal action by the leadership abuses of power by the minority. Although each side credited the other with malicious intentions, it is more likely that both sides improvised, responding to events rather than initiating them. It seems that the right-wing leadership advocated the postponement of the planned party congress both in the hopes that the Marxist Left's popularity had peaked and to see what the next move from that quarter would be.

While the Czechoslovak Social Democrats were quarreling among themselves, the German Social Democrats held their second party congress at Karlsbad. The party's own increasing internal problems provided the main topic of discussion. Dissension within the party was in part generational. Opposition leaders Hahn, Kreibich, and Neurath were ten to twenty years younger than most of the other party leaders. Their supporters included at least one former prisoner of war radicalized by experiences in Soviet Russia. One delegate reported the following exchange between Kreibich and party chairman Seliger. Kreibich rejected the argument of the party left's "youthful inexperience" noting that Napoleon was not yet thirty years old when he defeated the "old generals." Seliger retorted that Napoleon had, however, lost the war. The discussion ended when a member of the audience called out, "When he went to Moscow!"[68]

Seliger and Kreibich negotiated a short-lived compromise. Kreibich proposed the adoption of the so-called "Action Program" (*Aktionsprogramm*), one of the most radical and comprehensive political programs of the time in Czechoslovakia.[69] According to the program, in multinational states, seizure of power by the proletariat could succeed only when the proletariat of all nations was united in struggle.[70] Thus, the next battle would not be for national autonomy, but for the destruction of the bourgeois Czechoslovak state. An assumption implicit in the Action Program was that nationality problems would somehow resolve themselves in the "natural" course of events following the revolution. Opponents of the

Action Program objected precisely to this vagueness on the nationality issue.

Seliger believed that the method employed in the class struggle should depend on developments in the country in question, and in any case, social democratic parties were obliged to win the majority of citizens over to socialism, because dictatorship in the sense of the Communist Manifesto had to be the dictatorship of a majority. Further since the party was a democratic one, no group should dominate the rest and the party should be independent of outside pressure. Seliger countered with a five-point proposal that involved the creation of a standing proletarian congress to include both the Czechoslovak and German Social Democrats and their affiliated trade unions as the basis of the solution to the nationality program. The proposal seems to have been lost in the shuffle that soon followed, however, as the social democratic parties of Czechoslovakia divided. Seliger's proposal was accepted by a vote of 293 to 144.[71]

Details of the proposal were worked out by a commission that included Kreibich. The resulting compromise, which really was not much of a compromise at all, was then unanimously adopted by the party congress. Party dissidents could express their views within the party, but no other concessions were made. It was hoped that the compromise would maintain party unity.

Kreibich was content, for the time being, to remain in the party. He realized that acceptance of the compromise was not necessarily a true reflection of party sentiment. He believed that, in time, a majority of the party would support his proposal. Kreibich's reasoning was sound insofar as support from elected county (*Bezirk*) delegates, approximately 40 percent, was higher than support from the appointed delegates, about 15 percent. The Action Program received unanimous support from the delegates elected by the Reichenberg county and district organizations. Only the appointed delegates from the Reichenberg district—two trade union representatives, three parliamentary deputies and one senator—supported Seliger's proposal.[72]

Party unity was maintained for three short weeks. Then leaders of the Reichenberg faction declared that for them, the Karlsbad compromise had no significance other than the provision for possible further activity within the party on behalf of the Third International.[73] The DSAP left wing continued to maneuver within the confines of the party, attempting to win as many members as possible over to the left-wing point of view.

Party chairman Seliger died shortly after the Karlsbad Party Congress. Both the position Seliger would have taken on the nationality problem and the course he would have taken to maintain party unity remain an open question.

Seliger's successor as party chairman was deputy chairman Ludwig Czech, long time party leader in Brünn but a relative unknown among the Bohemian party members. A Moravian Jewish lawyer, Czech was born in Lemberg, Galicia, where his father, a member of the Habsburg civil service, had been posted to the railroad. Czech studied law in Vienna, where he joined the Austrian Social Democratic Party. Upon his return to Brünn in 1893, he was active in the Moravian provincial social democratic organization while maintaining a legal practice in which most of his clients were fellow party members.

That a Jew named "Czech" led a German party is one of the ironies of Czechoslovak interwar political history. Although Jewish domination of the upper echelons of the German Social Democratic Party resulted in anti-Semitic propaganda, particularly from nationalist German political quarters, during the interwar period, it became a major political issue only during the mid-1930s, following the rise of both Adolf Hitler and the radical nationalist Sudeten German Party (*Sudetendeutsche Partei,* the SdP). Many Jews in the former crownlands, like assimilated Jews elsewhere in Central Europe, were members of the parties of the political left: both the Czechoslovak and German Social Democratic Parties and later, the Czechoslovak Communist Party. In any case, Jewish members of left-wing parties tended to be Jewish in origin only, having exchanged their religious beliefs for the tenets of socialism or communism.

In principle, Czech (but not German) political parties, excepting those allied with the Roman Catholic Church, accepted Jewish members. Among the more nationally-oriented Czech politicians, however, many Jews were mistrusted because they spoke German. The Jewish alliance with the liberal, centralizing forces of the Habsburg Monarchy during the late nineteenth century, in opposition to the federalist aspirations of most Czech nationalists, provided grounds for anti-Jewish animosities that existed in some Czech political circles into the interwar period. As concerns the German non-socialist political parties, Jews played a major role only in the Brünn and Prague-based and Jewish-dominated German Democratic Freedom Party (*Deutschdemocratische Freiheitspartei*), and in its short-lived successor, the German Labor and Economic Association (*Deutsche Arbeits- und Wirtschaftsgemeinschaft*, the DAWG).[74]

The Division of the Social Democratic Parties

The questions under discussion within the Czechoslovak and German Social Democratic Parties—workers' councils, methods of class struggle and membership in the Third International—were also the subject of discussion within their affiliated youth groups, Czech Social Democratic Youth (*Česká sociálně demokraticka mladež*) and the Union of Social Democratic Working Youth (*Verband der sozialdemokratischen Arbeiterjugend*). At their second congress in late October 1920, the majority of the young Czech Social Democrats accepted the 21 Points of the Third International and approved a proposal to join the Communist Youth International founded the year before in Berlin. This led to a split within the group that paralleled the one within the Czechoslovak Social Democratic Party itself. The young Czech Social Democrats, however, delayed a definitive decision on participation in the Communist Youth International until after conferring with the Marxist Left leadership.

Following the example of the Austrian, Czech, and Weimer German Social Democratic youth organizations, representatives of the DSAP youth group voted 82 to 22 at their 21 October-1 November congress to join the Communist Youth International. The 30,000 member strong youth organization then united with the Union of Slovak Communist Youth (*Sväz komunistické mladeže Slovenska*) on the basis of the Communist Youth International. The young Czech Social Democrats (Left) were invited to join them, which they did in February 1921. Thus, the youth groups became the first social democratic organizations to make the division between the left-wing and the rest of the party final.[75]

The majority's acceptance of the 21 Points did not mean, of course, that all social democratic youth supported the Third International. Indeed, a social democratic opposition briefly remained in the former German Social Democratic youth organization until its members were expelled for agitation against the Communist Youth International. A youth international was an attractive idea, and at the time, no social democratic alternative existed.

Social restiveness, in addition to taking the form of intraparty political differences, was also played out in nationalist conflicts. Czech-German/ Jewish conflicts culminated in November with the defacing of statues commemorating Josef II in the town squares of Eger and Teplitz. In Prague, various German communal and university buildings were occupied; German and Jewish stores on Am Graben (Na Příkopě) were damaged and Jewish communal records in the Jewish city hall in Josefstadt (Josefov), the former ghetto, were destroyed. German newspapers reported cries from Czechs up and down Meiselgasse in Josefstadt, "String up any German or Jew on the next lamp post."[76]

Czech public reaction to the events appears to have been mixed. Indeed, they found some support among the Czech nationalists. The right-wing leadership of the Czechoslovak Social Democratic Party condemned the events, fearing that they could lead to a military dictatorship and noting that in the republic, German property had the same rights as Czech property.[77]

Just as excitement over the recent nationality conflicts was dying down, the Marxist Left called a general strike on 10 December 1920, in response to a police attempt the previous evening to remove them from the party headquarters which they still occupied. The strike provided the actual impetus for the division of the DSAP. The right-wing party leadership of the Czechoslovak Social Democrats, citing a court order obtained the previous September giving it possession of party property, relied on police aid for the return of party headquarters. Resistance to military and police efforts to clear the building resulted in some bloodshed.

The Marxist Left published an eight-point proclamation demanding the removal of police from the Lidový dům and the building's return to the workers, the release of those arrested during the clearing of the building, and an end to the "persecution."[78] General demands included the resignation of the Černý government, a thirty percent increase in workers' salaries, and the formation of workers' councils. Not all of the demands were specifically Marxist; they expressed the heterogeneous nature of the leadership of the Marxist Left as well as an attempt to appeal to the widest possible audience for support.

The general strike received broad support in Smíchov and Libeň, two of the industrial suburbs of Prague, as well as in Brünn, Kladno, Brüx, and elsewhere. The Marxist Left mobilized factory workers in the capital, who marched on the parliament in the Altstadt (Staré Město) from the working class suburbs in eastern Prague. The most radical activity took place in the Kladno area and in Brünn. Under the leadership of Muna and Antonín Zápotocký, long-time Kladno party and trade union secretary; a district-wide central revolutionary council was formed in Kladno to confiscate some 80 estates, and the railroad stations were occupied. In Brünn, the municipal electrical plant and water works were occupied and public transportation was halted.

Among the Sudeten Germans, support for the Marxist Left was limited primarily to Reichenberg, where some two-thirds of the German workers followed Hahn's and Kreibich's call for an immediate strike. Interpreting the events in Prague not as a fight over a local assembly house, or as an argument between Šmeral and Tusar, but as a call for class struggle, the two demanded the creation of workers' councils. Their position was opposed by the German Trade Union Council (*Deutscher Gewerkschaftsbund*, the DGB), headquartered in Reichenberg, as well as by the German Social Democratic Party executive committee, which rejected the call for a general strike on 12 December. In contrast to Hahn and Kreibich, the party executive declared that the events in Prague were simply a struggle within the Czechoslovak Social Democratic Party over control of the Lidový dům, and were of only local significance; the German working class had no reason to become involved.[79] The Reichenberg left, breaching party discipline, called a strike in support of the Marxist Left.

The general strike was brief; by 14 December, the government had taken action, and by 16 December, it was officially over. The government, with permission from Masaryk, had taken measures that limited or rescinded some civil liberties in several districts, including Kladno. The final toll from the strike was 13 dead, scores injured, and some 3,000 arrested.

German Social Democratic Party leaders considered the general strike a failure. The DSAP had supported neither the Czechoslovak Social Democratic leadership nor the Marxist Left. On the one hand, German Social Democratic leaders had consistently opposed what they considered the non-socialist coalition policies of the Czechoslovak Social Democratic right, and further condemned both the heavy-handed tactics of the Czechoslovak Social Democratic leadership and the strong-arm tactics of the police that had led to bloodshed. On the other hand, they stressed the Marxist Left's lack of clear goals, and accused it of abusing the weapon of the general strike.[80]

The Czechoslovak Social Democratic leadership saw the events that led to the general strike as merely the return of illegally expropriated property to its rightful owners and felt the Marxist Left had no valid reason for calling the strike. The party leadership further believed that the Marxist Left's actions could not be tolerated lest other groups believe that they too could commit such "anarchic" acts as the arbitrary appropriation of property. It was the actions of the Marxist Left, not those of the party leadership, that precipitated the December violence.[81]

Asserting that it represented the majority of the party, the Marxist Left claimed both the printing press and the party headquarters, and condemned the tactics of the Czechoslovak Social Democratic Party leadership. From the point of view of the Marxist Left, its social democratic opponents had allied themselves with the "bourgeois" courts and the police against the working class; in partnership with the state, the Czechoslovak Social Democratic Party leadership was responsible for the strike's failure.[82]

Government failure to crack down on excesses by Czech nationalists, particularly Legionaries, during anti-German, and in Prague, anti-Jewish, demonstrations a few weeks earlier had led many to underestimate the government's strength. Indeed, the Marxist Left had interpreted the Czech-German excesses as a symptom of general social unrest connected with the "revolutionary character of the time."[83] This is a partial explanation for the call for a general strike by the weak, fragmented and unprepared Marxist Left. The Marxist Left assumed that its actions would also be tolerated without governmental resort to armed force.

The December general strike was not an unqualified failure. It revealed some mass support for the Marxist Left and the Reichenberg left, however diffuse the two groups were. It was officially estimated that some 160,000 persons throughout the country participated in the strike.[84] The government's need to use extraordinary laws and the military to end the strike speaks for its strength. And, with the decision to call a strike in the Reichenberg area, the December events constituted the first supranational action by the organized working class since the formation of the Czechoslovak state.

The strike was a failure if its only goal was revolution. This had been the desire of some of its leaders, but revolution in Czechoslovakia was unlikely. While many strikers were protesting against government policies and certainly some government ministers, most do not appear to have

been protesting against President Masaryk or the existence of the Czechoslovak state.

The German Social Democratic leadership's reaction to the strike was
swift. When it became clear that the party leadership and the Reichenberg left could not come to terms, the party executive voted, in an extraordinary meeting on 17 January 1921, to expel the Reichenberg district
from the party without consideration of the personal political loyalties
of the German Social Democrats there. The district organization, encompassing some 16,000 members,[85] seven county and 169 local (*Ort*) organizations,[86] was one of the largest and wealthiest in the party. The party
executive justified its action on the grounds that the Reichenberg district
organization's participation in the December general strike constituted
a gross breach of party discipline. The expulsion left a legacy of ill will
in the Reichenberg area that the German Social Democrats were never
able to overcome, especially among those who had remained loyal to
the Karlsbad compromise but had been expelled anyway.[87] The loss of
Kreibich, recognized by other DSAP leaders as a major political figure
of his generation, was a great one (his survival of various inter- and postwar Czechoslovak Communist Party purges is a measure of his political
skill). The party later missed both his journalistic and oratorical talents.

The party executive's action left Kreibich and his colleagues with the
entire district organization political structure intact, including the district newspaper, the influential *Vorwärts*. The German Social Democratic Party faced the difficult task of recreating a party organization in an
area that was to become a stronghold of Sudeten German communism.

Previously, the development of the German Social Democratic left-wing
had been influenced by similar, earlier events within the Czechoslovak
Social Democratic Party and the SPD in Weimar Germany. From this
point, however, Kreibich and the Reichenberg left took the lead in moving toward the formation of a communist party in Czechoslovakia.

Kreibich's political behavior at this time was the subject of considerable discussion in the German Social Democratic press, which vilified
him as opportunistic and worse.[88] Kreibich himself had provided a partial
answer to the apparent contradictions in his political behavior in a speech
at the Teplitz Party Congress of 1919, noting that he spoke in a different
tone when he spoke as a party representative than when he spoke at an
assembly or wrote an article.[89] Kreibich later expressed his growing

conviction that a unified working class, not the nationality question, was the most important issue facing the working class.[90] His belief that any national minority party, even one with the support of the majority of the nationality group, lacked power, led him to call for the unification of the Czech and German working class. Kreibich's belief that unification would best be achieved under the auspices of a communist party placed him at the far left politically among the leaders of the organized working class in Czechoslovakia.

Possible reasons for the change in Kreibich's political point of view are numerous. Kreibich and other German Social Democrats from the Reichenberg district organization were in contact with members of the KPD. They had been affected by the continuing unemployment and hunger among the Germans in the border area, sometimes exacerbated by the apparently indifferent attitude of the Prague government, as well as the apparent inability of the German Social Democrats to do anything to alleviate the problems. In addition, some of the Hungarian communist leaders fleeing the "White Terror" of the post-Kun era had made their way to Reichenberg, where they served as advisors to leaders of the Reichenberg left.

Beginning in January 1921, Kreibich attempted to pressure the Marxist Left into forming a communist party, sometimes engaging in angry polemics against its leader, Šmeral. He criticized the Marxist Left for failing to accept Lenin's 21 Points and joining the Third International at its conference in early January. The Marxist Left had chosen to delay consideration of the Third International until May in order to allow the local organizations a chance for in-depth discussions of the issue.[91] Kreibich believed the delay was due, in part, to descriptions of communism in the press of the Czechoslovak Social Democratic Party right as an enemy of the Czechoslovak state, which made the Marxist Left apprehensive about taking decisive action.[92]

Revolutionary ardor had cooled somewhat in the aftermath of the December strike when Kladno strike leaders Muna and Zápotocký, and 3,000 strikers were arrested and many given prison terms. In addition, trade unions affiliated with the Czechoslovak Social Democratic Party, with their wealth and reformist tendencies, played an important role in restraining the more radical members of the Marxist Left. Although some trade unions, to be sure, accepted the communist point of view with alacrity, for the most part, they stood politically closer to the Czechoslovak Social Democratic Party leadership than to the Marxist Left. Membership in social democratic and communist-affiliated trade unions was consistently larger than membership in the respective social democratic and communist parties. Working class political parties, dependent on the trade unions for monetary and voter support, had to remain in the good graces of the union leaders, who tended to be more concerned with improving the economic lot of their rank and file than with revolution.

After the March 1921 formation of the Communist Party of Czechoslovakia (German Section) (*Kommunistische Partei der Tschechoslowakei [Deutsche Abteilung]*) in Reichenberg, Kreibich's political model was the KPD. His small, disciplined group attempted to force Šmeral and his colleagues to the left and then to unite with them. In a move to isolate the social democratic right in Weimar Germany, the Spartacists (*Spartakusbund*) had pressured the USPD in much the same way.[93] The attempt was made in both cases to apply the Leninist concept of using a politically conscious elite, the "vanguard of the proletariat," to lead the "uneducated masses," rather than the social democratic idea of educating them to lead themselves.

Šmeral and Zápotocký moved within a larger and more varied political milieu than did Kreibich, who, along with Neurath, dominated the newly-formed Communist Party of Czechoslovakia (German Section). Šmeral continued to try to win over as many Czechoslovak Social Democrats as possible to his point of view, leading Kreibich to accuse the Marxist Left of harboring centrists and opportunists within the organization.[94] Kreibich's attitude should be seen within the context of a 24 September 1920 *Pravda* article, in which Lenin called for the "cleansing" of both the USPD and the Italian left of counter-revolutionary elements.[95]

The reasons for Šmeral's attitude were numerous. First, although his political ideas were changing—he seems to have been favorably impressed by his spring 1920 trip to Soviet Russia—it appears clear that he hesitated to place his organization under the auspices of the Comintern. Secondly, the leaders of the Marxist Left were not immediately pressured from within to form another political party as the expelled German Social Democrats had been, for the Marxist Left was already a separate organization. Nor did the Marxist Left need the German communists to form an effective political party. This is not to imply, however, that Šmeral was immune to the pressure exerted by the diverse members of the Marxist Left, by the small, independent communist parties clamoring for Comintern recognition or by Moscow itself, for he was not. Finally, Zápotocký, a trade unionist, did not want to move so fast as to alienate his trade union support, much of which was politically far more conservative than the leaders of the Marxist Left.

It was not until its congress in mid-May 1921 that the Marxist Left, with representatives of the Ruthenian and Slovak Social Democrats also in attendence, voted to form a communist party and join the Third International. Šmeral rejected Kreibich's call for immediate unification of the Czech and German wings of the party on the grounds of national sensitivities and organizational problems. Šmeral also cautioned that Kreibich ought not be too zealous in his calls for purification of the party.

Disagreements between Kreibich and Šmeral continued until the Third Congress of the Communist International met in late June. Lenin himself attempted to solve the Czechoslovak question, calling for the unification of the Czech and German sections of the Czechoslovak Communist Party along with the newly-formed Zionist and Polish Communist Parties of Czechoslovakia. His advice to the Czechoslovak communist leaders included the now famous dictum that Šmeral should take two steps to the left and Kreibich one step to the right, to form a unified Czechoslovak Communist Party.[96] Lenin defended Šmeral's behavior to Kreibich, saying that the leader of a mass party must be cautious, especially in a revolutionary situation.

The various communist parties of Czechoslovakia were officially united at a 30 October-2 November congress at which Kreibich and Šmeral were the main speakers. The Czechoslovak Communist Party celebrates the anniversary of its foundation, however, on 16 May, the date on which the Czechoslovak branch of the party was formed.

The initial effect of the formation of the Czechoslovak Communist Party on the Czechoslovak and German Social Democrats at the parliamentary level—the first place it could be quantitatively measured—varied greatly. The left-wing had been poorly represented among the 31 German Social Democratic deputies elected to the parliament in 1920. Thus, the DSAP lost only three deputies to the communists. The Czechoslovak Social Democrats, on the other hand, suffered major losses in both chambers: 22 of 77 deputies and 7 of 44 senators elected in 1920 moved to the Czechoslovak Communist Party.

The attractiveness of the Czechoslovak Communist Party, a political movement with support in both rural and urban areas as well as supranational appeal, became apparent with the results of communal elections in Bohemia, Moravia, and Silesia in 1923 and was confirmed by the results of the 1925 parliamentary elections. The Czechoslovak Communist Party attracted an estimated fifty percent of the Czechoslovak Social Democratic constituency, decimating the Ruthenian and Slovak branches of the organization, and about one-third of the German Social Democratic Party's membership.[97] In contrast to other parts of Europe, the Communist Party in Czechoslovakia received relatively more votes in rural areas than in more industrial areas. Support increased proportionally moving eastward from the Czech lands, peaking in Ruthenia, one of the most backward areas in Europe.[98] A partial explanation for this phenomenon is that the Hungarians and Jews who dominated the Ruthenian and Slovak branches of the Czechoslovak Social Democratic Party had been radicalized by the Slovak Soviet and Kun's Jewish-dominated Hungarian Soviet Republics. Eastern Slovakia had been briefly occupied by troops of the Hungarian Soviet Republic. One German Social Democrat from Slovakia explained that the high illiteracy rate among the Slovak and Ruthenian peasants made it easy for the communists to manipulate them with promises of "immediate revolution."[99]

The Situation in the Trade Unions

In Czechoslovakia, trade unions, like political parties, were divided along national lines. Most trade unions were affiliated with, although not part of, political parties. At the end of the First World War, the majority of Czech trade unions in the Bohemian Crownlands were affiliated with either the Czech Social Democratic (*Odborové sdružení československé*) or the Czech National Socialist (*Československá obec dělnická*) trade union centers in Prague. Most German trade unions belonged to the Austrian Social Democratic-affiliated trade union center, *Gewerkschaftskommission Österreichs,* in Vienna. In June 1919, the former Bohemian, Moravian, and Silesian provincial branches of the Austrian organization founded a new trade union center in Reichenberg affiliated with the German Social Democrats. Following a drastic loss of support during the war, the social democratic-affiliated trade unions of of Czechoslovakia experienced a massive increase in membership during 1919 and 1920, especially among unskilled workers, who were organized for the first time.[100] The social democratic trade unions were, of course, affected by the postwar internal problems of the respective social democratic parties.

Although the German Social Democratic trade unions opposed the policies of the Prague government, while the Czechoslovak Social Democratic trade unions supported them, the ability of the trade unions to work together somewhat more harmoniously than their political counterparts was reflected as early as the summer of 1920 in a joint boycott of arms shipments to Poland. The Czechoslovak and German trade union centers were encouraged by officials of the Amsterdam-based International Federation of Trade Unions (IFTU) to cooperate on policies initiated by the IFTU. Soon after its foundation, the German Social Democratic trade union center had applied for membership in the IFTU, with which the Czechoslovak Social Democratic trade union center was associated, but was not accepted due to IFTU policy that permitted the affiliation of only one trade union center per country, a policy that differed from that of the Second International.[101] Thus, while in the prewar period, only the Austrian Social Democratic trade union center in Vienna, and not the separatist Czechoslovak Social Democratic trade union center in Prague, had been part of the IFTU, in the postwar period, the situation was reversed. The IFTU recognized the Czechoslovak Social Democratic trade union center in Prague, not the German Social Democratic trade union center in Reichenberg. The trade union center in Reichenberg did follow the principles of the IFTU, however, and cooperated with Amsterdam, which eased relations between the two trade union centers somewhat.[102] This cooperation was not duplicated between the Czechoslovak and German Social Democrats, in part because they belonged to different social democratic organizations, the Second International and the Vienna Union, or "2½" International, respectively, until the two merged in May 1923.

Efforts by left-wing socialists to take over the social democratic trade unions began in early 1921, even before the formal creation of the Czechoslovak Communist Party, and continued throughout 1922. One reason for the lack of a coordinated attempt to take over the social democratic trade unions can be found in the trade union tradition of pre-revolutionary

Russia, which had been far weaker than in Western Europe or Cisleithania. Although there had been a great increase in trade union membership following the February Revolution, the soviets, which included soldiers and peasants, had played a more important role in worker organization than the trade unions. Moscow initially sent mixed signals regarding the role of trade unions, and as late as 1921, jealousy persisted in Soviet Russia between trade unions and soviets at the local level, with some provincial leaders believing that the soviets made trade unions superfluous. This attitude had been shared by some members of the KPD and the USPD left. There was no international "revolutionary" or communist trade union organization until July 1921, when the "Red" International Trade Union Commission (*Internationaler Bund revolutionärer Gewerkschaften; Rudá odborová internacionála,* the ROI) was formed in Moscow. Although a communist trade union bureau was established in Reichenberg in March 1921, it was not until October 1922 that a Czechoslovak Communist branch of the Red International was formed, the International Federation of Trade Unions (*Internationaler Allgewerkschaftlicher Verband,* the IAV; *Mezinárodní všeodborový svaz*).

Because neither the Czechoslovak nor the German Social Democratic trade union centers had supported the abortive December general strike and the Czechoslovak Communists considered this a decisive factor in the failure of the strike, the communists had good reason to want to discredit the social democratic trade union leadership.[103] Their call for a trade union unity front was met with skepticism from social democratic trade unions which claimed that responsibility for the fragmentation of the working class lay with the communists in the first place.

Although many trade unionists tended to be more conservative than the parties with which they were associated (and not all of them were party members), this was not always the case. Communist tenets appear to have been especially attractive to members of some of the newly founded trade unions, which lacked both social democratic tradition and property. The rhetoric of impending world revolution, while more appealing to unskilled workers, also made inroads among members of some of the skilled trade union: miners and textile workers, for instance, with their traditions of radicalism. In addition, the Czechoslovak Communist Party could, for example, attract the Czech members of a particular trade union, while gaining little or no following from the members of the corresponding

German trade union. The reverse was also true. This was a reflection of differing industrial development and economic circumstances among the trade unions of the various nationalities in Czechoslovakia.

In the spring of 1921, members of the communist trade union bureau in Reichenberg, led by former German Social Democrats Paul Brunner (former executive committee member and editor of the railroad workers' union magazine, *Der Eisenbahner*) and Anton Hanke (one-time DSAP representative for the Reichenberg district organization), began their offensive against the German Social Democratic trade unions. German Social Democratic leaders quickly condemned the communist effort to build cells within the social democratic trade unions. The attacks on the German Social Democratic trade unions were seen as part of a world-wide attempt on the part of the Third International to destroy the Amsterdam-affiliated trade unions.

Communist agitation among the Reichenberg area textile workers, which had begun almost as soon as the December general strike ended, resulted in the splitting of one of the largest German Social Democratic trade unions (some 90,000 members). The textile union expelled 86 functionaries, including trade union secretary Adalbert Hampl, from Grotzau, Kratzau, Neustadt, Warnsdorf, and Zwickau, all in the Reichenberg area, for breach of trade union discipline. Soon afterward, the first communist trade union in Czechoslovakia, representing textile workers, was formed in Reichenberg.[104]

Communist attempts to take power in the social democratic trade unions continued somewhat sporadically, perhaps reflecting Šmeral's attitude of not meddling in the trade union issue.[105] Although the communists made some headway in their attempts to gain influence, for instance, with the Czechoslovak Social Democratic agricultural and the chemical workers trade unions, they suffered defeat at the January 1922 Czechoslovak Social Democratic trade union congress. Only two of the fifteen delegates elected to the center's administrative board were communists and delegates rejected a proposal to join the Moscow-based ROI by a vote of 339 to 227, representing 338,447 and 222,027 organized workers, respectively.[106] The communist-dominated trade unions were then expelled. Leaders of the expelled trade unionists formed the Czechoslovak branch of the ROI in October of the same year.

Moscow criticized the Czechoslovak Communist Party for its lack of a methodical approach to the trade union issue at a 1922 meeting of the Communist International, where the party was advised to make a concentrated and systematic effort to take over the social democratic trade unions. There had been a recent exodus of workers from the trade unions in Czechoslovakia, reputedly due to "proletarian indifference." The Communist International's solution to the problem was to split the trade unions and provide the workers with the (communist) leadership they allegedly needed.[107]

The Czechoslovak Communist Party took over the Czechoslovak Social Democratic agricultural workers, stone mason and chemical worker unions, and gained support among some textile workers and miners in both the Czechoslovak and German Social Democratic trade unions. Other trade unions, although communist-dominated, did not join the ROI, but remained independent. The Czechoslovak Communist Party was not to achieve the influence with the trade unions that it had earlier gained within both the Czechoslovak and German Social Democratic Parties.

In the Wake of the Party Division

Because many European social democrats interpreted the Russian Revolution of 1917 as the first time the proletariat had dominated an entire country, some, though not all, initially greeted it with enthusiasm, even if they did not support the means by which the revolution had been achieved. Throughout the 1920s, most center and left-wing social democrats defended the existence of Soviet Russia against what they perceived as the imperialism of the Entente countries and their allies, many of which were slow in extending official recognition to the Soviet government. These same social democrats, however, rejected what they considered the exporting of Bolshevism to their own countries, in the form of national communist parties, increasingly dominated by Moscow. Further, they vociferously opposed attacks on their own parties by native communists.

The formation of the Czechoslovak Communist Party exacerbated the economic and nationality problems of the working class in Czechoslovakia. The existence of another working class party, one at odds with all of the other parties, further fragmented the organized working class, which was in any case growing more conservative as the unrest of the immediate postwar period subsided and other political groups consolidated their positions.

Many German Social Democratic leaders viewed the division of the Czechoslovak Social Democratic Party as the reasonable result of Czechoslovak Social Democratic rank and file opposition to what they termed the "non-social democratic" government policies of the right-wing party leadership. At least initially, DSAP leaders did not equate the Marxist Left with the Bolsheviks, considering the former's politics neither free of the nationalist attitudes of the Czechoslovak Social Democratic right nor particularly more radical than those of center and left-wing social democrats elsewhere in Europe.

The German Social Democrats viewed the division within their own party somewhat differently: it was the result of an attempt by renegade party members under the influence of Moscow to destroy the DSAP from within and then construct a communist party.

The German Social Democrats remained steadfast in their call for German national autonomy in Czechoslovakia as the primary issue on their political agenda. Like the Czechoslovak Social Democratic Party, the German Social Democratic Party was subject to pressure from the political right. Recognizing the attractiveness of nationalist appeals from other German political parties to their constituency, the German Social Democrats were reluctant to seek closer ties with the Czechoslovak Social Democrats, who were in any case unsympathetic to their national aspirations. Although their attitude toward the Czechoslovak Communists remained negative, the German Social Democrats encouraged "errant" social democrats to leave the communist party and return to the social democratic fold.

The rump Czechoslovak Social Democratic Party, influenced to some extent by the Czechoslovak National Socialists, moved further to the right. It participated in an increasingly moderate all-national coalition government until 1926. Although further social reforms were legislated under the auspices of the Czechoslovak Social Democratic Party, the losses caused by the division of the party prevented it from playing a decisive role in the government. There was little in the contemporary political situation to encourage the Czechoslovak Social Democrats to work more closely with the German Social Democrats, so long as the DSAP persisted in its national demands and its opposition to the government, on whatever grounds. Cooperation with the DSAP would have gained the Czechoslovak Social Democrats few adherents from the organized working class left so long as they remained in the all-national coalition, and would have alienated the party's more nationalist members.

Both the Czechoslovak and the German Social Democrats went on the defensive. They were attacked by both the communist left and the nationalist right. The defensive posture that both parties felt obliged to maintain gave them—especially the German Social Democrats as both a minority and an opposition party—little space to maneuver, allowing other political parties, particularly the Czechoslovak parties, to try to shape the Czechoslovak state according to their own economic and political views.

CHAPTER II

THE POST-REVOLUTIONARY PERIOD
1922-1926

The Political Situation in Post-Revolutionary Czechoslovakia

A period of increasing economic and political conservatism followed the division of the social democratic parties. The Republican Party of Farmers and Peasants (*Republikánská strana zemědělského a malorolnického lidu*) and the Czechoslovak People's Party (*Československá strana lidová*), popularly known as the Czechoslovak Agrarians and Clericals, gained strength at the expense of the Czechoslovak Social Democrats. Czechoslovakia's conservative domestic and foreign policy between 1922 and 1926 reflected European-wide trends that did not begin to change until late 1924.

After major gains in the tumultuous postwar period, most European social democratic parties had been weakened by internal divisions and growing economic uncertainty during the first half of the 1920s. This was certainly the case in Czechoslovakia, where the organized working class was divided not only between the communists and socialists, but also among the socialists of various nationalities.

Although the Czechoslovak Social Democrats remained in the government until 1926, their portfolios following the September 1920 demission of the Tusar government became increasingly peripheral. So did their role in the *Pětka* (Committee of Five), an informal indeed, extra-constitutional, consulting committee whose members were drawn from the five

Czechoslovak political parties that originally participated in the All-National coalition: the Czechoslovak Agrarians, Clericals, National Democrats (*Ceskoslovenská strana národně-demokratická*), National Socialists, and Social Democrats. *Pětka* members acted as liaisons between the coalition parties and the central government, exercising a great influence over parliamentary activities, because their responsibilities included convening the parliament, establishing the length of the session and setting the daily schedule. In addition to the *Pětka*, a loose, but influential group known as the *Hrad* (castle), after the president's official residence, the Hradčany, had grown up around President Masaryk. Members of the group included politicians from various parties as well as persons with no political affiliation. What members had in common was their support of Masaryk.

The Czechoslovak Agrarians and National Democrats, who occupied increasingly important ministerial positions, were not easily pressured into making further concessions to the working class. The few social reforms enacted during this time tended to reflect both the nationalistic policies of those two parties and their belief that perhaps too much social reform had been legislated already. Agrarian influence on Czechoslovakia's economic policy—both foreign and domestic—favored its primarily Czech and Slovak rural constituency at the expense of industrial workers in general, and of the Sudeten German workers, dependent on favorable trade tariffs for their luxury exports, in particular. Due to the economic problems of Czechoslovakia's two main trading partners, Austria and Germany, Sudeten German products also suffered on the international market. Further, the uneven development of the Czechoslovak economy during this period also adversely affected many sectors of the sensitive Sudeten German economy. The First Republic's inheritance of some forty-three percent of the prewar Monarchy's industrial force and just twenty-seven percent of its population was a mixed blessing; Czechoslovakia had an internal market of about 13 million people in contrast to Austria-Hungary's 52 million. In the immediate postwar period, many industrial workers, particularly German, were thrown out of work because the country could neither absorb nor export all that they produced.

Czechoslovakia's foreign policy goals, as envisioned by Foreign Minister Edvard Beneš, a nominal member of the Czechoslovak National Socialist Party, were generally at odds with the tenets of social democracy, in particular those of the DSAP. The Czechoslovak Social Democratic Party's continued support of Beneš's foreign policy was a point of contention between the Czechoslovak and German Social Democrats. The latter regarded Czechoslovakia's pro-French, pro-Entente foreign policy as imperialistic. They opposed the Versailles Treaty and the accompanying war reparations, not to mention the 1923 Franco-Belgian occupation of the Ruhr, as anti-German. They also considered the Czechs anti-Soviet for failing to recognize the communist government in Moscow.

The international situation eased somewhat during 1924 with the fall of Raymond Poincaré's conservative government in France and the adoption of the Dawes Plan in the same year, which fixed German war reparations and ended the Ruhr crisis. The replacement of Wilhelm Cuno's right-wing German government with one led by Gustav Stresemann and changes in other European governments, also eased tensions. Stresemann's foreign policies ushered in a new period of international cooperation, the high point of which was the signing of the multilateral Locarno Treaty in October 1925. The treaty provided for the rapprochement of France and Great Britain with Germany as well as the guarantee of Germany's western boundaries by Great Britain and Italy. The same formula was not applied to Germany's eastern border with Czechoslovakia and Poland. France, however, guaranteed Czechoslovak and Polish borders in case of German attack in two bilateral treaties signed at this time. The Czechoslovak-French treaty was to form the backbone of Beneš's foreign policy throughout the interwar era, and Czechoslovak policy remained officially pro-French and unofficially, anti-German.[1]

The German Social Democrats in the Post-Revolutionary Era

It was under these difficult conditions that the German Social Democrats undertook the complicated task of rebuilding the party following the events of 1920-1921. In addition to taking stock of its internal situation and attempting to recoup losses, the DSAP defined and developed its relationship with the other most important working class parties, the Czechoslovak Communists and Social Democrats, both at the local and the national level. The German Social Democrats also participated in the Socialist International, which had been reestablished in March 1923.

As members of a non-coalition minority party, the German Social Democrats had only limited ability to pursue legislation. Most of the party's parliamentary activity in this period thus was in opposing or attempting to modify legislation deemed harmful to its constituency. Special emphasis was placed on land reform and nationality rights.

The party's local organizations had begun concerning themselves with Lenin's 21 Points and membership in the Communist International during the first half of 1921. As early as February 1921, specially-called communal elections in the western Bohemian towns of Eger and Ober-Leutensdorf had shown that the division of the party and the subsequent formation of the Czechoslovak Communist Party cost the party both members and voter support. The DSAP lost mandates to parties on both its left and right. It was not until 1922 and 1923 that the party officially began to assess its losses. The extent of the damage caused by the internecine struggle within the working class became clear in September 1923, when communal elections were finally held throughout Czechoslovakia. These had been originally scheduled for 1922, but were delayed due to the social unrest that accompanied the economic downturn of 1922-1923.

Local losses in party membership are attributable to five causes: 1) the influence of local party leaders; 2) the impact of events in neighboring areas, i.e., proximity of radical Saxony to Reichenberg; 3) the difficult local economic and political situation; 4) the influence of local Czech communists; and 5) the general political indifference of the working class once the revolutionary period was over. There appears to be no direct correlation between the level of industrialization in a region and the size of German Social Democratic losses. The communists made gains at their expense both in highly industrialized areas and less industrialized ones. The organizational and political ability of communist agitators seems to have been more important. Outside the Reichenberg distrist (*Kreis*), which was entirely lost to the German Social Democrats, decrease in membership varied from county to county and, indeed, within the counties themselves. Figures on losses of party members are incomplete and losses can be only roughly estimated. District organization reports to the party congresses of 1921, 1923, 1925, and 1927 as well as membership figures listed in the proceedings of these congresses, provide the best basis for estimates, although it can be assumed that the social democratic organizations played down their losses as much as possible. The district organization reports sometimes included specific information on decline in membership: location, numbers, occupation, trade union affiliation. Total numerical losses suffered by the German Social Democrats were the subject of some dispute. Contemporary estimates range from the party's optimistic twenty-five percent to the communists' and other parties' gleeful predictions of its imminent demise. Membership dropped from an interwar high of more than 120,000 in 1920 to 103,000 in mid-1921, and stood at 78,000 by mid-1922, a loss of some thirty-five percent. The party never regained its overwhelming strength of the immediate postwar period.[2]

The primary explanation of the DSAP for its membership losses outside Reichenberg was that the majority of those who left the party during this period were not loyal, long-time party members, but "November Socialists" who had joined the DSAP in the immediate postwar period due to discontent with other parties. These people lacked political education and experience and were thus likely to change party allegiance.[3] Given the great increase in DSAP membership in the immediate postwar period, this assertion appears, in part, true. The German Social Democrats also accurately claimed that their membership losses were not solely to the benefit of the communists. Support for the budding KSČ often meant the destruction of local DSAP organizations, but not necessarily the creation or maintenance of the communist organization, merely the opportunity for other parties to gain a toehold in what had previously been German Social Democratic political territory.[4] First the internal tension between the party left and right-wings, followed by the division of the party, and finally the agitation of the communists were blamed for both the political indifference of some former social democrats and for defections to the "bourgeois camp."

The German National Socialist Party (*Deutsche nationalsozialistische Arbeiterpartei*, the DNSAP), which also claimed to represent the workers, benefited from the post-1920 social democratic losses as well. The German National Socialists had grown out of the prewar anti-capitalist, anti-Marxist German Workers' Party (*Deutsche Arbeiterpartei*). The anti-Semitism and anti-Czech attitudes of this radical nationalist party had a primarily economic and social rather than racial, basis.[5] The DNSAP's greatest support came from areas of northwestern and western Bohemia where Czech migration was perceived as endangering German jobs. The party was especially popular in the lignite coal region of northwest Bohemia, including Teplitz (see Tables 2-6, 2-7), where beginning in the 1870s, rapid expansion of the coal fields had led to a large increase in population, including a six-fold growth in the number of Czechs, over a fifty year period.[6] Following the demise of the party in 1933, many of the former members supported first the Sudeten German Party and later, Adolf Hitler's Nazis.

German Social Democratic losses were uneven; they varied regionally. In towns where party papers were published, editors played an important role in influencing local social democratic opinion. In Komotau, in western Bohemia, where the local *Volkszeitung* was under the influence of the left,[7] the district organization supported the demands of the Reichenberg left and later defected to the communists; a new German Social Democratic organization had to be founded. On the other hand, northern Moravia's regional German Social Democratic newspaper, *Volkswacht,* dominated by party loyalist Ludwig Morgenstern, played a decisive role in retaining a majority of the German Social Democrats for the DSAP in the face of strong communist challenge.[8] If members of the local party administration or other particularly respected party or trade union officials joined the ranks of the communists, sometimes the entire local organization followed. More often, the existing organization split as the dissident social democrats formed a separate communist organization.

In the cases of highly-industrialized Asch in western Bohemia and the paper factory-dominated town of Böhmisch Krumau in southern Bohemia, most members of the local party organization followed left-wing social democratic leaders over to the Communist Party. In Asch, eleven of the DSAP's twelve communal representatives joined the KSČ. Communist strength ebbed rapidly after 1921, however, and in the 1924 communal elections, Asch communists received only seven mandates as compared to eight for the DSAP.[9] Böhmisch Krumau remained a communist stronghold throughout the interwar period although communist support among both the Czech and German workers in the surrounding area was minimal. In the northwestern Bohemian district of Aussig, where both the social democratic organization and the party paper had been dominated by left-wing social democrats who later joined the Czechoslovak Communist Party, membership losses varied from 18.7 percent in the city of Aussig itself to 86.5 percent in the county of Leitmeritz-Lobositz.[10] The

Leitmeritz-Lobositz organization was smaller than the one in Aussig and the region was predominantly agrarian. Losses were mainly to the German Agrarian Party (*Bund der Landwirte*).

Events in the Reichenberg district organization which until its expulsion had been led by the highly-regarded Karl Kreibich, Otto Hahn, and Alois Neurath, influenced nearby areas, especially small, neighboring textile towns like Zwickau that had strong economic ties to Reichenberg. Revolutionary events in neighboring Saxony exerted some influence on workers in Bohemia. This was particularly true in areas where Sudeten Germans crossed the border to work in Germany. The *Sachsengänger* had experienced both Weimar Germany's initial postwar radicalism and its later hyper-inflation and mass unemployment; the last threatened their own economic existence. Workers in the Bodenbach region of the Teplitz-Schönau district organization, for example, were radicalized by the situation in Germany.[11] This fact was reflected in the influence of both the social democratic left and the independent left in the immediate postwar period.

The local economic situation often played an important role in the workers' enthusiasm for Lenin's theory of immediate revolution. Poorer areas of industrialized Bohemia, which had long suffered from chronic unemployment in the Habsburg Monarchy, and now from mass unemployment in the postwar period, were particularly susceptible to Bolshevik ideology. This was often the case with some of the long-industrialized trades where workers were organized along traditional craft lines and industry was old-fashioned in structure and marginal in profit, but which had been protected from foreign competition by the high customs tariffs of the Habsburg Monarchy. The small textile-producing villages surrounding Reichenberg, where *Heimarbeit* predominated, and a high percentage of female employees—often unorganized—could be found, and nearby Tannwald and Gablonz, where traditional glass blowers worked side by side with modern glass industries, were examples of workers that found communist ideology attractive.

Due to local circumstances, the communists were sometimes unable to penetrate occupational groups that they had radicalized elsewhere. Social democratic trade union members in the mining industry, for example, outnumbered communist trade unionists two to one. In the ethnically-mixed coal-mining area of Ostrau on the Moravian-Silesian border, the communists originally made headway, and badly damaged both the local Czechoslovak and the much smaller German Social Democratic organizations in Schlesisch Ostrau. The Czechoslovak Social Democrats were influenced by the left-wing trade union official Petr Cingr, a former member of the Czech Social Democratic Worker Party, and the miners initially formed the backbone of the Communist Party there. In the larger Mährisch Ostrau, an administrative and steel center as well as a mining area, German Social Democrats were primarily skilled workers who found the Czechoslovak Communist Party less attractive than had the miners of Schlesisch Ostrau. The majority of the Czechoslovak Social Democrats in Mährisch Ostrau, many of whom were also miners, remained in the party, influenced by the moderate Czechoslovak Social Democratic trade unionist Jan Prokeš.

In the Brüx-Dux lignite coal-mining region of northern Bohemia, many of the Czech miners who predominated in the German-administered mines had early come under the influence of the Czech anarcho-communists, for whom Czechoslovak Communist Party discipline was anathema. They supported the Czechoslovak National Socialists in the initial postwar period. Some joined the KSČ, however, after their leaders left the Czechoslovak National Socialists in 1923. German Social Democratic losses in this area tended to be to other German parties rather than to the communists.[12]

Local areas of Czechoslovak Communist Party strength among the Czech and German workers did not necessarily correspond. Czechoslovak Social Democratic leaders in Reichenberg, for example, while sympathizing with Kreibich in 1920, informed him of the lower levels of worker consciousness and sophistication among the Czechs than the Germans there. They pointed out that Czech workers in Reichenberg continued to support the Czechoslovak Social Democratic Party right-wing leadership. That the majority of Czechoslovak Social Democrats from that area continued to support their party becomes clear when the relative loss of voter support among the Czechoslovak and the German Social Democrats in Reichenberg in the 1920 and 1925 parliamentary elections is compared. The German Social Democrats received 22,445 votes, the Czechoslovak Social Democrats 4,208 votes, in the first elections. In 1925, however, support for the German Social Democrats dropped to 6,170 votes, a loss of some seventy-two percent, while support for the Czechoslovak Social Democratic Party dropped to 3,073, a loss of only twenty-seven percent, well under the average of Czechoslovak Social Democratic losses in the election.[13]

Czech workers in Brünn for the most part supported the Czechoslovak Communist Party, while German workers in and around Brünn do not appear to have found the KSČ particularly attractive, although Iglau in neighboring southwest Moravia was considered a communist stronghold among the German workers. According to German Social Democratic reports, however, some eighty percent of the KSČ's German membership in Brünn was neither formerly social democratic nor worker, but students and academics.[14]

In addition to losses in membership, the German Social Democratic Party suffered a significant drop in voter support. This was reflected in the communal elections of 1923, and later in the parliamentary elections of 1925. In general, the DSAP gave the same explanation for electoral losses as it had given for membership losses: the attacks by the communists, the indifference of the workers, and the influence the bourgeois parties exerted on unenlightened workers. Party leaders admitted that their success in the first communal elections had come as a surprise and did not reflect the natural growth of the party. Many who voted for the DSAP in 1919 and 1920 had previously been either politically indifferent or supported bourgeois parties until the end of the Monarchy and were neither socialists nor convinced supporters of class struggle.[15] Finally, German Social Democratic electoral losses were considered a part of a European-wide growth of political reaction.

Far more people voted for German Social Democratic candidates than were members of the party. In the 1920 parliamentary elections, for example, when the party membership was estimated at 120,000, German Social Democratic candidates received 689,589 votes. Party members accounted for slightly more than seventeen percent of the vote, a relatively low membership-voter ratio. This ratio dropped slightly in the 1925 and 1929 parliamentary elections, but rose to twenty-seven percent among a much smaller number of voters in 1935, the last parliamentary election of the interwar period.[16]

The low membership-voter ratio of the DSAP provides a striking contrast to the Austrian Social Democratic Party. In Austria's first postwar elections, some sixty to eighty percent of the votes cast for the Austrian Social Democrats came from party members, and in some places, this figure reached ninety percent. Although the membership-voter ratio had dropped by the 1923 parliamentary elections, almost forty percent of the 1,311,870 votes were still cast by party members, with the percentage rising higher in some areas of Vienna.[17]

Among both Czech and German voters, the respective agrarian parties replaced the social democrats as the most popular political party in 1923. In the case of the Czechoslovak Social Democrats, the replacement was permanent. Both social democratic parties claimed that political infighting and internal disorganization enabled the other parties to gain strength at their expense. This is correct; intra- and interparty strife appears to have repelled the voters of Czechoslovakia throughout the interwar period.

The majority of the Czechoslovak Social Democratic losses were at the hands of the Communist Party. This was not the case with the German Social Democrats, however, whose former constituents were as likely to move into the nationalist as the communist camp. This phenomenon was diagnosed in *Bohemia* as follows:

> As concerns the increase in KSČ votes, one can include the nationally saturated, but economically dissatisfied Czech worker, while the German worker, who has recognized that the international parties can bring him neither national nor economic help, due to the chauvinism of the Czechs, has turned his back on the Marxist parties altogether.[18]

Bohemia also asserted that many Germans supported the German Social Democrats in the earlier elections because the party had presented itself as a bridge between the Czechs and Germans,[19] due to its connections with the brother Czechoslovak Social Democratic Party. There had, however, been little cooperation between the two parties in the early postwar period.

While association with the Czechoslovak Social Democratic Party may have helped the German Social Democratic Party in 1919 and 1920, it was perceived as a hindrance later. Following the communal elections of 1923, the German Social Democrats complained that they had been hurt not only by the political reaction of the time, but also by the Czechoslovak Social Democratic Party's continued participation in the government coalition. The other parties attempted to tie the German and Czechoslovak Social Democrats together and to make the DSAP responsible for the actions of the Czechoslovak Social Democrats.[20]

In 1919, the German Social Democrats alone among the German political parties had extensive regional organizations—dating from the creation in
1907 of a system of provincial representation for the SDAPÖ in Bohemia—
and thus had an advantage over the other German political parties in the
first elections after the war. Although the other German parties, with the
exception of the Agrarians and the DNSAP, had tended to couple lists in
1919 to obtain the maximum possible number of votes, they did not do so
in the communal elections of 1923. The other German parties recovered
from their initial disarray, developing their own regional organizations and
new parties were also formed. The other German parties tended to campaign against the fomerly all-powerful German Social Democrats, whom
they perceived as their main electoral opponent and they attacked the
DSAP's performance in communal administration in particular.

German Social Democratic electoral losses in 1923 varied from area
to area, but did not necessarily correspond to party membership losses.
Social Democratic voter support, as could be expected, dropped noticeably in Reichenberg and surrounding communities, but election figures
appear to support the German Social Democratic contention that the
popularity of the KSČ among the German electorate had peaked between
the 1920 parliamentary elections and the 1923 communal elections. This
assumption is based primarily on the fact that during 1921, numerous
left-leaning German Social Democratic communal officials had defected
to the Communist Party, but their mandates had not necessarily remained in communist hands after the 1923 elections. The contention is supported by a drop in KSČ membership between 1921 and 1923, a drop
likely to be accompanied by a corresponding drop in voter support.[21] The
claim cannot be fully substantiated, however, because the 1923 elections
was the first time that communist candidates participated in general
elections.

The German Agrarians declared themselves the most popular German
party following the communal elections of 1923. The German Social
Democrats disputed this assertion, claiming that the elections did not
accurately reflect DSAP strength, because they had not been held throughout the country. In some of the larger German towns, where the DSAP
could expect to do the best, elections were not to be held until 1924.
In fact, the German Social Democrats lost votes in urban areas to the KSČ

and other German parties (but not to the German Agrarians) in 1924, and Agrarian claim to being the largest German political party would be vindicated in the parliamentary elections of 1925.

A comparison of the communal election results for 1919 and 1923 from the communities of judicial districts (*Gerichtsbezirk, soudní okres*) Reichenberg and Teplitz, both in northern Bohemia, although incomplete, provides a detailed picture of German Social Democratic voting losses. (See Tables 2-1 to 2-7.) Reichenberg, with a population of about 35,000 was the second largest German city in Czechoslovakia. The Reichenberg judicial district, located on the Czech-German language border, included one community with a Czech majority, Ober-Rosenthal. Teplitz, a heavy industry and coal mining center, had a population of some 28,000. Most German Social Democrats in Teplitz, home of former party chairman Seliger, had supported the party leadership at the 1920 Karlsbad Congress. A relatively large city by Sudeten German standards, Teplitz and the surrounding communities that made up the judicial district all had German majorities.

In the 1919 elections, the German Social Democrats scored overwhelming victories in both judicial districts. They won a majority of the German mandates in 20 communities out of 31 in Reichenberg and in 18 out of the 28 in Teplitz for which figures are available.

The German Social Democrats suffered major losses in both Reichenberg and Teplitz in 1923, where they received only six percent and twenty percent of the vote, respectively. In judicial district Reichenberg, the Czechoslovak Communists made obvious inroads at the expense of the German Social Democrats, while the German bourgeois parties and the German National Socialists made lesser gains. As the figures for the Czech parties are less specific, it is difficult to assess parallel Czechoslovak Social Democratic losses in Reichenberg. The DSAP, however, won a majority of mandates in just one of the twenty-five communities for which statistics are available. The KSČ gained a majority in three and a plurality in nine of the communities in the district.

More Czech and German political parties campaigned in Teplitz in 1923 than in 1919. The German Social Democrats gained a majority of mandates in only three of the twenty-two communities in which elections were held, and a plurality in seven. They maintained the same number of mandates as before in only one community, though they lost votes there. The

Czechoslovak Communist Party either did not campaign or failed to win mandates in eleven communities. According to available figures, where both parties campaigned, the KSČ received more mandates once, with an eight to seven ratio of communist-social democratic mandates.

The big winner in Teplitz appears to have been the German National Socialists, who in 1919 received mandates in only four of the 28 communities for which statistics are available, while in 1923, they won mandates in eight of the 22 communities where elections were held. Although the German National Socialists nowhere won a majority of mandates, they did win a plurality in Weisskirchlitz, where the German Social Democrats had previously won fifteen of thirty mandates.

In German-speaking areas of Moravia, where earlier support for the German Social Democrats had not been so strong as in Bohemia, the DSAP also lost ground; less to the KSČ or the more nationalist parties, the German Nationalists (*Deutsche Nationalpartei,* the DNP) and the German National Socialists, than to the German Christian Socialist People's Party (*Deutsche christlichsoziale Volkspartei*), popularly known as the German Clericals.

In Ruthenia and Slovakia, where communal elections were held for the first time in 1923, the Czechoslovak Communist Party was very successful. The KSČ remained a major political force in backward, rural Ruthenia throughout the interwar period and communist support there was primarily at the expense of the Czechoslovak Social Democrats. The DSAP had few voters in either Ruthenia or Slovakia, although it established a county organization in Pressburg, the provincial capital of Slovakia.

The German Social Democrats recognized that the Czechoslovak Communists were not their only, and in many cases, even their primary competition. The various German bourgeois parties and the German National Socialist Party, which continued to mount common assault on the DSAP, were attractive to some of the DSAP's constituency. In northern and western Bohemia, the German National Socialists and the German Agrarians, in southern Bohemia and especially in Moravia, the German Social Democrats' traditional opponents, the German Clericals, provided effective opposition to the DSAP.

That the German Social Democrats continued to lose voter support was reflected in the 15 November 1925 parliamentary elections in which the agrarian, clerical and communist parties triumphed at the expense of the social democratic parties, following the pattern established in the 1923 communal elections. Some 907,379 more ballots were cast in the 1925 elections than in the 1920 elections, as Czechoslovak citizens voted for 300 deputies rather than the 281 elected in 1920 (the first parliamentary elections had taken place in Ruthenia in March 1924). The Czechoslovak Communist Party emerged as the second strongest party overall, with 13.2 percent or 934,223 votes and 41 mandates, just 35,000 votes and four mandates fewer than the Czechoslovak Agrarians.[22] Its gains, like those in the 1923 elections, were primarily at the expense of the Czechoslovak Social Democrats.

The communists and the social democrats vied for the support of the same constituency. The combined parliamentary support for the communist and social democratic parties in the former crownlands corresponded closely to the number of votes the social democrats had received in 1920. In absolute figures, the vote rose in proportion to the increase in the size of the electorate. A breakdown of the vote by nationality, though not fully accurate, shows communist strength in Bohemia to be the greatest in Czech judicial districts, where the KSČ won 13.6 percent of the vote. In the German judicial districts of Bohemia, the KSČ averaged 9.6 percent of the vote.[23]

The combined percentage of the vote won by the German political parties in the 1920 and 1925 elections was 25.5 and 24.0 percent, respectively. The German bourgeois parties, except the German Democratic Freedom Party, which did not campaign in the 1925 elections, increased their percentage of the votes, supporting the contention that German Social Democratic voting losses were to the right rather than to the left.[24]

The Party Organization

Although the inauspicious economic and political situation slowed the recovery of the German Social Democratic Party following its division, regrouping was further hindered by structural problems specific to the DSAP. Unlike the Weimar German Social Democrats, who had Berlin; the Austrian Social Democrats, who had "Red" Vienna; or the Czechoslovak Social Democrats, who had Prague; the Sudeten German Social Democrats lacked a geographic center. The decision to move the party headquarters from Teplitz to the Weinberge (Vinohrady) district of Prague following the death of party chairman Josef Seliger reflected the city's importance as the center of Czechoslovakia's political life. Only a fraction of the DSAP's constituency lived there, however, mainly department store and party employees, as well as officials of the German insurance company, rather than industrial workers. Relocating the party headquarters in the nation's capital isolated, to a certain extent, the party administration and leadership from the daily concerns of the party members. Often party functionaries were too busy in Prague to make the trips to the border regions necessary to keep them in close contact with their constituency.

A central party newspaper, *Sozialdemokrat,* designed to replace the Viennese *Arbeiter Zeitung* began appearing in Prague in September 1921. A central party paper had been mandated at both the 1919 and 1920 party congresses, but the division of the party provided the actual impetus for the founding of the paper. German Social Democracy saw its party newspapers—many of which folded due to financial troubles in the period following the party's division—as an important means of combating the other political parties, which also attempted to influence public opinion by means of their respective political presses. In 1924, the leaders of the DSAP voted to unify the entire German Social Democratic press as a defensive measure against attacks from the other parties. This action enforced press uniformity and hindered heresies or even constructive criticism, such as occurred during 1920-1921. Each newspaper, however, continued to provide local news.

While the party headquarters and the main newspaper were located in Prague, the trade union center was in Reichenberg. Some trade unions also maintained headquarters in Reichenberg, with others located in Aussig and Teplitz, near their members.

The central party secretary was one of the most powerful persons in the party, not least because he held the purse strings of the central organization. He directed party functions through the secretaries of the various district organizations. One-time Teplitz *Freiheit* editor Karl Čermak was party secretary until his death in 1924; he was succeeded by the Moravian-born Siegfried Taub, director of the Brünn Workers' Heath Insurance Fund, who held the post for the rest of the interwar period.

District organizations, which corresponded roughly to national electoral districts, dictated the activities of the smaller county and local organizations, each district secretary functioning similarly to the party secretary, but with a more limited area of competence. The role of the district secretary was important, because parliamentary campaigns were organized at that level. The district secretary had to be well acquainted with party members in his organization as he helped choose the delegates to party congresses and recommended promising local members for party positions. The district secretary was not necessarily the most important political figure in his area. Reichenberg, for instance, was dominated throughout the interwar period by parliamentary deputy Anton Roscher, head of both the central trade union commission and the textile workers union as well. Since half of the officials in the district were members of the textile union and the others were personally obligated to Roscher, it was not a good idea of ambitious local party functionaries to come into conflict with him.

In addition to the party organization, district offices housed the local German Social Democratic women's and youth organizations and other party-related activities that had been established there. Many district organizations published a local party newspaper, and its offices, as well as those of social democratic trade unions, were also found in the party district headquarters.

Although women in Czechoslovakia gained the right to vote under the free, equal franchise enacted in 1918, their participation in prewar Austrian politics had been limited; until 1912, paragraph thirty of the Austrian organizations law (*Vereingesetze*) forbade participation in political groups by foreigners, juveniles, and women. Such restrictions were not limited to the Monarchy; similar laws had also existed in Wilhelmine Germany until 1908. Exposure to social democratic ideas was mainly limited to those females who worked in factories in cities or industrial areas.

The influence of the "Kirche, Küche und Kinder" ideology prevalent in middle class Austria-Hungary was also dominant in many poverty stricken working class families. It served to discourage female participation in working class politics. The working class family, its structure often rent by the stress of alcoholism, low life expectancy and venereal disease, remained patriarchial. So did the work place, where women had less desirable, less well paying jobs. Although socialist theory was committed to the emancipation of women, the attitude of many social democratic men seems to have been ambivalent. Complaints were made that cheap female labor was a major obstacle to the economic advancement of the working class; there were even calls for the exclusion of women from the work place. The law, prevalent social attitudes, and familial demands on their time appear to have discouraged female participation in social democratic politics.[25]

The German Social Democrats championed abortion, equal pay, health care, public housing, and child and youth welfare. The party condemned prostitution, alcoholism, and other social problems that played havoc in the family life of their proletarian constituency, especially the females. Although consistently comprising some 28 to 30 percent of the German Social Democratic Party rank and file, women were seldom moving forces within the party. The few women in the upper echelons of the party did not have the political influence of the male social democratic leaders. Women's names were found on party voting lists far less often than their numbers would have warranted; when they did appear, women almost never led the lists or were even ranked among the first five candidates. Three women served in parliament during the interwar period, where they voted as a bloc with the rest of the party deputies. The Czechoslovak Agrarian, Communist, National Socialist, and Social Democratic parties also elected female parliamentary representatives.

Women were seldom found in the middle level of the German Social Democratic Party administration. Party county and district secretaries were almost exclusively male, as were the majority of the delegates to party congresses. Women delegates tended to be appointed rather than elected; they were often party parliamentary representatives and high-level officials who automatically attended the congresses by virtue of their position. Some women active in the party were the wives of high party officials, including Lilly Czech, who shared her husband Ludwig's interest in youth welfare. Long-time German Social Democratic youth leader Karl Kern met his wife at a social democratic youth group outing and during the early years of their marriage, one of their shared responsibilities was spending one evening a week working at the local social democratic bookstore. Women participated in party activities except the party defense organization, *Republikanische Wehr*. Two women's magazines, *Frauenwelt* and *Gleichheit,* designed to appeal to female party members were published throughout the interwar period.

The three former provincial organizations of the SDAPÖ that had been fused in 1919 to form the DSAP had little or no prewar tradition of co-operation; during the Monarchy all party business had been conducted through the Vienna headquarters. The amalgamation of the provincial parties required recognition of and sensitivity to the various regional problems faced by the DSAP's constituency. The postwar integration of the provincial organizations was complicated by the deaths of several experienced party leaders between 1920 and 1926. In addition to Seliger and Čermak, Wilhelm Kiesewetter—senator, long-time editor of the *Trautenauer Echo,* and party warhorse—died in 1925; and Oswald Hillebrand, Silesian-born parliamentary deputy and party executive committee member, died after a long illness in 1926.

With the deaths of Čermak, Hillebrand, and Seliger, upper level party leadership passed into the hands of German Social Democrats from Moravia, especially from Brünn. In addition to party chairman Ludwig Czech and party secretary Taub, former typesetter Wilhelm Niessner, also from Brünn, served as editor of the *Sozialdemokrat* from 1921 to 1935. Niessner, along with Czech, was a leader of the SDAPÖ Moravian provincial organization in the prewar period. Trade unionist Theodor Hackenberg, a Brünn-born parliamentary deputy who had served in the *Reichsrat,* was also influential in the party. The upper echelon of the party was not limited to Moravians; lawyer Carl Heller, scion of a wealthy Teplitz Jewish family, as well as senator and party treasurer, rounded out the inner group of the DSAP leadership.

As German-Czech relations were better in Moravia than in Bohemia, what effect, if any, the leadership's Moravian background had on German Social Democratic politics, particularly nationality politics, has been the subject of some discussion. Since the Second World War, some former party members have asserted that the Moravians were not so sensitive to the nationality problems in northwest Bohemia as they should have been, or as Bohemian politicians would have been. Particularly those disparaging Czech's leadership have expressed regret at the untimely deaths of Čermak, Hillebrand and Seliger, which allowed the leadership of the DSAP to "fall into the hands" of the Moravians. It is incorrect to speak of the party leadership as passing from a Bohemian triumvirate (Čermak [he was Viennese], Hillebrand, Seliger) to a Moravian one (Czech, Niessner, Taub), because all of these men were products of the much larger prewar SDAPÖ.

One thing did differentiate the Moravians in the DSAP from their Bohemian counterparts; they were much more often able to speak Czech.

It is true that many leading German Social Democratic politicians, especially in the 1920s, came from outside the provinces in which they now lived. In the Austrian Social Democratic Party, where the older party leaders had begun their careers, it was not uncommon for functionaries to move from one province to another, with Vienna rather than Prague, the center of their political world. Many outstanding Austrian Social Democratic leaders, including Victor Adler, Anton Hueber and Karl Renner, had originally come from Bohemia or Moravia. The reverse was also true: a number of important German Social Democratic politicians, including Čermak, were natives of Vienna.

Throughout the 1920s the Austrian Social Democratic Party was an intellectual and political focal point for the DSAP, which did not have any social democratic intellectuals comparable to Bauer or Renner. The Austrian Social Democratic publication, *Der Kampf,* remained the theoretical periodical of the German Social Democrats until 1928, when the DSAP began publication of *Tribüne.* Further ties existed because party members who had been trained in a trade had often apprenticed in Vienna and a number of those in the free professions had studied there.

Although the former Moravian and Silesian organizations were well represented in the party executive committee during the interwar period,[26] party attention tended to focus on northern Bohemia. This region, with its large industrial working class, political explosiveness and underlying nationalist animosities, possessed more, larger, better organized, and usually wealthier county organizations than elsewhere. Northern Bohemia also provided a majority of the party's middle-level functionaries, including those giving educational and organizational assistance to poorer and less well organized groups in other parts of the country. This well-intended assistance was not always appreciated. According to a party member from a small town in Moravia:

> He is perhaps more able than we. But when a comrade from northern Bohemia comes to us in the rural southern Moravian communities, he hinders us more than he helps us. It is the same as if a Prussian were to be sent to Bavaria.[27]

Communal Administration

Within the German Social Democratic Party, the value of a social democratic majority or plurality in a commune became a topic of discussion. Following the 1919 elections, the DSAP had recognized that the election of social democratic communal representatives was of limited value at a time when the administrative competence of the community was shrinking.[28] The DSAP's calls for communal autonomy were in vain against the centralizing tendencies of the Czechoslovak government, which the party perceived as having a pro-Czech, anti-working class bias. Governmental restrictions on communal autonomy were interpreted as an attempt to offset any possible radical changes legislated by working-class administrations elected from industrial suburbs or villages. The restrictions also provided the central government with the means of controlling rebellious minority administrations if necessary.

In 1919, the German Social Democrats had a majority in some communes and DSAP mayors were elected in Aussig, Bodenbach, Rothau, Fischern, and Warnsdorf in Bohemia, as well as Freiwaldau and Jägerndorf in Silesia, and Sternberg in Moravia.

The achievements of the social democratic administration in the "socialist Mecca" of Vienna were emulated by the local German Social Democratic officials. In Aussig, strides were made in housing construction as well as in cultural and educational matters under German Social Democratic mayor Leopold Pölzl. The improvements in social welfare that could be made by a social democratic communal administration were demonstrated in Altrohlau, a small community near Karlsbad. Between 1919 and 1927, a DSAP majority built public housing, modernized the water supply system, installed electricity, and renovated and expanded the schools.

A fortnightly periodical, *Die freie Gemeinde,* was founded in 1919 in an attempt to coordinate social democratic policies at the local level. It was to provide German Social Democratic communal representatives with information on the party's attitude toward and policies for communal administration. Nevertheless, the DSAP lacked a coordinated plan for approaching communal politics between 1919 and 1921; a common program for communal administration was adopted only at the December 1921 party congress. Not all German Social Democratic communal representatives subscribed to *Die freie Gemeinde* and this remained a point of contention within the party. Further, some communal representatives elected on the German Social Democratic list failed to follow party policy at all.

The German Social Democrats faced major financial problems in communal administration during the first electoral period: the miserable financial situation inherited by many communes, especially Sudeten German ones, due to wartime purchases of imperial war bonds, and the loss of further communal assets held by Viennese banks through Czechoslovakia's currency reform of February 1919.

Local social democratic power was further curtailed by the right of the politically-appointed provincial administration to dissolve communal administration under a variety of circumstances. This measure was used when the refusal of the bourgeois parties to cooperate with social democratic representatives led to a stalemate in communal administration, a not uncommon occurrence. The German Social Democrats sometimes cooperated on the local level with representatives of the various working-class parties and even with some of the bourgeois parties, but administrative and legal limitations, combined with a lack of administrative experience, did not enhance the DSAP's performance in governing at the local level.

The German Social Democrats and the All-National Coalition

The entry of German political parties into the government coalition was delayed until October 1926. Czechoslovakia's first multinational government was formed only after three tasks, all reflecting Czech national interests, were complete. They were: land reform, enacted most extensively between 1923 and 1926; regulations for the enforcement of existing language laws in February 1926; and the transfer of the civil service into overwhelmingly Czech hands, a process that occurred primarily between 1923 and 1926.

By late 1924, some Germans began to consider participation in the coalition. This willingness was signalled by the division of the German Union (*Deutscher Verband*), a body that included all the bourgeois German parties represented in parliament, into two groups. Those willing to work with the government became part of the "Association for Work" (*Arbeitsgemeinschaft*), the Activists; those opposed to cooperation with the government became part of the "Association for Struggle" (*Kampf-gemeinschaft*), the Negativists. The German Social Democrats belonged to neither group. They maintained that participation in a bourgeois coalition was a violation of Marxist principles, but they tried to distinguish their position from that of the Negativists, who opposed the existence of the Czechoslovak state.

The German Social Democrats favored land reform both in theory and in practice. Recognizing the necessity of transfering the estates of the church and the nobility into the hands of small landowners and landless peasants, they had stressed the need for land reform at party congresses. Party leaders were not, however, in favor of land reform as carried out in Czechoslovakia between 1923 and 1926, which they interpreted as an attempt to colonize the country's non-Czech regions.[29]

Government application of the land reform law of April 1919 had two objectives in addition to the redistribution of land: retribution for the land seized from the indigenous Bohemian nobility after its defeat at White Mountain in 1620 and provision for strategic defense. The government did not want forests on the Czechoslovak borders to remain in the hands of German and Hungarian estate owners whose loyalty was questionable, especially in the eyes of the conservative, nationalist members of the coalition.

Those of Czech origin were the main beneficiaries of the land redistribution. The officials in charge do not appear to have taken into consideration the fate of those—both small farmers and factory workers—who had long rented land on the former German and Hungarian estates. In many areas, German workers from industrial villages kept a pig or a few chickens on small plots of land rented from the local large landowners. These people were often displaced by the postwar sale of German estates. The dislocation of the German small farmer caught the attention of all German political parties, as did the migration of Czech peasants into formerly German or Hungarian areas as a result of the land office's activities. Opposition was, however, of little avail.

The Czechoslovak language law of February 1926 provided for the expansion of "Czechoslovak" as the state language. Language provisions had been laid down on 28 October 1918 and detailed in a series of laws between that date and 29 February 1920. The original decrees had not extended to all branches of the government. Some Czech nationalist politicians believed that the failure to apply this law to the defense, education, foreign, post, railroad, and welfare ministries signified noncompliance with the original law, which called for common regulation of all government officials. The law of 1926, in addition to expanding language regulations to include all areas of the government, designated some heretofore private professions as organs of the government. These included surveyors, authorized civil and mining engineers, and community and district doctors.[30] Only those who spoke Czech or Slovak could be employed by the government. In addition, Czechs and Slovaks living in communities with over 3,000 residents could demand that petitions and announcements be made in their own language, while the same right was extended to members of the national minorities only if at least twenty percent of the residents of a community were members of that minority.[31] This requirement excluded the 40,000 Germans residing in Prague and some ten percent of the German population in Czechoslovakia was thus unable to conduct official business in its native tongue. Czech and Slovak politicians correctly noted, however, that the nationalist laws and practices of the First Republic were still more tolerant than those of neighboring countries.

The expansion of the language law and other "reactionary" measures of the goverment met with protests throughout the Sudeten lands. As had been the case in the demonstrations of March 1919, complaints were both national and social in nature. The German Social Democrats opposed the language law as a "torment" for civil servants, one that placed extraordinary pressure on the communities, especially minority ones. It was pointed out that some 980 German communes in which no votes had been cast for Czech political parties in the most recent commnal elections in 1923 would be obliged to provide the required services for Czechs and Slovaks in their own tongues.[32] German Social Democratic newspapers condemned the curtailment of the use of minority languages as an unconstitutional attack in the sphere of civil rights, one that was intolerable for the nation's minorities.[33] In sharp criticism of the Czechoslovak Social Democrats' support of the law, the DSAP central organ, *Sozialdemokrat,* commented that it was difficult to understand why axioms that applied to Czech workers did not apply to German workers or why the Czech worker's struggle to use his native tongue was a socialist battle, while the Sudeten German worker's struggle for the same privilege was a nationalist one.[34]

In 1923 and 1924, the government began to reduce the bloated bureaucracy of the civil service and to place it overwhelmingly in the hands of Czechs. At the end of 1924, a law reducing the number of state employees was passed. Provisions were made for the paid retirement of civil servants with more than ten years' service, but those employed less than ten years could be summarily dismissed. During this period, postal and railroad workers were tested for their knowledge of the state language. Those who failed to exhibit the required level of proficiency lost their jobs. Combined with the general reduction of civil service positions, this caused the loss of some 16,000 German railroad jobs over a four year period. Between the end of 1921 and 1925, the number of German railroad employees dropped from twenty-two to sixteen percent, well below the percentage of Germans in the general population.[35] The reduction of civil service positions, as well as the exclusion of those Germans who did not speak the state language from the civil service, was interpreted by the Germans as another government attack on minorities. Although the position of the minorities in the civil service was later to improve somewhat, the increased influence of the Germans never approached their proportion of the population.[36]

Writing in the mid-1960s, lawyer-historian Johann W. Brügel, long-time secretary to DSAP chairman Czech, claimed that there had been no rigid or automatic replacement of German officials by Czech ones. Due to their general lack of knowledge of the Czech language, Germans were more affected by the overall reduction of civil servants in the mid-1920s. His assertion contradicts the opinions German Social Democrats expressed at the time, and in fact, the comprehensive application of the language law guaranteed the dismissal of many German civil servants.[37]

An added source of Czech-German friction during this period was a government decision to rationalize the educational system in Czechoslovakia, which involved cutting the number of German classrooms and closing some German schools. The process, which had already begun in 1919, was accelerated in 1925. The primary reasons given for the government's actions were the drop in the postwar German birthrate and the desire to make reparations for the inferior status of the Czech schools under the Habsburg Monarchy.[38] All of the German political parties opposed this attack on German cultural life. It was a sensitive point for the German Social Democrats because Education Minister Ivan Marković was a Czechoslovak Social Democrat.

It is true that many of the German schools affected were grammar schools, often old and poorly attended, and in what had by then become purely Czech areas. Closure was resented as a tool of "denationalization," however, because it was sometimes accompanied by the building of new Czech schools for only a few Czech children in predominantly German areas.[39]

Throughout the life of the all-national coalition, the German Social Democrats, along with the other German political parties, opposed the majority of the legislation enacted. Pains were taken, however, to differentiate DSAP policy from that of the other German parties, with the DSAP always attempting to couch its position in terms of its obligations as a social democratic and international working class party.

Interparty Relations: The German Social Democrats and the Czechoslovak Social Democrats

The last year before the breakup of the all-national coalition in 1926, with growing strain between the various Czechoslovak parties, and converse rapprochement of bourgeois parties of differing nationalities, did not result in a corresponding rapproachement between the Czechoslovak and German Social Democrats. German Social Democratic accusations of non-internationalist behavior were met by counter-accusations of nationalist and reactionary alliances. Czechoslovakia's two major social democratic parties charged each other of the same crime using the same party rhetoric.

The German Social Democrats, taking the point of view that a strong, united socialist opposition would be more successful politically than the fragmented movement that then existed, called on their Czechoslovak counterparts to go into opposition. The Czechoslovak Social Democrats declined, enumerating their achievements and arguing that their presence in the government coalition had hindered attempts by "nationalist and capitalist" elements to pursue more extreme measures at the expense of the working class.[40] They felt that through their influence on the writing of the nation's constitution, which had in fact been primarily the work of Czechoslovak Social Democratic lawyer Alfréd Meissner, they had been able to demand more concessions for the national minorities than would have otherwise been the case.[41] Finally, the Czechoslovak Social Democrats asserted that the rights of the national minorities were defended by the Minority Treaty of the Paris Peace Conference, not to mention that minorities had the recourse of complaint to the League of Nations. The Czechoslovak Social Democrats said they would have been happy had they had such rights under the Habsburgs.[42]

The parallel growth of Czech Social Democratic politics and Czech national consciousness is clearly reflected in the Czechoslovak Social Democrats' continued support of the government. They felt themselves a part of the state and believed that their presence in the government coalition was necessary, even at the expense of a break with the other social democratic parties in Czechoslovakia.

The Czechoslovak Social Democrats accused the German Social Democrats of widening the gap between the two parties through cooperation with the most reactionary political parties in the republic, the German Negativists. The accusation was unfair as the principled Marxist opposition of the DSAP to the politics of the government coalition was not the same thing as the categorical opposition of the German Negativists to the existence of the Czechoslovak state.

Although speeches by some leading Czechoslovak Social Democrats at their April 1924 party congress in Ostrau showed their willingness to improve relations with the German Social Democrats, rapprochement did not occur at this time. Relations, in fact, worsened. The two parties were constantly at odds over the question of continued Czechoslovak Social Democratic participation in the coalition government.

The low point for Czechoslovak-German Social Democratic relations during this period, perhaps during the entire interwar era, began in autumn 1924, a time of economic and political tension in Czechoslovakia. The dismissal of German workers, in part due to the stiff language law requirements, in part due to the general streamlining of the civil service, was made worse by an unrelated, but noticeable increase in the cost of living.

The German Social Democratic parliamentary deputies chose not to participate in the planning of the next year's national budget in protest of the dismissal of some 7,000 German railroad employees. The other German political parties followed their example.

Bitter polemics became the daily fare of the respective social democratic party organs. The Czechoslovak Social Democrats felt that the task of the German Social Democrats was to work for economic and social reform and to imbue the proletariat with a sense of class consciousness and socialism.[43] The DSAP tactic of passive opposition in parliament was condemned in *Právo lidu* as the final step in the alienation of the Czech and German Social Democrats. The passive opposition of the DSAP was, somewhat unfairly, compared with the obstructionist, inkwell tossing tactics of the reactionary parties in the *Reichsrat* during the Habsburg Monarchy.[44] That both the Czech parties of all political persuasions and the Austrian Social Democrats had also indulged in such behavior in the *Reichsrat* went unmentioned.

The above is but one illustration of the gulf that separated the Czechoslovak and German Social Democrats, due primarily to their divergent attitudes toward the Czechoslovak state and, consequently, toward the nationality problems within it. The Czechoslovak Social Democrats consistently reminded the German Social Democrats that the German position in Czechoslovakia was not nearly so difficult as the Czech position had been in Austria. They do not appear to have taken into consideration that most Germans perceived their position in "democratic" Czechoslovakia to be worse than it had been in "nondemocratic" Austria. The Germans in Czechoslovakia were obliged to regard themselves as a minority within a Czechoslovak state, and they did not like it.

In terms of working class solidarity, the Czechoslovak and German Social Democratic trade unions were ahead of their affiliated parties. Beginning in October 1924, leaders of the two trade union commissions, under the auspices of the Federation of Trade Unions, began negotiations for the creation of a single social democratic trade union commission. Meetings continued sporadically and resulted in the creation of a single national trade union center in Prague by February 1927.

The International

An important step in the long-term rapprochement of the two social democratic parties was the May 1923 creation of a new Socialist International in Hamburg through the unification of the Second International and the Vienna Union. The reunification of the rump USPD with the SPD in Weimar Germany in late 1922 had provided the impetus for its foundation. The formation of the new International followed failed negotiations between the Second International, the Vienna Union, and the Moscow-based Third International in 1922.

Strained relations between those parties that had been represented in the Second International—they tended to be more conservative and included the Czechoslovak Social Democrats—and the Vienna Union—to which the DSAP belonged—were not immediately eased.

Party Secretary Čermak, one of the German Social Democratic delegates to the Hamburg Congress, did not hesitate to accuse publicly the Czechoslovak Social Democrats of grave offenses against the cultural, economic, and political interests of the entire organized working class of Czechoslovakia.[45] His speech reflected the frustration of German Social Democratic leaders with Czechoslovak Social Democratic refusal to heed their calls for a united working class opposition to the "anti-proletarian, capitalist, imperialist, militarist" government of Czechoslovakia.[46] DSAP representatives felt that the Czechoslovak Social Democrats had committed a long list of sins against the basic obligations of any social democratic party to working-class solidarity. Two were of especial significance: one involved foreign, the other domestic, policy.

The Czechoslovak Social Democrats, alone among Europe's social democratic parties, had rejected decisions by both Internationals and the Federation of Trade Unions and had supported the French imperialist occupation of the Ruhr. In so doing, Czechoslovak Social Democracy supported the policy of Foreign Minister Beneš, who had recently signed a bilateral treaty with France. In addition, Czechoslovak Social Democrats had supported the Law for the Defense of the Republic, enacted during April 1923 in the wake of the assassination of Finance Minister Alois Rašín. This law, with its long list of capital crimes, had been opposed by the German Social Democrats, who considered it neither socialist nor democratic, as well as by the Czechoslovak Communists, who had perceived it as aimed at themselves.

The German and Hungarian Social Democrats of Czechoslovakia presented a joint memorandum to the newly-created International criticizing the relationship of the Czechoslovak Social Democratic Party to the other social democratic parties in the country. The memorandum focused on the splintered Czechoslovak working class, a large part in the communist camp, another in various social democratic opposition parties and the rest, separate from the others, in a government party. The contradictory situation was viewed as pushing more and more workers into indifference, with the same situation existing in the cooperatives and the trade unions.[47]

The Czechoslovak Social Democrats considered the memorandum to be an inappropriate airing of dirty domestic laundry in an international forum. They argued that Czechoslovak domestic policy was not the business of other members of the International, who because of their distance from Prague, could not accurately assess the domestic situation. They further believed that the German Social Democratic Party had taken advantage of the fact that Czech was not a world language to misrepresent the internal situation in Czechoslovakia.[48] The Czechoslovak Social Democrats defended their participation in the government to the International in the same terms that they had used to defend it to the DSAP: their presence had helped to improve the situation of the entire working class of Czechoslovakia, including Germans, Magyars, Poles, and Ruthenians, especially in a time of increasing world reaction.[49]

Czechoslovak Social Democratic complaints about German Social Democratic behavior at the International were exaggerated. The German Social Democrats believed that Czechoslovakia's problems, especially minority problems, were international problems like the Ruhr occupation, on which the International had taken a position: against the use of force on foreign peoples and for the unlimited right to self-determination. Further, the DSAP felt that the Czechoslovak Social Democrats ought to recognize that as members of an international working class organization, they should act voluntarily within the bounds acceptable to the organization.[50]

If the Czechoslovak Social Democrats were displeased with the behavior of the German Social Democrats at the Hamburg Conference, they were also unhappy at the sympathetic reaction of international social democracy to the Germans' complaints. Following the conference, a series of articles appeared in the Czechoslovak Social Democratic press that made it clear that the Czechoslovak Social Democrats felt the International should have limited itself to a celebration of unification, rather than become involved in Czechoslovak domestic affairs.[51]

An international commission on the problem of Czechoslovakia was formed at Hamburg as a result of the dispute between the two parties. Following several postponements, the committee met with the concerned parties in late October 1923. It concluded, not surprisingly, that the fusion of the social democrats of Czechoslovakia was impossible at that time. The Czechoslovak and German Social Democrats did agree to begin making the preliminaries necessary for such an agreement.[52]

Interparty relations had not improved noticeably by the Marseilles Congress of the Second International in August 1925. On the one hand, distribution of two brochures by the German Social Democrats, one concerning ethnic discrimination, the other about political and social reaction in Czechoslovakia, were not calculated to improve relations between the two parties. On the other hand, the Czechoslovak Social Democrats' opposition to Point Three of the International's "Resolution on the Danger of War in the East" confirmed the feeling among German Social Democrats that the Czechs were remaining intransigent on the question of national minorities. Point Three of the resolution called for national autonomy for large minority groups in geographically enclosed areas and for equality, particularly in the use of language for cultural and educational development for small, geographically fragmented minority groups.[53]

Relations between the Czechoslovak and German Social Democrats were not improved by the exchanges at the Hamburg and Marseilles Congresses. An international forum had been created, however, that could be used for airing of various problems that arose between the two parties. This forum was used far more by the Germans than by the Czechs. In addition, the International could, and did, attempt to bring moral pressure on the two parties to mend their differences. It would have notable success in this area only after the Czechoslovak Social Democrats had left the all-national coalition.

TABLE 2 - 1
MANDATES, COUNTY REICHENBERG 1919

COMMUNE	DSAP	BdL	DBrg	Czech
Alt-Habendorf	20			7
Alt-Harzdorf	15		15	
Alt-Paulsdorf	17		4	3
Berzdorf	11		4	
Buschullersdorf	12		6	
Dörfel	19		7	4
Eichicht	9		5	10
Einsiedel	10		4	Unk[1]
Franzendorf	20		5	5
Friedrichswald	9		4	5
Gränzendorf	(Information not available)			
Heinersdorf	(Information not available)			
Hermannsthal	11		7	
Hluboká	(Information not available)			
Jaberlich	(Information not available)			
Johannesthal	17		7	
Karolinsfeld	15			
Katharinberg	10		8	
Kunnersdorf	9		9	
Langenbruck	8	3	5	2
Liebenau	8	11	11	
Maffersdorf	23		11	2
Münkendorf	(Information not available)			
Neu-Paulsdorf	13		10	1
Nieder-Hanichen	12		6	
Ober-Hanichen	12		6	
Ober-Rosenthal	11		7	18
Pelkowitz	(Information not available)			
Ratchendorf	15		3	
Reichenberg	15		22	5
Röchlitz	17		7	12
Rosenthal	14		10	6
Rudolfsthal	7		5	
Ruppersdorf	16		13	1
Saskal			9	3
Schimsdorf	(Information not available)			
Schönborn	11		7	
Schwarau	(Information not available)			
Voigtsbach	11		4	

NOTE: [1]Number of mandates illegible in source.

SOURCE: *Vorwärts*, 17, 18 June, 1919.

TABLE 2 - 2
MANDATES, COUNTY TEPLITZ 1919

COMMUNE	DSAP	DBrg	DDem	BdL	DNSAP	Jdsh	Czech
Boreslau	6		6				
~~Dreihunken~~	~~13~~	~~2~~					~~3~~
Eichwald	5[1]						
Graupen	17	10					3
Grünwald	(Information not available)						
Hertine	13	5					6
Hundorf	10			2	2		4
Jüdendorf	8	4					
Klein-Augezd	19	3					8
Kosten	(Information not available)						
Kradrob	8	4					3
Liessnitz	8	3					4
Moldau	(Information not available)						
Neustadt	(Information not available)						
Niklasberg	7	2		6			
Ober-Graupen	15						
Pihanken	19	2					9
Probstau	12	5					13
Rosenthal	10			5			
Schallan	11			3			1
Serbitz	(Information not available)						
Settenz	14	6					10
Soborten	(Information not available)						
Suchey	9			6			
Teplitz-Schönau	15	14	2		2	2	5
Tischau	5[1]						
Turn	17	7			2	1	9
Ullersdorf	(Information not available)						
Voigtsdorf	6	2		7			
Webeschan	10	3					3
Weisskirchlitz	15	8					7
Weschen	6			9			
Wisterschan	17	7					6
Wistritz	16	5					9
Zinnwald	(Information not available)						
Zuckmantel	14				6		10

NOTE: [1]No other information available.

SOURCE: *Freiheit*, 16 June 1919; *Die freie Gemeinde*, 16 May 1924.

TABLE 2-3
COMMUNAL ELECTION RESULTS,
COUNTY TEPLITZ 1919

COMMUNE	DSAP	DBrg	DDem	BdL	DNSAP	Jdsh	Czech
Boreslau	149		154				
Dreihunken	416	60					112
Eichwald	(Information not available)						
Graupen	1099	683					195
Grunwald	(Information not available)						
Hertine	470	208					244
Hundorf	329			56	81		121
Jüdendorf	132	64					
Klein-Augezd	486	75					209
Kosten	(Information not available)						
Kradrob	247	123					103
Liessnitz	192	80					108
Moldau	(Information not available)						
Neustadt	(Information not available)						
Niklasberg	(Information not available)						
Ober-Graupen	(Information not available)						
Pihanken	719	80					337
Probstau	471	197					543
Rosenthal	253		124				
Schallan	319		107				39
Serbitz	(Information not available)						
Settenz	600	270					454
Soborten	(Information not available)						
Suchey	232		142				
Teplitz	5354	4870	642		623	1001	2222
Tischau	(Information not available)						
Turn	3644	1623			502	200	1851
Ullersdorf	(Information not available)						
Voigtsdorf	173	81		199			
Webeschan	218	75					66
Weisskirchlitz	1182	633					516
Weschen	93		140				
Wisterschan	1146	445					416
Wistritz	607	186					340
Zinnwald	(Information not available)						
Zuckmantel	754				340		498

SOURCE: *Freiheit*, 16 June 1919; *Die freie Gemeinde*, 16 May 1924.

TABLE 2 - 4
MANDATES, COUNTY REICHENBERG 1923

COMMUNE	DSAP	KSC	DNP	BdL	DNSAP	DGew	WIP	DWah	DCl	Fest	Czech
Alt-Habendorf	7	10		2	2	5		4			
Alt-Harzdorf	(Information not available)										
Alt-Paulsdorf	2	9						12			1
Berzdorf		10						5			
Buschullersdorf		7		3		4	4				
Dörfel	5	11		2	3	3			3		3
Eichicht		5						9			10
Einsiedel		7	7	4							
Franzendorf		13						12			5
Friedrichswald	(Information not available)										
Gränzendorf	(Information not available)										
Heinersdorf	(Information not available)										
Hermannsthal		7		4	2	1			1		
Hluboká	(Information not available)										
Jaberlich	(Information not available)										
Johannesthal	1	10						12			1
Karolinsfeld	(Information not available)										
Katharinberg	8	4			3						
Kunnersdorf	(Information not available)										
Langenbruck		6			6			5			1
Liebenau	3	4			3			14			8
Maffersdorf	2	14	2¹	4		4			5	3	2
Münkendorf	(Information not available)										
Neu-Paulsdorf	1	8			5			9			1
Nieder-Hanichen	(Information not available)										
Ober-Hanichen	4	4						6			1
Ober-Rosenthal	1	6			2			9			18
Ratchendorf		12						6			
Reichenberg	3	6	2		5			20			6
Röchlitz	3	10		1	7	3			4		8
Rosenthal		8						16			6
Rudolfsthal	5	5						5			
Ruppersdorf	1	13	6					12			1
Saskal	(Information not available)										
Schimsdorf	(Information not avaiable)										
Schönborn		6		4		4			1		
Schwarau	(Information not avaiable)										
Voigtsbach		9						6			

NOTES: ¹This party, referred to as *deutschsoziale* in the *Trautenauer Echo*, appears in *Vorwärts* voting results only one time. The mandates are usually credited to the German Nationalist Party.

SOURCE: *Bohemia, Trautenauer Echo*, and *Vorwärts*, 18 September 1923.

TABLE 2 - 5
COMMUNAL ELECTION RESULTS, COUNTY REICHENBERG 1923

COMMUNE	DSAP	KSC	DNP	BdL	DNSAP	DGew	DWah	DCl	Fest	Czech
Alt-Habendorf	312	467		117	102	221		174		
Alt-Harzdorf	(Information not available)									
Alt-Paulsdorf	109	379					477			51
Berzdorf		263					139			
Buschullersdorf	(Information not available)									
Dörfel	424	830	151	192	248			229		257
Eichicht		231					391			452
Einsiedel		323	320	170						
Franzendorf		620					602			248
Friedrichswald	(Information not available)									
Gränzendorf	(Information not available)									
Heinersdorf	(Information not available)									
Hermannsthal		285		161	76	54		65		
Hluboká	(Information not available)									
Jaberlich	(Information not available)									
Johannesthal	59	429					501			67
Karolinsfeld	(Information not available)									
Katharinberg	275	150			128					
Kunnersdorf	(Information not available)									
Langenbruck		209		223			217			81
Liebenau	161	240		161			775			433
Maffersdorf	279	1501	211[1]	428		363		535	350	211
Münkendorf	(Information not available)									
Neu-Paulsdorf	67	395		242			466			79
Nieder-Hanichen	(Information not available)									
Ober-Hanichen	181	157					247			40
Ober-Rosenthal	145	603		253			825			1829
Ratchendorf		539					272			
Reichenberg	1559	3442	983		2655		9934			2962
Röchlitz	251	883		81	677	310		346		748
Rosenthal		562					1149			467
Rudolfsthal	(Information not available)									
Ruppersdorf	79	863	404				838			89
Saskal	(Information not available)									
Schimsdorf	(Information not available)									
Schönborn		246	133			167		55		
Schwarau	(Information not available)									
Voigtsbach		287					206			

NOTE: See Note 1, TABLE 2-4.

SOURCE: *Bohemia, Trautenauer Echo,* and *Vorwärts,* 18 September 1923.

TABLE 2 - 6
MANDATES, COUNTY TEPLITZ 1923

COMMUNE	DSAP	KSC	DNP	DDem	BdL	DNSAP	DGew	DWir	DWah	DCl	Jdsh	Czech
reslau	5			10								
eihunken	9	2							6			1
hwald	(Election held 4 May 1924)											
aupen	13				5	4				5		3
inwald	(Information not available)											
rtine	(Information not available)											
ndorf	(Information not available)											
lendorf	5							7				
ein-Augezd	17							6				7
sten	7	5			5		5					14
adrob	7			5								3
ssnitz	8			3								4
ldau	2			8	4							1
ustadt	(Information not available)											
lasberg	(Information not available)											
er-Graupen	7							5				
anken	13	4				9						4
bstau	8	2							8			12
senthal				3	3				6[1]			1
aallan	6			5		3						1
bitz	(Election held 16 March 1924)											
tenz	11	2			3				7			7
orkin	(Election held 16 March 1924)											
hey	6			6								3
olitz-Schönau	6	2	9	2	4	1	3			6	3	6
chau	(Election held 4 May 1924)											
rn	11	3	1		3				11			6
ersdorf	(Information not available)											
igtsdorf	(Information not available)											
beschan	(Election held 16 March 1924)											
isskirchlitz	10	3			11	2				2		3
schen	(Election held 16 March 1924)											
sterschan	7	8							13			2
stritz	11	4							9			6
nwald	(Information not available)											
ckmantel	10	3							10			7

TES: [1]Socialists through Compromise.

URCE: *Trautenauer Echo*, 18 September 1923.

TABLE 2 - 7

COMMUNAL ELECTION RESULTS, COUNTY TEPLITZ 1923

COMMUNE	DSAP	KSC	DNP	DDem	BdL	DNSAP	DGew	DWir	DWah	DCl	Jdsh	Ca
Boreslau	108			212								
Dreihunken	317	86								197		
Eichwald	(Election held 4 May 1924)											
Graupen	993					378	299			401		1
Grünwald	(Information not available)											
Hertine	(Information not available)											
Hundorf	(Information not available)											
Jüdendorf	107									143		
Klein-Augezd	551									200		
Kosten	613	427				439		395				1
Kradrob	227			170								
Liessnitz	217			102								
Moldau	67			233	120							
Neustadt	(Information not available)											
Niklasberg	(Information not available)											
Obergraupen	143									118		
Pihanken	554	160				387						2
Probstau	410	109							384			
Rosenthal	(Information not available)											
Schallan	182			138	106							
Serbitz	(Election held 16 March 1924)											
Settenz	560	112				154			367			Ul
Soborkin	(Election held 16 March 1924)											
Suchey	170			167								
Teplitz-Schönau	2490	803	3657	751		1472	387	1257	2606		1284	23
Tischau	(Election held 4 Mary 1924)											
Turn	2684	621		303		701		2617		229		13
Ullersdorf	(Information not available)											
Voigtsdorf	(Information not available)											
Webeschan	(Election held 16 March 1924)											
Weisskirchlitz	893	254				948	224			224		3
Weschen	(Election held 16 March 1924)											
Wisterschan	529	633							973			2
Wistritz	486	168							409			2
Zinnwald	(Information not available)											
Zuckmantel	638	177							628			4

NOTES: [1]Number of votes cast illegible in source.

SOURCE: *Trautenauer Echo*, 18 September 1923.

ABBREVIATIONS

The following acronymns and abbreviations have been used in the preceding tables.

BdL *Bund der Landwirte;* German Agrarian Party

Czech Czechoslovak parties

DAWG *Deutsche Arbeits- und Wirtschaftsgemeinschaft;* German Labor and Economic Association

DBrg Joint voting list, German bourgeois parties

DCl *Deutsche christlichsoziale Volkspartei;* German Clerical Party

DDem *Deutschdemokratische Freiheitspartei;* German Democratic Freedom Party

DEin *Deutsche Einheitsliste;* German Unity List

DGew *Deutsche Gewerbepartei;* German Small Trader Party

DNP *Deutsche Nationalpartei;* German National Party

DNSAP *Deutsche nationalsozialistische Arbeiterpartei;* German National Socialist Party

DSAP *Deutsche sozialdemokratische Arbeiterpartei in der Tschechoslowakei;* German Social Democratic Workers' Party in Czechoslovakia

DWah *Deutsche Wahlgemeinschaft;* German Voting Group

Fest *Festbesoldeten;* German Salaried Group

Jdsh *Jüdische Partei;* Jewish Party

KSČ *Komunistická strana Československá;* Communist Party of Czechoslovakia

WlP *Wahlliste ohne Partei;* Independent list.

CHAPTER III

THE GENTLEMEN'S COALITION
1926-1929

Formation of the Coalition

Following losses at the hands of the Czechoslovak Agrarians and Communists in the parliamentary elections the previous November, the Czechoslovak Social Democrats and National Socialists left the government coalition in March 1926. Elections had been held following the breakup of the coalition over a government decree on sliding tariffs that the Agrarians had secured against socialist opposition. Czechoslovak Social Democratic electoral losses had been so great that the coalition could no longer govern as a majority without the addition of other parties, so the Czechoslovak Small Trader Party (*Československá živnostensko-obchodnická strana středostavovská*) joined the coalition. The Czechoslovak Agrarians, who had become the strongest party in the country, were no longer satisfied with the sliding tariff and demanded high fixed tariffs on grain and other agricultural products. The Czech Clericals, who had also made gains in the November elections, called for government salaries (Congrua) for the clergy. Both the tariff and the Congrua were opposed by the anticlerical Czechoslovak Social Democrats and National Socialists.

Disagreements over these two issues led to the downfall of the restructured coalition, which lasted until March when it was replaced by a second government of officials that governed through October 1926. Passage of the grain tariff in June 1926 over the strenuous objection of the opposition was a milestone of sorts in Czechoslovak political history.[1] It marked the first parliamentary vote in which the political parties of Czechoslovakia voted according to economic and class interests, rather than national political interests. With the exception of the intransigent national minority parties, which sided with the opposition, the debate pitted the bourgeois parties of all nationalities against the social democrats and the communists.[2]

After the six month interregnum, minority parties participated in the Czechoslovak government coalition for the first time. Three German parties, the Clericals, Agrarians and Small Traders (*Deutsche Gewerbepartei*) joined the coalition in October; Hlinka's Slovak People's Party (*Hlinkova slovenská l'udová strana*)—the Slovak Clericals—followed suit in January 1927. The German Agrarians were represented in the cabinet by party chairman Franz Spina, a Slavic literature professor at the German University in Prague; the German Clericals by Robert Mayr-Harting, a member of the law faculty at the same university. The former was appointed Minister of Public Works; the latter held the portfolio of the Ministry of Justice. Spina used the expressions "Equal among equals" and "No cabinet without Germans" in defense of his party's participation in the Czechoslovak government.[3]

The formation of the so-called "Gentlemen's Coalition" (*panská koalice*), which excluded the working-class parties, reflected both the Czechoslovak Social Democrats' loss of power and the recognition of common interests by some of the bourgeois parties of different nationalities. The Czechoslovak National Socialists and Social Democrats had worked out a program for a socialist government, but they lacked the majority support necessary to realize it. Due to the electorate's swing to the right, as well as to the weakening of the working class through the communist opposition, the government coalition moved solely into the hands of the bourgeoisie.

The number of German Social Democratic parliamentary representatives dropped: from thirty-one deputies and sixteen senators to seventeen deputies and nine senators. Sixteen of the seventeen deputies had served during the previous parliamentary period; only Eugen de Witte, editor of the Karlsbad *Volkswille,* had been newly-elected. In the senate, seven of the nine senators had also served during the previous parliamentary period. In addition, former deputies Troppau district secretary Hans Jokl and long-time Aussig politico Franz Beutel had moved to the senate.

The Slovak People's Party joined the coalition following adoption of a provincial government reform which party chairman Andrej Hlinka interpreted as "the first flash of autonomy" for Slovakia.[4] The party's participation in the government was negotiated by Karel Kramář. His conservative, nationalist Czechoslovak National Democrats had left the coalition in 1926—"Germans in the government, we're in the revolution"[5] — rather than share governing responsibilities with any German political parties, but returned to the coalition in April 1928.

The tariff and Congrua laws benefited at least a part of the German Agrarian and Clerical constituency, but they had been enacted prior to these parties' entry into the coalition. In fact, the benefits the German parties accrued through participation in the government were limited. The armed forces were disenfranchised, preventing Czech and Slovak soldiers garrisoned in mixed-nationality regions from tipping the balance in elections in these areas. There was some redress of the lack of German representation in the civil service. The January 1928 accord with the Vatican, however, was of more significance to the Czech than the German Clericals, for it only smoothed pontifical feathers ruffled by the Czechs' lavish commemoration in 1925 of the execution of their national Protestant martyr, Jan Hus.

German nationalists condemned the three German coalition parties as traitors to the German people. The German Social Democrats attacked them for placing profit motives above concern for the "legitimate" national demands of the Germans of Czechoslovakia, especially with regard to revision of the language law. The German Social Democrats believed that these parties' entry into the coalition would force them to reveal their "bourgeois-reactionary" class character to the German people. They claimed that as members of the opposition, the German Agrarians and Clericals had been able to pose as "friends of social progress," knowing that their Czech political counterparts in the coalition would look after their class interests.[6]

At the time, German Social Democratic Party chairman Czech addressed one of the paradoxes of Czechoslovak political history: why the nationalist bourgeois parties had been able to come to an understanding sooner than the international working class parties. He asserted that economic motives, including the desire for increased agricultural profitability, rather than a consensus on the nationality question, provided the basis for these parties' cooperation. Czech doubted that the solution to the German question in Czechoslovakia was to be found in an understanding among the members of the bourgeoisie; it had to be found in an understanding among people of all classes.[7] Certainly the Czechoslovak and German Agrarians, Clericals and Small Traders had come to agreement on certain economic legislation whose enactment could be obtained only through mutual cooperation.

The Czechoslovak Social Democrats had a political program with goals they believed were best met by coalition participation. Cooperation with the German Social Democrats in opposition did not necessarily further their aims. The German Social Democrats considered national equality, which they did not believe they had, a presupposition for their socialist aims. So long as the Czechoslovak Social Democrats supported the political status quo, which they continued to do after leaving the coalition, there was little basis for cooperation between the two parties.

The duration of the Gentlemen's Coalition corresponded to the period of greatest economic prosperity in interwar Czechoslovakia. This prosperity was less a reflection of particularly sound economic practices on the part of the Prague government and more a part of a European-wide economic and political sense of well being.

The acceptance of Weimar Germany into the European concert of nations under the sponsorship of Aristide Briand's French government had begun with the evacuation of the Cologne zone of occupation, included German membership in the League of Nations and culminated in 1929 with a new reparations program, the Young Plan, and the evacuation of the Rhineland. The high point of the "Spirit of Locarno" was reached in August 1928 with the adoption of the Kellogg-Briand Pact, which rejected war as an instrument of policy.

The Prague government used this period of relative economic prosperity to legislate a series of economic and social measures that in less felicitious circumstances might have been difficult to enact. The German Social Democrats opposed what they considered dangerous coalition attempts to limit or to disband all together previously legislated social welfare measures.

German Social Democratic Response to Coalition Politics

The major legislation of the Gentlemen's Coalition was a series of laws concerning the military, a tax reform advantageous to business interests, including changes in communal finances, and a government reform involving the creation of four provincial governments. An attempt in early 1928 to dismantle a large part of the social welfare system was stymied by determined working class opposition. Finally, parliament elected T. G. Masaryk to his second term in office during this period.

The military laws, legislated beginning in 1927, made permanent the existing eighteen month military obligation and created a standing peacetime army of 140,000 men as well as a discretionary armaments budget.[8] At this time, the army was also disenfranchised both to stop its politicization and to end communist agitation within it. The social democrats as well as the communists opposed the military laws and their passage was met with large-scale demonstrations by the Czechoslovak and German Social Democratic youth organizations.

The attempt to dismantle the social welfare system—which the German Social Democrats already considered inadequate—by changing the coverage of the 1924 social security laws, denying seasonal farm workers access to insurance, and weakening worker influence over sick funds and hospital administration through government appointment of administrative officials, was defeated in a rare show of cooperation between the social democrats and communists. At their first meeting in November 1927, officials of the joint social democratic trade union center went on record against government efforts to amend the law. Throughout that winter and the next spring, the German Social Democrats cooperated with the Czechoslovak Communists, National Socialists and Social Democrats in a series of strikes and demonstrations throughout the country.[9] This included a nationwide trade union protest in late March that resulted in violence in Prague when gendarmes forcibly prevented workers from attending an assembly in the Altstädter Ring (Staroměstské Náměstí) and the police beat some of the demonstrators. The government confiscated editions of *Právo lidu* and *Rudé právo* carrying reports of the events.[10] The Czechoslovak National Socialists and Social Democrats began negotiations with the Czechoslovak Agrarians over the social security law only when the Czechoslovak Communists attempted to turn the protests into a struggle for power. The negotiations resulted in legislation that was disadvantageous to the working class, but not the degree originally anticipated.

The June 1927 tax reform had three main components: direct taxation, self-government financing, and budget stabilization. The German noncoalition parties and, to a lesser degree, the Czechoslovak Social Democrats, criticized the second portion of the reform due to the centralizing, bureaucratic tendencies it embodied. Prior to the reform, communes had automatically received five to ten percent luxury and sales tax receipts; the reform did away with this. The previously autonomous finance commission was also placed under the auspices of the Prague bureaucracy.[11] Communes lacked authority to raise levies. With the abolition of the automatic return of sales and luxury tax revenues, as well as the other means of revenue production, they had to depend on handouts from the state financial administration in Prague. The communes were obligated to honor legal and contractual responsibilities that they had no way of fulfilling. Following the loss of many previously available sources of revenue production, some of the smaller communes were left without means of raising revenue, because the remaining possibilities were not practical for them.[12] Writing in the mid-1930s, the historian Harry Klepetař noted that the ensuing world economic crisis had demonstrated that Czechoslovakia's tax reform, the work of the Czechoslovak National Democrat Karel Engliš, was based on the incorrect assumption that the economic situation would remain static. With the advent of the Great Depression, the law had to be amended. In 1930, the section concerning self-government was changed.[13]

Indeed, the situation of communal finances was so grave that German Social Democratic discussion of communal government centered not on how to create socialist government at the local level, but on how to escape the economic impasse in which many communes found themselves.[14] This problem was never solved to the satisfaction of the DSAP. Despite the 1930 amending of the tax laws, the financial situation of the communes became more and more acute during the depression. The centralizing, bureaucratic tendencies of Prague vis-à-vis the communes adversely affected social welfare measures during the 1930s.

The governmental reform aimed at further centralization of the Czechoslovak administration has received the most attention of the legislation enacted during the years of the Gentlemen's Coalition. The creation of four provincial diets for Bohemia, Moravia-Silesia, Ruthenia, and Slovakia, standardized administration for the first time throughout Czechoslovakia. During the Habsburg Monarchy, the Austrian Crownlands had been governed through a series of provincial administrative units, while in Hungary, a system of counties was used. In 1920, the Czechoslovak government had adopted a general prefectural system, closer to the former Hungarian system than to that of Austria. The system was implemented only in Slovakia, in 1923. It was never used in the former crownlands, mainly because the Germans would have had a majority of two of the twenty-one planned prefectures, Karlsbad and Böhmisch Leipa, despite gerrymandering by the central government.[15] Analogous to the *Landtage* of the Monarchy, Czechoslovakia's provinical diets (*Landesvertretung*) had a purely administrative function and their competence was limited to cultural and economic issues. Two-thirds of the representatives were to be elected and one-third were to be appointed by the government. The latter were to be "specialists" selected for their expertise in economic, cultural, national or social matters. The centralizing measures employed in this law involved the transferring of the Commission on Communal Government from the autonomous communes to the state. In addition, beginning in 1928, many provincial departments then under communal auspices, including public hospital administration and street maintenance, were placed in the hands of state officials.

The passage of the reform was a prerequisite for Slovak Clerical participation in the government and was a case of Prague wooing the Slovaks at the expense of the Germans. It was enacted with the reluctant consent of the German coalition parties. Indeed, two German Agrarian parliamentary deputies were expelled from the party for failure to maintain discipline on the issue. The application of this system presupposed a Czech-Slovak majority in the diets, which was insured by the union of Moravia and Silesia. Although the abolition of Silesia as an independent province on administrative grounds was reasonable, its primary goal was to prevent a non-Czechoslovak majority in a provincial diet.[16] The Germans, who comprised 40-45 percent of the population of Silesia, in cooperation with the Poles, who made up some 15 percent of the population, could have formed a majority in an independent Silesian provincial diet.[17] Combined with predominantly Czech Moravia, the provincial diet would be safely in Czech hands.

The German non-coalition parties opposed the proposed unification of Silesia and Moravia, not least because of the anticipated loss of German jobs in Troppau, the provincial capital of Silesia, when provincial government offices were moved to Brünn, the capital of Moravia. The German coalition parties supported the union of Moravia and Silesia on the weak grounds that it would create a German population large enough to make its political presence felt in Moravia-Silesia.[18]

Both the Czechoslovak and the German Social Democrats interpreted the appointment of one-third of the provincial diet representatives as the coalition's first attack on the republic's free, equal and universal franchise, which was based on proportional representation.[19] The right to vote in the provincial dietary elections was limited to those over twenty-four years of age who had lived in the particular province for more than one year. The government's reason for imposing the high age requirement was the need for diet members with the experience or expertise necessary to raise the quality of government. A voter had to have attained a certain level of maturity to recognize such qualities in candidates due to the vast quantity of campaign literature disseminated.[20] Of course, older voters were less likely to support left-wing—non-coalition—candidates.

The major nonlegislative parliamentary event during the life of the Gentlemen's Coalition was the re-election of the president in May 1927. Masaryk, receiving 274 of 434 ballots cast, defeated the only opposition candidate, Czechoslovak Communist Party Senator Václav Šturc. The latter received 54 votes; the rest of the ballots had been left blank. The coalition parties, with the exception of the Slovak Clericals, supported Masaryk. The Czechoslovak National Democrats, future members of the coalition and generally supportive of coalition politics, cast unmarked ballots. The social democratic parties, all of which were in opposition, supported the president. Although Masaryk had been elected to a first term without the aid of German votes, he could not have won re-election without the help of the four German parties, which represented three-quarters of all German deputies and senators. German Social Democratic Party chairman Czech explained his party's vote: the blank ballots of 1920 had not been a protest against Masaryk personally, but against the governmental system of the time.[21]

A Move to the Left? The 1928 Elections

The communal elections held in 1927, the first opportunity for the electorate to show a change in political sentiment between parliamentary elections, had little effect on the government. Both Czech and German coalition parties maintained their positions fairly well. The Czechoslovak

Communist Party suffered some reverses, particularly in Czech urban areas, where the Czechoslovak Social Democrats made gains at its expense.[22] The elections, though nationwide, took place in only some seventy percent of the communes. They were not held in most of the cities and towns with historic charters, including Brünn, Mährisch Ostrau, Pilsen, Reichenberg, and Troppau and thus do not provide a complete picture of public opinion, especially in urban areas.

The national county and provincial dietary elections of December 1928 provided the first real test of the policies of the Gentlemen's Coalition. A good point of comparison for the latter is the deputies vote of 1925, because German voter turnout was approximately the same. In the 1928 elections, the thirteen coalition parties received a total of 48.16 percent or 3,211,203 votes, while the noncoalition parties received 51.83 percent or 3,456,526 votes.[23]

Johann W. Brügel's claim that the activist parties held their own against the intransigent national parties in the 1928 provincial dietary elections and the 1929 parliamentary elections is misleading.[24] The German political party making the biggest gains in both elections was the German Social Democratic Party. Although certainly not an intransigent nationalist party, it was an opposition party and not a part of the German bourgeois political parties' activist bloc. The German National Socialists increased their share of the electorate, as well. American political scientist Joseph Rothschild is correct in noting that the voters "punished" the German coalition parties in both the 1928 and 1929 elections.

With the exception of the Czechoslovak Agrarians, all coalition parties, particularly the German parties, showed losses in the percentage of the vote they received in the 1928 elections as compared with the 1925 elections. The German Clericals were especially hard hit, suffering a thirteen percent drop in support.[25] The German Clericals lost some of their working class constituency to the German Social Democrats, apparently a result of backing legislation detrimental to the working class.

The German Social Democrats received twenty-seven percent of the 1,493,364 votes cast for German parties in the former crownlands, while the major German government parties, the Agrarians and the Clericals, each gained seventeen percent of the German vote. Of 3,491,885 votes cast in Bohemia, fifty-seven percent and forty-six elective mandates went to the seven opposition parties (three German, two Czech, one supranational).

The seven government parties (four Czech, three German) received forty-three percent of the vote and thirty-four mandates. The German noncoalition parties won a majority of the German vote, with sixty percent of the 1,055,328 votes cast.[26] By far the most popular German party in Bohemia, the German Social Democrats polled twenty-nine percent of the vote. The German Agrarians followed with nineteen percent. Through manipulation of the twenty-two appointive mandates, however, a majority was created for the government parties in the Bohemian provincial diet.

Coalition parties won a majority of the vote in Moravia-Silesia, gaining fifty-one percent of the 1,627,095 votes cast. The German noncoalition parties received a majority of the German vote, with fifty-five percent and five mandates. The German Clericals were the most popular German party in Moravia-Silesia, winning twenty-three percent of the vote, closely followed by the German Social Democrats with twenty-two percent. The German Agrarians, the fourth largest party behind the German Nationalists (campaigning as the German National Union), had fifteen percent of the vote.

An overview of the election results in formerly independent Silesia indicates that German voters cast ballots against the German government parties and voted both for "loyal opposition" parties like the DSAP and for the irreconcilable nationalist parties. If the vote is interpreted as a referendum on government policies in general, and on governmental legislation for the elimination of Silesian autonomy, in particular, then the majority of Silesian German voters rejected coalition policies. Combined support for the three German coalition parties, the Agrarians, Clericals and Small Traders, reached the Moravian-Silesian average of forty-five percent in just eight of Silesia's twenty-three judicial districts. German Social Democratic support in Silesia, almost 22.5 percent, was slightly higher than the average support for the party in all of Moravia-Silesia, 21.5 percent, but lower than in Bohemia. In Troppau, the predominantly German former provincial capital of Silesia, the German National Socialist Party with thirty-seven percent and 4,395 votes was the most popular German party; the Clericals with twenty percent and 2,435 votes were a distant second. The combined vote of the two negativist parties, just over fifty percent of the German vote, was a pattern repeated in Troppau in all national elections during the 1920s.[27]

Had the appointed deputies been apportioned strictly according to the number of votes each party gained, one deputy would have been appointed for every two deputies elected. This was not, however, the case. The German coalition parties received nine of twelve or three-quarters of the German deputies appointed in Bohemia.[28] Although coalition parties had won just six of eleven of the German parties' elected mandates in Moravia-Silesia, they received three of the four appointed mandates. The German Social Democrats, who had elected two representatives, received the final mandate. Because the coalition parties had a dietary majority in any case, manipulation of the composition of the provincial diet through appointment of deputies was not so blatant in Moravia-Silesia as in Bohemia.

German Social Democratic representatives in the provincial diets were not among the party's inner circle of political leaders. Although party leaders had chosen not to use their brightest political talent in a body with limited competence, they still felt that the DSAP had deserved at least one and probably two more appointed deputies. *Sozialdemokrat* complained that lack of expertise in provincial affairs was not the reason for Prague's failure to appoint more Social Democratic deputies to the diet.[29]

During the 1928 campaign, German social democratic politicians had depicted the elections as a referendum on the government's role in the increase of the cost of living and the decrease in living standards as well as on reforms in finance and provincial government that the German Social Democrats interpreted as effectively limiting self-government.[30] A post election evaluation by young party executive committee member Wenzel Jaksch provides some good insights into the election results. In the party theoretical monthly, *Tribüne,* he wrote of the DSAP's double election goal: to inflict a noticeable loss of mandates upon the bourgeois parties, especially the German ones, and to bring their former supporters into the German Social Democratic camp. Jaksch believed that the party had been more successful with the former than the latter. The DSAP gained some votes at the expense of the government parties, but not as many as those parties lost despite a major offensive effort.[31]

This was in part because the previously existing prefectural governments, despite having a potentially great economic and social significance for the population, had worked *in camera* and, in Moravia and Silesia, with practically no observable results. Thus, although the DSAP had campaigned hard, the party should not over-estimate the interest in the recent election.[32]

The Czechoslovak and German Social Democrats

Closer cooperation both in parliament and without began to charact-erize Czechoslovak and German Social Democratic relations as a result of their common status during this period as part of the "loyal opposition." The slowly warming attitude of the Czechoslovak Social Democrats to-ward the German Social Democrats was colored, however, by their role as an opposition party. The Gentlemen's Coalition was the only time in the history of the First Republic that the Czechoslovak Social Democrats did not participate in the government and they were sensitive to other Czechoslovak political parties' criticism of their improving relations with the German Social Democrats. Two events marked this era of increased contact between the two parties: the unification of the trade union cen-ters affiliated with the Czechoslovak and German Social Democrats and the first joint meeting of the social democratic parties of Czechoslovakia.

That the soured relations between the two parties did not immediately improve is illustrated by the results of the meetings that continued to be held under the auspices of the Socialist International. The German Social Democrats felt that solution to Czechoslovakia's nationality problem lay in the development of a program for national autonomy that would create a political situation separating the Czechoslovak Social Democrats from the other Czechoslovak political parties. This would, in turn, lead to im-proved relations between the Czechoslovak Social Democrats and the other social democratic parties of Czechoslovakia.[33] Though the Czechoslovak Social Democratic minority commission representative František Soukup had responded positively to German proposals for autonomy, the Czecho-slovak Social Democratic executive committee quickly distanced itself from his remarks.[34] At the request of the minority commission of the International, the DSAP proposed guidelines for a program of democratic autonomy in Czechoslovakia in 1926. It contained four points: national and cultural self-administration, school administration, regulation of the language question, and defense of the work place. Points one and two were similar to proposals that Josef Seliger had put forth at the party's founding congress in 1919. The last two points were in response to government language measures then being instituted in the public sector. Participants of the DSAP party congress at Teplitz in 1927 adopted these principles in the form of an executive committee proposal "Our Struggle for Self-government and National Self-Administration" ("Unser Kampf um Selbstregierung und nationale Selbstverwaltung"). The proposal remained, however, simply a basis for discussion between the two parties.

A conference marking the unification of the trade union centers was held in 1927. The first joint meeting in more than twenty years, the congress was hailed as ending thirty years of strife between the trade union centers. The common headquarters facilitated common activity, including coordination of strikes and trade union cooperation against governmental attempts to change the social welfare laws. Czechoslovak Communist reaction to the joint social democratic trade union center was one of contempt; the KSČ claimed that its constant pressure for a united front and unified proletarian action was responsible for the unification of the two organizations. Articles in *Vorwärts* derided the negotiations as laughable, claiming the reason they had been kept quiet was fear of opposition from both the reformist, nationalist trade union rank and file and some trade union officials.[35]

In a country with numerous trade union centers (thirteen to sixteen during the interwar period) affiliated with the various political parties represented in parliament, the importance of the unification of the social democratic trade union centers remained somewhat symbolic. Their combined membership represented one-third of the First Republic's organized workers, and even with the addition of the Czechoslovak National Socialist trade unions, representation hovered at one-half of all organized workers. Membership in the social democratic trade unions had shown dramatic increases in 1919 and 1920 (supra), with membership rates beginning to drop by 1921 and continuing to drop through the mid-1920s. Although losses were initially blamed on communist agitation and worker apathy, later reports assessed the problem as follows. Many of those who had joined German Social Democratic trade unions in the immediate postwar period soon left, when they felt they had obtained the concessions they deserved from their employers.[36] German Social Democratic public sector trade unions suffered further membership losses between 1924 and 1927 due to governmental dismissal of personnel not meeting language law requirements.

Initiated by Czechoslovak Social Democratic Party leaders Alfréd Meissner and Leo Winter, the social democratic parties of Czechoslovakia held
their first joint congress in Smíchov in January 1928. Friedrich Adler,
attending as a representative of the Socialist International, noted that the
congress could not have occurred as a *Diktat* from above or from the
International, but only due to the initiative of the parties themselves.[37]
In fact, he commented that the International's attempts to impose a solution had been rejected. Little substantive change in relations among the
social democratic parties resulted from the congress, though all sides manifested conciliatory attitudes, adopting a resolution that called for the
entire Czechoslovak working class, regardless of ethnicity, to strive for the
destruction of the coalition.[38] The nationality problem continued to
separate the Czechoslovak and German Social Democrats. Although
Meissner, for one, recognized that the two parties should solve their national differences themselves, rather than allow others to propose solutions and then criticize these efforts, the unification committee failed to
come to a concensus on a political program.[39] Further work in this area
was delegated to a joint committee on cultural, economic and national
problems that was to create the program necessary to successful unification of the various social democratic parties in Czechoslovakia.[40] Mention of the nationality problem, which German Social Democratic Congress participant Ernst Paul correctly labeled the "cardinal problem of
the republic" was limited to a resolution demanding that the Czechoslovak state form not only an economic and political entity but also
develop in a culturally and nationally equitable form. Paul has written
that the failure to address national demands was something both parties
later regretted.[41] The inability of the delegates to come to agreement at
the Smíchov Conference adumbrated the futility of cooperation between
the Czechoslovak and German Social Democrats which would be witnessed
again in the crisis years of the 1930s.

The Demise of the Gentlemen's Coalition

Internecine quarrels among the various Slovak political parties caused
the decline of the Gentlemen's Coalition. The issue that forced new elections, however, was Czechoslovak Agrarian Premier František Udržal's
insistence on transferring the Defense Ministry portfolio to another
Czechoslovak Agrarian politician over the protest of the other coalition
parties.

Results of the October 1929 elections showed a dramatic increase in voter support for all of the socialist parties in Czechoslovakia. A colorful series of possibilities for government coalitions followed: Red-Green (Socialist-Agrarian), Red-Black (Socialist-Clerical), Red-Green-Black (Socialist-Agrarian-Clerical), or a return to an all-national coalition. The last option was rejected, as German participation in the government had been accepted as the norm during the short span of the Gentlemen's Coalition. The first option, a Socialist-Agrarian Coalition, was chosen, thus providing the German Social Democrats their first real opportunity to participate in governing Czechoslovakia.

CHAPTER IV

THE RED-GREEN MULTINATIONAL COALITION
1929-1935

The 1929 Parliamentary Elections

Although hailed by the German Social Democrats as a swing to the left, the results of the 1929 parliamentary elections reflected rather a movement toward the political center as the parties of both the far left and far right lost popularity. This continued a trend begun with the communal elections in 1927. Support for the Czechoslovak Agrarians increased. The party received 15 percent of the vote and 46 mandates, maintaining its position as the most popular political party in the country. The Czechoslovak Social Democrats, with 13 percent of the vote and 39 mandates, became the second largest political party, followed by the Czechoslovak National Socialists with 10.5 percent and 32 mandates. Meanwhile, the Czechoslovak Communist Party had slipped to fourth place, with just over 10 percent of the vote and 30 mandates. The Czechoslovak Clericals were the fifth largest party, and the German Social Democrats were again the strongest German party in parliament, and the sixth largest party overall, with 7 percent of the vote and 21 mandates.[1]

Both the Czechoslovak and the German Social Democrats improved their showing over the 1925 elections; the gains of the Czechoslovak Social

Democrats were larger than those of the Germans, but then their losses in 1925 had also been larger. Support for the Czechoslovak party increased by 52 percent, while German support increased by 23 percent. The Czechoslovak National Socialists showed gains of slightly more than 20 percent, an increase consistent with the earlier elections. The Czechoslovak Social Democrats, and to a lesser extent the German Social Democrats, considered this party a political ally, although it had not been permitted to join the Socialist International. Given the abundance of political parties in the First Republic, it was to their advantage to ally themselves with the Czechoslovak National Socialists, who shared their interest in legislation for the benefit of the working class. The three parties combined had won just 30 percent of the vote, closer to the 23 percent of the vote they had received in the 1925 parliamentary elections than to their total of 45 percent in 1920. Even with the inclusion of the Czechoslovak Communist Party, the organized working class parties tallied only slightly more than 40 percent of the vote in 1929, nowhere near a parliamentary majority. (See Table 4-1.)

German National, Slovak Clerical, and Czechoslovak Communist Party losses were due more to internal party problems than to particularly attractive campaign positions of the other parties. In the first case, the German Democratic Freedom Party, headed by Bruno Kafka, lawyer, professor and publisher of *Bohemia,* had joined with the big business arm of the German Nationalists led by lawyer-financier Alfred Rosche to form the German Labor and Economic Association, also known as the Rosche-Kafka Group. The gains of this activist party at the expense of the German Nationalists had already been visible in the 1928 provincial elections. The prolonged trial and subsequent conviction for treason of trusted Hlinka aide Vojtech (Béla) Tuka in 1929 led to far greater losses for the Slovak Clericals than those suffered by the Czech Clericals in the election. The German Clericals, campaigning with the German Small Traders, increased their share of the electorate in the 1929 elections as compared to 1925.

Dramatic Czechoslovak Communist Party losses were the result of purges ("reorganization") as Moscow increasingly dominated the party. The purges had begun in February 1925 with the expulsion of Prague district secretary Josef Bubník for "opportunism" and sharpened following the Fourth Party Congress in March 1927 when a new politburo was elected, whose radical members rendered the previous, primarily one-time

social democratic leadership, including Kreibich and Šmeral, almost power-
less. The party allegedly still included anarcho-communists and Trotskyites
—by the late 1920s, the latter term was applied to virtually any communist
whose views did not coincide with those of the party leadership—as well as
many former social democrats, who were "reformist" rather than "revolutionary." Trotskyite intellectuals were influential in the party youth
movement in Prague and in northern and western Bohemia, particularly
Asch and Gablonz, where former DSAP member Alois Neurath was active
until his expulsion from the party in 1929.

The Communist Party's chaotic internal situation was perhaps best reflected by the "Red Day" called for 6 July 1928 in Prague both to protest
the government's prohibition of the party's planned gymnastic and sports
festival (*Spartakiade*) and to demonstrate the party's strength. Young German Social Democratic journalist Emil Franzel aptly compared the events
of 6 July with those in Vienna ten days later:

> In Vienna, the revolutionary masses were there, but had no one to
> lead them; while in Prague, the leaders were there, but not the
> masses.[2]

Even Czechoslovak Communist Party members admitted that this was the
case.[3]

Internal conflict moved toward a climax following the Fifth Congress
of the KSČ in February 1929, culminating with the expulsion in June of
numerous high party officials following protests against the policies of
party chairman Klement Gottwald. Those expelled included parliamentary
deputy Alois Muna, and senator Josef Skalák, both of whom were among
the founders of the party. Soon afterward, in a renewed offensive against
social democracy, international communism adopted the slogan, "social
fascism," equating "bourgeois democracy"—and those who came to terms
with it—with fascism.

Czechoslovak Communists explained that electoral losses in 1929 were
the result of self-criticism. Further, a vote for the Communist Party was a
vote for revolutionary, Bolshevik-led class struggle. Communist leaders
noted that their electoral support came primarily from among the youngest and least skilled workers, while the party had suffered losses among the
petite bourgeoisie and the skilled workers.[4] The process of Bolshevization

virtually destroyed the Czechoslovak Communist Trade Union Commission; the remaining members joined the social democratic trade union center in 1930. Communist Party support had increased, however, in the predominantly German districts of Böhmisch Leipa and Karlsbad, reflecting both the leftward political drift in those areas and the fact that party purges had not yet occurred in northwest Bohemia. Czechoslovak Communist Party reaction to the electoral gains of the "social fascists" was predictable: the deplorable situation was similar to earlier "social fascist" victories in England, Germany, and France. The Czechoslovak Communists predicted that the prospective government would be one of "war, fascism, and hunger."[5]

The elections left František Udržal's government with only minority support in parliament, so it resigned. At Masaryk's request, as representative of the nation's largest political party, Udržal formed a new government reflecting the election results. He approached Antonín Hampl, who had become Czechoslovak Social Democratic Party chairman in the mid-1920s, to discuss forming a new government. Hampl informed him that neither that Czechoslovak Social Democrats nor the Czechoslovak National Socialists were willing to participate in a government coalition that did not include the German Social Democrats. Udržal initially attempted to construct another bourgeois coalition rather than share governing powers with the DSAP.[6] His attitude confirms the contemporary German Social Democratic view that the bourgeois and social democratic parties approached the building of the coalition from diametrically opposed positions. The former wanted a continuation of the previous coalition as much as possible, while the latter desired the creation of an entirely new coalition based on approximate parity between the bourgeois and socialist parties. Efforts to shore up the existing coalition failed, however, both because the small Hungarian Christian Socialist Party was not interested and because the price demanded by the Slovak Clericals—amnesty for Tuka—was too high.

Udržal was thus forced to approach Hampl again. The Czechoslovak Social Democrats initially did not reject Udržal's proposal to a return to an all-national coalition, but Masaryk opposed any coalition that excluded the national minorities. Therefore, on 23 November, the Czechoslovak Social Democrats refused to participate in an all-national coalition[7] and demanded that the German Social Democrats be included in the government.

Czechoslovak Social Democratic insistence on German Social Democratic participation in the proposed coalition was not so much a matter of loyalty to a fellow social democratic party as the desire not to be part of a hopeless minority in a bourgeois-socialist government. The Czechoslovak Social Democratic motives illustrated the secondary role of the German Social Democratic Party in the government and its weakness vis-à-vis the Czechoslovak party.

The coalition finally negotiated consisted of nine parties: six Czech, three German; six bourgeois, three socialist. In addition to the Czechoslovak Agrarians, National Socialists, Social Democrats, and the German Social Democrats, the Czech Clericals and Czechoslovak National Democrats as well as the German Agrarians and the DAWG participated. The failure to include the German Clericals in the coalition was a matter of political geometry—Czech reluctance to have more than three German parties in the coalition—rather than any unwillingness on their part to participate.

In an attempt to strengthen the position of the bourgeois parties, Udržal originally offered the socialists only five of fourteen governmental ministries, including the insignificant nutrition portfolio, earmarked for the German Social Democrats. Final allotment of portfolios found the bourgeois parties with eight ministries and the socialist parties with six. The Czechoslovak Agrarians held four, the Czechoslovak Social Democrats three, and the Czechoslovak National Socialists and Czech Clericals two apiece. The German Social Democrats and Agrarians as well as the Czechoslovak National Democrats and Small Traders had one ministry each. Socialist ministers and their portfolios were: German Social Democrat Ludwig Czech, Welfare; Czechoslovak Social Democrats Rudolf Bechyně, Ivan Dérer and Alfréd Meissner, Nutrition, Education, and Justice; and Czechoslovak National Socialists Edvard Beneš and Emil Franke, the Foreign and Post Ministries, respectively. The Czechoslovak Agrarians had retained most of the important Ministries, including Interior and National Defense.

Coalition negotiation and portfolio assignment had taken almost six weeks; members of the coalition were left with only twenty-four hours to create a program prior to the announcement of the cabinet. The program introduced was no program. As Czech Clerical coalition member Jan Šrámek commented, "We have agreed that we shall agree."[8]

The introduction of the cabinet to parliament in December provided a preview of the change in Czechoslovak Communist Party policies: unruly behavior on the part of the party's newly-elected parliamentary deputies. Czechoslovak Communist theatrics at the time resulted in the suspension of twenty-two deputies for ten parliamentary sessions. Similar scenes took place in the senate, though the senators were less obstreperous due to their more advanced age.[9]

The Gentlemen's Coalition had been only partially successful in implementing a vaguely-defined program of predominantly anti-working class legislation during a period of economic prosperity. The Red-Green coalition, doubly mixed by both class and nationality, also lacked a comprehensive governing program and was unprepared to meet the demands placed on it by the worldwide economic crisis, which began even as the coalition was being formed.

The German Social Democrats Join the Coalition

There had been discussion about participating in the future government at the German Social Democratic District Conference at Bodenbach in January 1929. Social democrats in Austria and Germany provided contrasting alternatives toward participation in government coalitions. The Austrian Social Democrats, despite increasing membership and representation in parliament—with forty-one percent of the vote in 1930, they would become the most popular party in the country—remained in opposition after 1920. According to party leader Otto Bauer, this was the "natural" position for social democrats in a "bourgeois" state. The SPD, on the other hand, had chosen to participate in the "Grand Coalition," with member Hermann Müller as chancellor, following its success in the elections in 1928.

DSAP treasurer Carl Heller, an advocate of closer relations with the Czechoslovak Social Democrats, admitted that the solidarity of the social democratic parties still did not equal that of the various bourgeois parties. Although he asserted that part of the fault lay in the nationalist influence the Czechoslovak National Socialist Party exerted on the Czechoslovak Social Democratic Party, Heller believed that the Czechoslovak Social Democrats themselves were unconvinced of the value of closer cooperation with the German Social Democratic Party.[10]

During the electoral campaign in 1929, leading German Social Democrats informed their constituency of the executive committee's willingness to join the coming government, stressing the importance participation would have for the workers.[11] Czech spoke in favor of participation in the government at an extraordinary party congress convened in Aussig in late November to discuss the prospect. Czech claimed that according to the Socialist International, the question was not one of coalition participation per se, but of appropriate tactics. He believed that participation in government coalitions was consistent with traditional German Social Democratic positions on the subject, because even during the revolutionary period of 1920, the party had not entirely rejected coalition politics, considering participation acceptable under some circumstances.[12]

Czech, describing the recent electoral campaign as a "struggle between the capitalist bourgeoisie and socialism," interpreted the domestic political situation as follows: although the working class had grown stronger again in recent years, the bourgeoisie had also gained strength both economically and politically. The contradictory interests of the bourgeoisie had lessened, at least as far as the working class was concerned. Even when divided, the bourgeois parties could still form a majority within the government. The German Social Democrats were obliged to participate in the coalition, even if only half measures were possible, in order to avoid a reactionary government.

Czech met with some opposition at the congress, particularly from delegates from the Bodenbach area, because entering the government required cooperation with bourgeois parties.[13] On the other hand, local party leaders from Teplitz-Schönau argued that it was necessary in their area, with its large Czech minority, to attempt the cooperation between Czech and German workers that had been discussed at the Smíchov Congress.[14]

The German Social Democratic Party joined the government 1) because the election results had deprived the ruling bourgeois parties of their majority; 2) because of the economic situation; 3) because of international developments; and 4) because of their party's relationship with the Czechoslovak Social Democrats. The latter clearly preferred governing powers and prerequisites to opposition. After the 1929 elections, the Czechoslovak Social Democrats had made it clear to the German Social Democrats that they intended to rejoin the government. The DSAP was left with the choice of joining the government or straining, if not breaking, the improving relationship between the two parties.[15] German Social Democrats entered the government with the intention of working with the Czechoslovak Social Democrats insofar as this could be reconciled with their own future—unspecified—goals. Party deputy Adolf Pohl's parliamentary speech on 13 December 1929 stressed both the premium the German Social Democrats placed on cooperation with the Czechoslovak Social Democrats—he believed the victory of the working class was possible only through the cooperation of the entire proletariat—and the recognition that entering the government marked a turning point in DSAP politics.[16] Some DSAP members had more specific aims; newly-elected deputy Wenzel Jaksch spoke of entering the government both on urgent economic-political and social grounds, and in order to solve the nationality problem.[17]

Like the German Agrarians and Clericals before them, the German Social Democrats entered the government unconditionally. According to Johann W. Brügel:

> It may have been tempting to show the other Germans that the social democrats—entering the government on the same terms as the bourgeois activists had earlier, i.e. without economic-political and social preconditions—were in a position to achieve more [than the bourgeois activists had].[18]

In fact, the German Social Democratic Party was no more in the position to lay down conditions for its participation in the government than the other German parties had been.

German Social Democratic optimism concerning cooperation with the Czechoslovak Social Democrats initially appeared justified. Several months after the formation of the coalition, at their party congress in September 1930, the Czechoslovak Social Democrats adopted a program that seemed to indicate a new flexibility toward the German minority, for it recognized the principle of cultural autonomy within the Czechoslovak state for the first time.[19] The Czechoslovak Social Democratic position was hailed by the Germans and condemned by the nationalist Czechoslovaks, but the question of cultural autonomy soon took a backseat to the economic problems which were looming on the horizon.

In the Shadow of Black Friday

The German Social Democrats assumed that by participating in the government they could insure the economic security of the German areas of Czechoslovakia, which, they believed, was generally ignored by Prague. Their failure to do so was primarily the result of the government's inability to deal with the large-scale economic crisis of the 1930s, rather than their own ineffectiveness. Czechoslovakia was saddled with an economy that—with the exception of a short upswing in the mid-1920s—had been stagnant since the end of the war. It had only slowly overcome the limitations of the Monarchy and gradually succeeded in gaining new markets in Western Europe and North America, which the Depression disrupted.

Although the effects of the economic crisis that followed the Wall Street crash of October 1929 were felt later in Czechoslovakia than elsewhere, they appeared initially and most severely in northwest Bohemia, particularly in the German-dominated glass and textile industries. In Zwickau, a textile village of some 4,800 persons, the unemployed numbered 1,500 by February 1931.[20] At the same time, some 1,500 glass blowers in nearby Haida-Steinschönau lost their jobs, due both to the closing of the factories where they were employed and to their refusal to work for reduced wages.[21] These industries had been in dire straits, however, even before 1929. The effect of the crisis on both industries was especially catastrophic because of existing structural problems. Rationalization in the 1920s, the introduction of the automatic loom and other improvements in productivity, had led to the dismissal of thousands of textile workers. With the aid of the new machinery, fewer workers could produce more goods at a lower cost than previously. The same was true in the glass industry where, for instance, with the Owens bottling machine, twelve workers could perform tasks that had previously required eighty to ninety.[22] Rationalization was the rule in industry throughout Czechoslovakia, and with the worsening economic situation, there was nowhere for the redundant workers to find new employment.

German Social Democrats objected less to rationalization than to the seemingly inhuman manner in which it was applied. Rationalization was particularly devastating in Sudeten German industrial villages, dependent as they often were on a single industry. A classic example was Rothau in

the county of Graslitz, a steel producing village of 3,692 in the Erzgebirge of western Bohemia. The Rothau ironworks were unified with the
Moravian Mining and Steelworkers Company in Witkowitz in the late
1920s, and shortly afterwards the unprofitable factory was Rothau was
closed, depriving the commune of more than eighty percent of its taxable
income as well as 1,800 jobs. The evaporation of the community's tax
base threatened a decade of improvements that had taken place under
German Social Democratic administration: electricity, running water,
worker housing.[23]

Unemployment in Czechoslovakia rose swiftly. Statistics for November
1931 showed a thirty-five percent increase over the previous month and
a one hundred percent increase over October 1930. In two years, unemployment had increased almost tenfold (figures for November 1931:
336,874; October 1931: 254,201; October 1930: 155,203; October
1929: 38,293).[24] Unemployment peaked during the winter of 1932-
1933 at 920,000 in a country of some fourteen million. (See Table 4-2.)

Exports dropped to twenty-eight percent of the level of 1929 (the high
point of Czechoslovakia's interwar prosperity) and the one-third of the
nation's industrial production destined for export suffered from both the
collapse of international trade and the subsequent rush to autarky. The
protectionist trade measures enacted in 1925 to aid the agrarian sector
of the Czechoslovak economy were increasing during the Depression in
response to pressure to support farm prices at the expense of industry.
In addition, during the early years of the Depression, the government, like
most others in Europe, pursued a deflationary policy.

Udržal was forced to resign in August 1932, when the social democratic
parties and others withdrew their support for his government, due to lack
of initiative concerning the economic situation. His successor, Czechoslovak Agrarian gentleman farmer Jan Malypetr, however, retained twelve
of Udržal's sixteen ministers and many of his economic policies. Despite
the Malypetr government's more active economic policy—some 240 legis-
lative measures were enacted—the Czechoslovak economy would not fully
recover by 1938.

Unemployment in the forty-seven predominantly German counties in
northwestern Bohemia rose about 23 percent during the month of February 1930 to 23,707.[25] At the end of the following April, 43 percent of
all unemployment in Czechoslovakia was in northwestern Bohemia.[26] In

September 1930, when the number of registered unemployed stood at 70,000 the unemployment rate among Germans was already higher than among Czechs.[27] The reasons lay both in the geographical structure of the German areas and in the export-oriented nature of their production.

The severity with which the economic crisis affected the Germans prompted the DSAP to hold an emergency conference, co-sponsored by the German Social Democratic Trade Unions. Criticism of the state's responsibility for the fate of German workers grew so heated that some Czechoslovak Social Democratic representatives left the conference in protest. The speeches made at the conference provide a comprehensive record of German Social Democratic attitudes toward Prague's employment practices. The leaders of the major German trade unions, including the chemical, mining, and textile unions, were uniformly critical. They condemned the use of lower paid, non-unionized Slovak workers on state jobs in Bohemia, despite the large numbers of local unemployed, and complained that the continued dismissal of German civil servants as a result of "Czechization" placed an additional burden on the economies of the German and mixed-population areas. Trade union leaders criticized Czech chauvinism and claimed that the battle for jobs was between German workers and the state, rather than between German workers and Czech ones.

Both the German and the Czechoslovak Social Democratic trade unions lost members during the Depression, but proportional losses were not as large as those of social democratic trade unions in other Central European countries. The decline in social democratic trade union membership in the First Republic during the early and mid-1920s—the latter exodus affected all trade unions in Czechoslovakia—had never been recouped, though membership again increased between 1927 and 1932. Gains in the early 1930s were primarily due to the adherence of the rump communist trade union center to the social democratic trade union center in 1930.

Prague's policy of filling state services almost exclusively with Czechs caused even greater resentment during the Depression than it had previously. The employment of Czechs in German areas was particularly resented because in branches like the postal system, which was only 7.5 to 18 percent German, positions were fairly secure, if not always well-paying.[28]

It is difficult to interpret data available on unemployment precisely. Discussion of unemployment is complicated by the plethora of material and statistics were seldom uniform. Unemployment was measured by job sector or by county, by the number of residents, by the number of employable persons, or in absolute figures. Statistics are available for the four provinces and for specific areas of each province. In most cases, the figures reflect only the registered unemployed. They do not include the large minority of unemployed who were not trade unionists, those working part-time (often at reduced wages), or persons of working age who had never been employed due to the Depression. Because Czechoslovakia had neither obligatory unemployment insurance nor reemployment aid, many of the unemployed never appeared in the statistics. Thus, the official unemployment figures, high as they were, tell only part of the story. Given these reservations, a general picture of unemployment in the Sudeten lands can be drawn. (See Table 4-3.)

Throughout the 1930s, unemployment was proportionally higher in German than in Czech counties, and with the exception of Brünn, Pilsen, and Prague, it was also absolutely higher. The ten counties with the highest proportional unemployment varied slightly, but were inevitably predominantly German. (See Table 4-4.) The ten counties with the lowest proportional unemployment also varied, but they were equally inevitably Czech. On the average, unemployment in German counties was two times higher than in Czech ones.

During the mid-1930s, the following counties were among those with the highest proportional unemployment: Graslitz, Elbogen, and Karlsbad in western Bohemia; Friedland and Rumburg in northwest Bohemia; Sternberg in north central Moravia, and Freudenthal in Silesia. Karlsbad, the largest of these, was also one of the counties with the highest absolute unemployment. Unemployment in all seven rose quickly at the beginning of the 1930s and remained high throughout the decade. The percentage of Germans in these counties in 1930 was: Elbogen, 96.45 percent; Freudenthal, 87.33 percent; Friedland, 94.37 percent; Graslitz, 98.88 percent; Karlsbad, 95.20 percent; Rumburg, 95.28 percent and Sternberg, 67.20 percent.[29]

In Friedland, for example, unemployment was 1,364 in January 1930. It increased by 113 percent during the next month to 2,905, and by January 1931 stood at 4,690, an increase of more than 340 percent.[30] In

January 1934, unemployment in Friedland was around 6,800,[31] fivefold higher than four years earlier. In July 1934, unemployment in Graslitz stood at over thirty percent, absolutely and proportionally the highest in the country. During the same month, unemployment in twelve counties was between twenty and thirty percent. They included Sternberg, 30 percent; Rumburg, 29.1 percent; Neudek, 25.4 percent; Friedland, 23.4 percent; Freudenthal, 22.7 percent; Elbogen, 21.4 percent and Karlsbad, 21.3 percent.[32]

Friedland, Graslitz, Rumburg, and Sternberg were textile producing centers. In Graslitz, and the surrounding small industrial textile villages, two-thirds of the residents were employed in industry. *Heimarbeit* predominated among the 13.5 percent of the population working in textiles, particularly in the sewing notions, embroidery, and lace producing branches.[33] Graslitz was also the center of Czechoslovakia's musical instrument industry, in which small-scale firms with one to five employees predominated and more than forty percent of the output was still by hand in 1930. The mining, porcelain, and glass industries of western Bohemia were concentrated in Elbogen and Karlsbad. In Karlsbad, famous for its spas, 13.8 percent of the population was involved in "luxury" commerce.[34]

By the mid-1930s, but particularly by the late 1930s, unemployment was generally lowest in central Bohemia, within a hundred kilometer radius of Prague, well within the Czech language border. The local economy in these areas varied, but included the clothing and the food and drink industries as well as branches of the machine industry: for instance, railroad repair, and automobile and motor production.[35] Some of the regional industries were connected with armaments production, which the Prague government was unlikely to locate in the border areas near an increasingly hostile Germany.

Ludwig Czech Serves as Government Minister

Ludwig Czech was an active Minister of Social Welfare, both because of the worsening economic situation and his own interests. An able administrator, he was involved in both major and minor decisions, attempting to use the ministry so far as possible—one of only two senior German civil servants, for example, was a German National Socialist—as an instrument of social progress. German Social Democratic policy had two priorities:

increased support for the unemployed and renewal of the housing law due to expire in March 1931.

Probably the farthest-reaching reform undertaken by Czech was the improvement of the provisions of the Ghent system of unemployment compensation, which had been enacted in 1925. Briefly, in this system, support from the trade unions evenly matched by state funds superceded direct support from the state. Compensation was insufficient for an economic crisis on the scale of that of the 1930s. The period of compensation thirteen weeks, was far too short, and the one-to-one ratio of state to trade union payments placed too great a burden on the trade unions. The Czechoslovak version of the Ghent system came under strong criticism during the 1930s because it excluded non-union members who were unemployed from compensation. Beginning on 1 January 1931, the compensation period was doubled, and in designated areas tripled. In the first-named areas, the contribution of the state was tripled, and in the latter areas, the ratio of state-trade union payments was increased to seven to one.[36]

Czech extended benefits to non-union workers not covered under the provisions of the Ghent system through the development of a nourishment program (August 1930) and a milk program (December 1930). The bourgeois press, particularly the Czechoslovak Agrarian press, engaged in a propaganda campaign against abuse of the food ration cards, known as "Czech cards." The unemployed were accused of organizing balls and of using their ration cards to buy liquor and to gamble.[37] Although the provisions of the cards were hardly generous—single persons received ten crowns per week and married unemployed received twice that amount, regardless of the number of children they had—the agrarian-dominated Interior Ministry attempted to exclude homeowners and those receiving war invalid compensation from the meager benefits. The Czechoslovak Communists ridiculed the cards as "Beggars' Money." The cards were distributed at the district level, and non-socialist local officials had some success in sabotaging the efforts of the Social Welfare Ministry. On the other hand, as a German Social Democratic official in Eger reported, the commissions were a positive influence for card distribution where the social democrats were in a position to apply pressure.[38]

Czech's call for the creation of work, a German Social Democratic tenet for overcoming the economic crisis, was accompanied by demands for a new trade policy, state guarantee of exports, greater availability of credit, and liberal capital expenditures. The bourgeois parties opposed all of these demands. Neither Czech's efforts, nor those of his Czechoslovak Social Democratic successor to obtain funds for public works from outside the ministry met with notable success.

When the government was reshuffled in February 1934, Czech took over the Ministry of Public Works, where his attempts to use investment to create employment opportunities were limited by the government's spartan tendencies. The Czechoslovak Agrarian press criticized his efforts to apportion work in needy German areas. The Prague bureaucracy's tendency to pass over German firms when work was divided did not help matters. When Minister Czech reviewed the apportionment of public projects, however, he discovered that German firms were as expensive as, or more expensive than, Czech firms. The DSAP minister nevertheless sought to guarantee that the Czech firms working in German areas employed Germans.[39] At the senate budget meeting on 20 November 1934, he complained that attempts to promote industrial production and thus to alleviate the crisis had failed. His efforts to meet the increasing demand for public works had been stymied by lack of money. The budget of his ministry had been cut some forty-five percent in three years.[40]

During his tenure as minister, Czech faced criticism from all sides. While the nationalist Czechs condemned his efforts on behalf of the workers, the communists attacked him for having done too little for them, and the German nationalists derided Minister Czech as the Jewish Marxist who had sold off the Germans to their arch-enemy, the Czechoslovak government.

The Internal Situation of the German Social Democratic Party

The number of German Social Democratic local organizations continued to increase through 1931; between 1926 and 1930, the party had a net growth of 193 organizations. By 1931, however, the number of party members had begun to drop, at least in northwest Bohemia, although the number of party organizations continued to increase.[41] The Karlsbad region with an increase of thirty-four organizations and a decrease of just one, showed the largest net increase. Although not reaching its pre-1921 level, Reichenberg also had sustained growth, with the number of local organizations almost doubling from nine to seventeen. In rural southwest Bohemia, the DSAP lost organizations, mainly in Bergreichenstein and Ronsberg. There was also a drop in organizations in the Dux-Brüx-Bilin-Ober-Leutensdorf coal-mining region and in Arnau and Trautenau in northeast Bohemia.[42]

Unemployment does not seem to have had an immediate effect on party membership, as statistics for the Karlsbad district, which included Elbogen, Graslitz, Neudek, and Weipert, indicate. Membership remained strong in this area, and indeed increased during the early 1930s.

The DSAP was only occasionally successful in attracting former communists into the social democratic fold. German Social Democrats claimed that inept Communist Party policies had led to the destruction of the KSČ's organization and trade union movement in northwest Bohemia. The German section of the party had remained relatively unified for a long time. The factionalism and purges that racked the Brünn and Prague local organizations did not occur in northern Bohemia. The communist workers there had, however, been so thoroughly schooled against the German Social Democratic Party that when a division finally did occur, and they became disenchanted with the Communist Party, the German Social Democrats were unable to recruit them. Many former communists moved to either the German Clerical or German National Socialist camp. Another reason for this, according to Karl Kern, was that the "anarcho-bolshevistic" ideology of the KSČ was closer to that of the National Socialists than to that of the German Social Democrats.[43]

The Exiled Brother Parties:
Social Democrats from Austria and Germany

Adolf Hitler's seizure of power in January 1933 and the *Gleichschaltung* measures that followed, led the SPD executive committee to decide in May 1933 to move the party headquarters to Prague, where they founded the exile organization "Sopade." Party functionaries and trade unionists followed, some of whom settled near the 1,500 kilometer-long Czechoslovak-German border to carry out underground work in Nazi Germany. Although SPD refugees were also to be found in the Saarland, Belgium, and elsewhere in Western Europe, they were most numerous in Czechoslovakia. Among the reasons for emigrating to Czechoslovakia were the large German community, the proximity to the homeland, and the possibility of crossing the border without valid papers.

Even as the civil war in Austria in February 1934 still raged, Austrian Social Democratic political refugees began pouring over the border into Czechoslovakia. Most members of the party executive committee were arrested, but Otto Bauer—aided by DSAP member Ernst Paul, who was in Vienna at the time—and paramilitary leader Julius Deutsch were able to escape to Czechoslovakia, where they founded the exile organization, "ALÖS" (*Auslandsbüro der österreichischen Sozialdemokratie*), with headquarters in Brünn. Austrian refugees lived mainly in Moravia-Silesia.

The Czechoslovak nationalist press launched a propaganda campaign against the influx of refugees,[44] but their numbers remained relatively small, especially in comparison with the number of permanent resident aliens in Czechoslovakia (the 238,808 aliens in Czechoslovakia in 1921 made up 1.7 percent of the population, rising slightly to 249,971, or 1.8 percent in 1930). There is no accurate record of the number of émigrés from Austrian and Reich Germany in general, or of social democratic émigrés in particular, but it has been estimated that between 8,000 and 10,000 German refugees from the Reich entered Czechoslovakia between 1933 and 1938. Many of them reemigrated, however, either immediately upon arrival or at a later date.

The SPD was no more united in exile than it had been in the last years of the Weimar Republic. There was conflict between the party and the trade unions, within the party over leadership and how the struggle against the Nazis was to be carried out, and occasionally with the Austrian exiles. The Austrian Social Democrats suffered less from factional disputes, in part because the middle and lower level officials who led the newly-formed *Revolutionäre Sozialisten Österreichs* had remained in Austria to engage in underground activities. DSAP relations with ALÖS and Sopade members were close; both Austrians and Reich Germans participated in daily affairs of the party.

Party secretary Siegfried Taub, aided by Paul, acted as liaison between the DSAP and Sopade, while Hampl was Sopade's main contact with the Czechoslovak Social Democrats. Numerous references in Sopade correspondence to Taub—who had good contacts throughout the Czechoslovak government—underscore the vital role he played as political troubleshooter for the social democratic exiles. According to former Sopade executive committee member Fritz Heine, relations with the Czechoslovak Social Democrats initially were not so warm as with the DSAP, but the former gave Sopade members pointers on how to conduct underground work, based on their own experiences during the First World War.[45]

DSAP aid to the refugees took many forms. By late 1933, more than two hundred Reich German Social Democratic émigrés had been provided with room and board and minimal pocket money. Sopade members used Sudeten German Social Democratic facilities in pursuing clandestine work, and following the Nazi occupation of Czechoslovakia, one of many DSAP members who would pay with his life for helping Sopade was Hans Ruppert, mayor of Neuern in southwestern Bohemia, who had kept a radio transmitter in his home. Party treasurer Heller and chairman Czech, both of whom were lawyers, provided legal advice. Czech helped political refugees gain Czechoslovak citizenship, including novelist Thomas Mann and social democratic theorist Karl Kautsky, whom Berlin had deprived of citizenship. Moravian-born Friedrich Stampfer, former editor-in-chief of the SPD daily *Vorwärts* and a friend of Czech's, did not need this aid: DSAP lawyers established that Stampfer had not lost his Czechoslovak citizenship upon becoming a naturalized German citizen.

Reich German displeasure with émigré activities in Czechoslovakia officially was expressed in diplomatic protests; unofficially, it took the form of kidnappings, the infiltration of émigré groups, and in the case of the noted professor Theodor Lessing, murder. Nazi complaints often resulted in Czechoslovak governmental pressure on the refugees. The Sopade headquarters was moved to Paris in spring 1938 due both to Prague's increasing limitation of activity in the border regions and to the worsening international political situation.[46]

The Czechoslovak Social Democrats provided little aid to the social democratic émigrés. Nor had the Austrian Social Democrats been willing to help the Reich German refugees in the period prior to February 1934, when they, too, were forced into emigration. Although the Matteotti Fund of the International Federation of Trade Unions in Paris provided some aid, the bulk of the responsibility fell on the Sudeten German Social Democrats. Despite their help, the funds available to the refugees have been aptly characterized as providing "too little to live and too much to die."[47] The care and feeding of the refugees, the mediation of their disputes with one another as well as with Prague, and the support for their clandestine work, fell to the DSAP, placing financial and political strain on the party.

Internal Opposition

Following the division of the DSAP in 1921, party leaders had attempted to avoid further internal dissension, and intraparty disagreements received little publicity. The executive committee played down dissent through control of the party papers which did not exercise an independent editorial policy. The deemphasizing of internal disputes had been useful during the process of rebuilding of the party in the early 1920s, and there was relatively little dissent to repress during the stable years after 1925. By late 1930, however, members had begun complaining about the party's lack of goals and there was increasing disagreement on how to combat the Depression and the growth of radical right-wing politics that accompanied it. The DSAP had no means of positively channeling the disagreements which arose over these issues and others.

Complaints about party policy were voiced beginning at the DSAP congress at Teplitz in 1930, and more strongly at Prague in 1932. At the Teplitz Congress, there was criticism of the decision to join the government, but none of Czech's leadership or record as minister. Delegates from northwest Bohemia, particularly from Bodenbach—which, led by mayor Fritz Kessler and communal representative Richard Reitzner, formed a sort of institutional opposition within the party—opposed the unqualified participation of the DSAP in the coalition. Reitzner, a school teacher, who had flirted with Bolshevik ideas while a POW in Russia and supported Kreibich's Action Program a decade earlier, but never joined the Communist Party, had a reputation as a leftist, without really doing much to substantiate it, except make fiery speeches at party congresses.

Some party leaders interpreted the somewhat favorable results of the 1931 communal elections as reflecting support for German Social Democratic coalition politics, but there was mounting criticism of the DSAP's continued presence in the government at the party congress in 1932, especially from the Asch, Aussig, and Bodenbach organizations. Czech was also attacked, although his achievements in the Welfare Ministry were recognized. Reitzner was particularly critical, claiming that after three years in the coalition, there had been no progress on economic or national questions and that the party was unable to combat the fascist threats it now faced. Some delegates demanded that the DSAP leave the coalition (in order, claimed their opponents, to avoid responsibility for unpopular governmental measures).[48] The heated debate, however, was curtailed and the party majority behind Czech and Heller supported a resolution recognizing the need to remain in the coalition to aid the almost 600,000 unemployed in the country.[49] The executive committee would later use this same argument to the frustration of the opposition at a joint trade union-party conference in Trautenau in December 1934. The comments of parliamentary secretary Robert Wiener appear to mirror the attitude of the party executive: there had been no surprising successes since the party joined the coalition, but none had been promised. The party was, however, helping to uphold parliamentary democracy in a time of increasing fascist threat.[50]

Prior to the party congress in 1932, Franzel had advocated a new political program to attract younger members, to clarify the party's position on national-cultural matters, and to address the numerous political problems that had arisen since the existing program had been adopted in 1919. His proposals incorporated ideological borrowings from the Czechoslovak and the Austrian Social Democratic parties. Because Franzel believed that the DSAP had no political theorist capable of developing a program alone, he proposed appointing a committee. Franzel suggested that participants should come from among the younger party members who would have to deal with the new program in future years, rather than from among the older Austromarxists.[51]

The twenty-member commission charged with creating a new party program appointed at the 1932 congress included older party leaders as well as some younger representatives as Franzel had recommended. Among the participants were chairman Czech, secretary Taub, party executive committee members Josef Hofbauer, Jaksch, Kern, Paul, and Emil Strauss as well as Franzel. Czech, Franzel, Hofbauer, Strauss, and other appointees had the academic and intellectual credentials for membership on the committee. The inclusion of Jaksch reflects the growing influence of this self-educated young man from a small village in the Böhmerwald, who had been trained as a stone mason. A member of the party executive committee since 1921, until his election to the parliament in 1929 he had been active mainly at the periphery of the party, first as an official of the Small Farmers Union, and later as the editor of the provincial social democratic newspaper in Komotau. He was now beginning to make a name for himself throughout the party.

To the intraparty critics, the need for a new political program was self-evident. The existing program, adopted almost fifteen years earlier at the party's founding congress, was based on the Brünn Program of 1899 and the Vienna Program of 1901, which called for an eight-hour day (legislated in Czechoslovakia in 1920) and the universal, equal franchise (legislated in the Cisleithania in 1907). Although the development of a new program had been mandated at previous party congresses, no further action had been taken, in contrast to the Austrian, Czechoslovak, and Weimar German Social Democratic parties, all of which had produced new political programs since the First World War. The program committee seldom met—almost forty years later surving members Franzel, Kern, and Paul could not remember a single meeting[52]—and in spring 1935, its members declared themselves unable to fulfill their task.[53]

Opposition was also developing within the German Social Democratic youth organization. It was treated in a heavy-handed manner heralding behavior within the party itself—the expulsion of dissenters. In autumn 1933, the young socialists began work on a new political program. When the "principal declaration" of the program appeared in the youth organization's newspaper, *Sozialistische Jugend,* the following March, internal party critics dismissed the declaration as "pitiful."[54] They claimed that party leaders, objecting to the program originally worked out by the young socialists, had simply quashed it.

The conference of the young socialists a month later at Komotau was the scene of stormy discussion between the group's executive committee and the opposition. The suggestion of a delegate from Brünn that one of the younger conference participants replace Otto Bauer as speaker sparked the controversy. In the uproar that followed, the delegate who made the proposal was removed from the speaker's platform and no other representatives of the opposition were allowed on the podium. At the next meeting of the young socialists, the executive committee presented a motion to expel the errant delegate for insulting Bauer. Those present were informed that anyone who opposed the disciplinary action could also consider himself expelled from the organization. In the end, only two people—both from Brünn—were expelled in addition to the delegate who caused the row, although about one-third of those in attendance abstained from voting on the issue.[55]

There were continuing references to dissent among the young socialists, including the organizational success of the opposition in the Karlsbad area under the leadership of district representative Michael Walter. They were met with a terse announcement by the executive committee of the youth organization, of which Walter was a member, that young socialist successes in Karlsbad were neither due to dissenting stances by Walter nor to an opposition there, but to the hard work of all the young socialists of the Karlsbad district.[56] Despite the denials, Walter's activities had been of enough concern to party leaders that an official of the young socialists in Prague had written to the party secretary for the Eger district, where Walter was active, for information on his behavior.[57]

The youth movement, which had never made a recovery comparable to that of the parent party after 1921, was where the German Social Democratic lack of appeal to the younger generation was most apparent. Young socialist membership had dropped from more than 30,000 in 1920 to about one-fifth of that in 1926. A 1930 campaign, "Youth, We Are Calling You" ("Jugend, wir rufen Dich"), increased membership to 8,500, the highest number since 1920 and one not to be equaled again.[58] Both the Czechoslovak Communists and the German National Socialists proved attractive to young Germans. Although DSAP leaders claimed not to have lost younger party members to the German National Socialists, as had the other German parties, they recognized that many of the younger members of the DNSAP came from working-class backgrounds.[59] The movement Kern and Paul rebuilt after 1921 appears to have been inspired by bourgeois German youth movements, with folk music, folk dancing, and stress on clean living overshadowing political activities. The differing emphasis of the youth movement was indicated by the changing of the name of the group's magazine from *Sozialistische Jugend* (Socialist Youth) to *Das Junge Volk* (Young People) in the mid-1930s.[60]

The disagreements within the youth organization provided some of the impetus for the publication beginning in June 1934 of *Sozialistische Aktion,* a fortnightly periodical representing what would prove to be the first sizeable, cohesive, intraparty opposition after 1920. Its founders, believing that party members were increasingly dissatisfied with the party leadership

but lacked a focal point for their dissent, attempted to build a united opposition. The chances for the dissenters to make themselves heard were
limited to local meetings, because at larger conferences, their comments
were either dismissed or not elicited at all, primarily due to the excessive
fears of some party leaders that any opposition could lead to a situation
similar to that of 1920, resulting in another division, and the possible
destruction of the party.

The opposition centered around three young social democrats from
Brünn, Georg Hammerschlag, Karl Rybnicky, and Hans Torn. Both Ham-
merschlag and Torn were students; Torn studied in Prague and knew
Franzel.[61] Rybnicky was a member of the Brünn DSAP organization.
Ferdinand Loew, a liquor manufacturer in Brünn, provided seed money
for *Sozialistische Aktion.*[62] Franzel and the "Bodenbacher," Kessler and
Reitzner, gave moral support. Franzel regularly wrote lead articles for
Sozialistische Aktion, some of which reflected his increasingly unorthodox
views, and he publicized the group's efforts in other journals, in both cases
anonymously. Jaksch, however, remained aloof.[63]

Comments in *Sozialistische Aktion* highlighted the dissatisfaction of
many members with the press, policies, and administration of the party.[64]
Dissenters wanted decisive changes: they called for the open discussion of
problems and for the integration of the members of the opposition, with
their energy and new ideas, into the party. They demanded that the DSAP
program committee meet immediately and that opposition members be
added to it. A new program should be formulated stressing the interde-
pendence of the Czechs and Germans in Czechoslovakia, rather than class
struggle, with a political orientation toward Prague, rather than Berlin and
Vienna. Although a thinly-veiled insult to the party's leaders, who had
been schooled in Austromarxism, the last demand made sense, given the
political situation in Austria and Germany. The opposition deemed the
convening of a congress especially important; according to party statutes,
one was to be held every two years. The political upheavals that had taken
place since the 1932 party congress—the destruction of the Weimar Republic, the defeat of the Austrian Social Democrats, the high point of the
Depression—made holding a congress all the more important.

At least initially, the opposition attacked the party leadership primarily
because of its lack of a program and its negative reaction to internal opposition, rather than because of its coalition policies.[65] The response of

the party leaders was to bring the three culprits before the five-member party arbitration committee, under the leadership of Jaksch, which threatened them with expulsion. A personality clash between Jaksch and Torn, as well as Jaksch's apparent unwillingness to damage his political career for possible allies, apparently played a role in the inability to negotiate a tolerable compromise with the three, who were thus expelled in autumn 1934.[66]

When Hammerschlag, Rybnicky, and Torn continued to publish *Sozialistische Aktion,* they were derided in the party press as "a handful of intellectuals and students, rich men's sons."[67] Both the party leadership and the opposition betrayed a strain of anti-intellectualism with each side belittling the arguments of the other as "academic and intellectual."[68] The party leadership attempted to dismiss the opposition as insignificant, which was incorrect.[69] That *Sozialistische Aktion* was widely distributed and read in some areas of Bohemia was attested to in a letter addressed to party secretary Taub blaming the recently-elected Eger district leader Martin Benda for the opposition's influence there, because he distributed the periodical (Benda denied the accusation).[70]

A proposal for a party program appeared in *Sozialistische Aktion.* Probably the work of Torn, and influenced by Franzel,[71] it was designed to appeal to farmers and the petite bourgeoisie, as well as to workers, reflecting the opposition's belief that the DSAP needed to expand its base of support. This "economic offensive against fascism," was divided into economic and political sections. Economic proposals included a five-year economic plan, a state monopoly on foreign trade and agricultural production, the nationalization of banks and insurance companies, and tax reform benefiting the working class and small landowners. Among its mixed political demands were the reform of parliament and the political parties, the creation of a "republican militia," and the separation of economic and political administration.[72]

Some party members interpreted the decision in spring 1934 to discontinue publication of *Tribüne,* the party's theoretical periodical which provided a forum for discussion of political topics, as another attempt to silence the internal opposition. This was because Franzel, a frequent *Tribüune* contributor, was dismissed from his post as head of the office for cultural and educational matters that summer and replaced by the DSAP loyalist Paul. The ostensible reason for party maverick Franzel's removal was his presumed responsibility for the undesirable conditions within the party, including the publication of *Sozialistische Aktion*. [73]

In May 1934, *Tribüne* was replaced with a new periodical, *Der Kampf*, edited by party executive committee member Hofbauer and ALÖS leader Bauer. The opposition feared that the creation of a joint periodical for the DSAP and the Austrian exiles would limit discussion of problems specific to Czechoslovakia, particularly the nationality problem, but this was not the case.

In memoirs written some thirty-five years later, Franzel complained that on the whole, the émigrés employed in the German Social Democratic press during the 1930s hurt the party more than they helped it. What could be discussed in the party press became itself a political problem. Franzel claimed that the émigrés shifted the emphasis from questions of vital concern to DSAP members to Reich German questions and later, to Austromarxist questions. [74]

As parliamentary elections neared in the spring of 1935, *Sozialistische Aktion* began criticizing the party's electoral practices as well as the qualifications of its parliamentary representatives: the advanced age of the party leaders, especially those in parliament; the performance of parliamentarians, and the method of selecting candidates. [75]

The opposition claimed that the party's method of apportioning mandates resulted in a general lack of specialists in fields such as social policy and workers' rights in parliament. Deputies were supposed to represent the entire party, but mandates often went to executive committee members and other party functionaries. In addition, the opposition charged that mandates were "sold." If a particular interest group or trade union contributed enough money to a campaign, its leader had the opportunity to be highly placed on a party voting list for parliament. Although the complaints of unfair political practices appear to have been exaggerated, they did have a basis: throughout the interwar period, the German Social Democratic parliamentarians were mainly trade union leaders or party officials. [76] Criticism of the overlap between the party executive committee and parliament was not new, since proposals at the party congress in 1932 had included limiting the number of deputies and party employees on the executive committee to fifty percent.

The final complaint concerned the "intellectual strength" of the party, which varied from region to region, but which was concentrated in cities and industrial areas. The opposition claimed that only local candidates stood for election, and thus, the use of some of the party's best minds was lost.[77] This was incorrect. Following SDAPÖ tradition, the DSAP placed candidates for parliament according to where they had the best chance of being elected, not according to where they lived. Beginning in 1925, Czech stood for election in Bohemia rather than in Moravia for symbolic reasons, leading the list earlier headed by first party chairman, Josef Seliger.

As these complaints make clear, the problem of opposition within the party was in part generational. Many of the party leaders had been in their forties and fifties at the end of the First World War, when the German Social Democratic Party was formed. More than ten years later, a majority of them still held high positions within the party, a situation that allowed little space for newer, younger political faces and ideas. The average age of party executive members was just over forty-three in 1920; by 1932, it was almost fifty. The original party executive committee had been composed of sixteen members, seven of whom still served on the thirty member executive committee in 1932. An additional seven members had been serving on the party executive committee since 1921.

During the third parliamentary period (1929-1935), German Social Democratic representatives were among the oldest of the German political parties. The average age of the DSAP deputies in 1929 was almost fifty-two years, and of the senators, fifty-eight years. Thirteen of the twenty-one deputies were over fifty years of age and three of them were more than sixty. While it was true that most DSAP parliamentarians were somewhat older than those of other parties, the problem was not so much that they were old as they had held their positions for a long time. Fifteen of twenty-one deputies and seven of eleven senators had served in all three parliamentary periods; two more senators had also served since 1920, first as deputies and later as senators. The average age of the eleven deputies elected in the fourth parliamentary period (1935-1938), was slightly higher than those elected in the third period. In the early 1930s, the deputies of the much smaller DAWG were close to the DSAP in age; one-half of them were more than fifty and one-quarter were over sixty years old. The deputies of the other German political parties tended to be younger, although, for example, the German Agrarian Party chairman Franz Spina was older than Ludwig Czech. While only 15 percent of the German Social

Democrats were under the age of fifty in 1934, some 40 percent of the German Agrarian deputies and 35 percent of the German Clerical deputies were. The German National Socialists were still younger, with almost 75 percent of their deputies were in their thirties and forties. The Czechoslovak Communist deputies were the youngest of all, with more than 90 percent under the age of fifty.[78]

Generational problems were not limited to the German Social Democrats. The Czechoslovak Social Democrats traced their origins back to an 1878 congress in which the average age, at least of those participants arrested had been twenty-three, and the oldest thirty.[79] The leaders of the Czechoslovak Social Democratic Party until 15 March 1939 assumed their positions around 1910, when they were about thirty years old. Members of the next generation would have been closer to fifty when, under normal circumstances, they would have taken over party leadership. Fifteen Czechoslovak Social Democratic deputies served in parliament during all four voting periods and nine of them had participated in the constituent National Assembly as well. Among the other political parties of the republic, multiple parliamentary terms—a sign of political stability—was also the rule, rather than the exception. Only parties suffering internal upheavals, like the Czechoslovak Communist Party, had a large turnover in parliamentary deputies.[80]

In Czechoslovakia, as in Great Britain, Germany, and elsewhere, members of the so-called "Lost Generation," who in ordinary circumstances would have succeeded the preceding generation of political leaders, had died in the First World War. Among the peoples of the Habsburg Monarchy, the Germans had suffered the highest proportional losses. This provides a partial explanation for the relatively advanced age of the First Republic's parliamentarians in general, especially of the German parliamentarians, but not for those of the DSAP in particular.

Occupational descriptions were often subjective, however, sometimes making it difficult to classify the parliamentary representatives by occupation. Often, a journalist or the administrator of a party-related organization, an insurance scheme, for example, was a former worker. His position in the party bureaucracy was a reward for loyal service. The term "worker" was also politically loaded. Expediency dictated that Czechoslovak Communist Party parliamentarians describe themselves as "workers," when they were in fact administrators. By the same token, a parliamentarian listing himself as an official (*Beamter*) could be in the public or the private sector, a trade union official or a party employee. In addition, representatives could list several occupations and or change them during their term in office.

The percentage which the two largest occupational groups, trade union leaders and party functionaries, represented among the German Social Democratic parliamentarians is thus difficult to determine exactly, but during the interwar period, some three-quarters of all DSAP representatives were either trade union leaders or party functionaries. Up to 1933, forty to fifty percent of the deputies were trade union leaders, while party officials were in the majority among the senators. Party functionaries represented one-quarter to one-third of the deputies during the first three parliamentary periods, while in the politically precarious period after 1935, more than half of the deputies were party functionaries. There was a noticeable difference between those heading lists for parliamentary elections and those heading lists for local elections. The latter varied more and included many workers as well as landless laborers.

Following the parliamentary elections in May 1935, the German Social Democratic Party executive committee would officially condemn *Sozialistische Aktion:* its editors were accused of publishing two issues immediately before the elections that damaged the party and provided its opponents with anti-party propaganda. The publication of *Sozialistische Aktion* was declared to be against the interests of the party and any association with it, including its purchase, was to be punished with expulsion from the party.[81] The last issue of the paper—publication had been planned to coincide with the German Social Democratic Party congress in June 1935—was confiscated by the police. The paper allegedly contained statements that were damaging to Czech personally and that libeled him as a public official in the exercise of his office.[82] In any case, due to the German Social Democratic Party's loss of political significance as a result of the elections, the group's original goal, a change in the intellectual and structural direction of the party, had become irrelevant. Therefore, *Sozialistische Aktion* would no longer appear as a fortnightly periodical, but as an occasional circular. This was the end of *Sozialistische Aktion* as a paper and as a group. Torn worked for the Spanish Republicans in Paris, while Hammerschlag and Rybnicky simply disappeared from the Czechoslovak political scene.

The demands voiced in *Sozialistische Aktion* were neither "left" or "right"; they were an attempt to breathe new life into an excessively bureaucratic party through open discussion about party direction. Opposition leaders envisioned themselves as part of a larger movement to revitalize international social democracy. In contrast to the intraparty social democratic opposition in other lands, however, they opposed cooperation with the communists, an attitude they shared with the party leadership.

What, if any, positive effect *Sozialistische Aktion* had on the German Social Democratic Party remains an open question. Letters published in the periodical initially reflected the desire for a new party program and widespread dissatisfaction with the party bureaucracy, and later with the party leaders. Executive committee members overreacted to the criticism, and their campaign against the group, spearheaded by deputy Eugen de Witte, seems to have engendered sympathy for the opposition and focused attention on its political demands. Certainly, some of the complaints were valid—and had been made previously—particularly those concerning the excessive bureaucracy of the party and the need for a party program. Others, however, appear to be a settling of personal political accounts. During the course of the debate, both sides adopted increasingly uncompromising positions. Despite the dissenters' call to maintain party discipline during the parliamentary campaign in 1935, *Sozialistische Aktion's* criticism of the DSAP leadership certainly provided the opposition with anti-party propaganda.[83] In the aftermath of the elections, party leaders would be more stubborn in their attempts to maintain the political status quo.

Domestic Politics, 1929-1935

In the early 1930s, there was an increase in political radicalism in Czechoslovakia. The devastating effect of the Depression on the Sudeten lands as well as the mounting influence of the Nazis in Germany clearly encouraged the growing activity of the German National Socialist Party, whose membership had more than doubled between 1930 and 1932. The shrunken Communist Party, by now little more than a Stalinist sect, continued its vocal campaign against the "social fascists." Members of the Slovak Clericals stepped up their demands for Slovak autonomy, and small

Czech fascist groups formed. The Czech fascists and the Slovak autonom-
ists, however, unlike the others, only represented a domestic problem. The
Czechoslovak government enacted legislation broadening its powers to
respond to the growing radicalism.

Both a law expanding press censorship and one enlarging upon the provisions of the 1923 Law for the Protection of the Republic were passed
in July 1933, the latter limiting, among other things, the freedom of assembly. The press law was regularly employed against the political left,
and *Rudé právo,* for example, was suspended more than thirty times in
1933 and 1934.[84] Prague used censorship not only against the parties of
the far left and radical right, but also to the social democratic coalition
participants. Sometimes, ostensibly non-political activities were prohibit-
ed, including a German Social Democratic youth organization's planned
cabaret evening.[85] In 1934, the government refused to permit demonstrations by the recently-formed Sudeten German Homefront (*Sudetendeutsche Heimatfront,* the SHF), in Karlsbad and Gablonz, or counter-
demonstrations sponsored by the socialist parties.[86] Sometimes these
attempts to limit public gatherings were thwarted. Following the refusal
to permit SHF demonstrations on May Day, the government attempted
to apply the same measure to traditional socialist-sponsored May Day
demonstrations in eastern Bohemia, but had to back down due to widespread protests. The socialist working class of eastern Bohemia marched
as usual.[87]

By 1931, the increasingly radical behavior of segments of the DNSAP
had led some of the organization's leaders to fear a crackdown by Prague
against irredentist activity. These fears proved justified, when the government began moving against the party in late 1932. Ultimately, both the
DNSAP and the DNP were disbanded in the autumn of 1933. One result
of the disbanding of the two parties was the division of their mandates.
The German Social Democrats demanded that the division of the mandates reflect the proportional strength of the remaining parties, but they
were often apportioned by the local government bureaucrats in a manner
reflecting their own political point of view, which was not usually social
democratic. In some places, newly-appointed local officials, although
designated "unpolitical," were not unpolitical at all, but were instead
former members of various other German parties. Because the redistribution of the mandates affected the strength of the remaining parties at the

local level, including influence on municipal contracts and employment, the German Social Democrats paid close attention to the process. Mandates were rarely distributed to their satisfaction, but German Social Democratic attempts to intervene with Prague were seldom successful.[88] As party deputy Franz Katz noted, the goal of the bureaucracy in distribution of the mandates was to weaken the social democrats in relation to the bourgeois parties.[89]

Even as the DNSAP and the DNP were dissolved, a new political force appeared on the Czechoslovak political horizon. Gymnastics instructor Konrad Henlein announced the formation of the Sudeten German Homefront at a meeting of the German Gymnastic Organization (*Deutscher Turnverband*) at Saaz in October 1933. Although Henlein's goals were nebulous, the SHF, with its *völkisch,* anti-Marxist rhetoric, quickly gained widespread support not only among former members of the DNSAP and the DNP, but also among the German Agrarians. Lesser gains were made among the German Clericals, the Social Democrats, and the German members of the Communist Party. The Sudeten German Homefront was not merely a replacement for the recently-disbanded nationalist German parties, nor was it simply a pawn of Hitler, although some of its leaders were Nazis. There were varying, even contradictory, political strains within the movement, and goals ranged from Sudeten German development as an independent branch of Germandom to the dissemination of Hitler's doctrine in the Sudeten lands.[90]

The German Social Democrats and the Czechoslovak Communists lost little time in branding the group as fascist and associating it with Nazi Germany. The political situation was initially complicated by the undefined status of the SHF: if it was not a political party, what was it? Although Henlein announced a political program calling for German cultural autonomy before a crowd of 20,000 at Böhmisch Leipa in October 1934, he would not transform his movement into a political party until just before the parliamentary elections in 1935.

German Social Democrats responded to Henlein's speech at Böhmisch Leipa with a counter-program and demonstrations in an offensive against "hunger, want, and Henlein fascism."[91] The demonstrations ("the advance of the 90,000"), which took place throughout Bohemia and Moravia on 4 November, were well attended, with the largest gathering of 25,000 people taking place at Karlsbad. German Social Democratic demands included more state investment in economically distressed areas and shorter working hours at the same salary.[92] Some DSAP demands appear to have been doomed from the start. One party senator admitted the government investment mandated in the program was impossible because the money simply was not there.[93]

The status of the SHF was still unresolved in spring 1935. Given Prague's treatment of the DNSAP and DNP, one could assume that the SHF would have been dissolved for seditious activity. The government, however, delayed making a decision about the Henleinists. The Sudeten German Homefront finally received permission to participate in the June 1935 elections in April, provided it constituted itself as a political party, which it did; becoming the Sudeten German Party.

The reason for the government's failure to crackdown on the Henleinists is not known. Some contemporary observers attributed it to the old and feeble President Masaryk, others to his son Jan, or both. Especially the Czech democratic left around Beneš agitated for the banning of the SHF on foreign political and on domestic grounds. They sought the same treatment for the parties of the Czech fascists associated with former Legionary Rudolf Gajda and former Czechoslovak National Socialist Jiří Stříbrný.[94] An early decision on the fate of the Henleinists had been delayed due to the disunity of the Czechoslovak Agrarians; those around the increasingly powerful Slovak Protestant Milan Hodža opposed the SHF, while more conservative party members were pro-Henlein. Some of the last asserted that if the SHF was dissolved, the KSČ should be as well. Other conservative Czechoslovak Agrarians opposed removal of the Czechoslovak Communists from the political scene on the grounds that it would benefit the social democrats.[95]

At the time, British diplomat Sir Joseph Addison wrote that he believed the younger Masaryk was acting for his father—"probably actively"—in preventing the disbanding of the SHF.[96] An article published in the Czechoslovak Clerical *Lidové listy* in 1938 also advanced this thesis. All of the Czechoslovak coalition members, save the Czechoslovak Agrarians, opposed Henleinist participation in the elections.[97] They supported German Agrarian Franz Spina's negotiations with the SHF and his dual hopes of drawing off some of Henlein's support and of damaging the German Clericals and Social Democrats. The SHF would then join a coalition to be dominated by the Czech-German "Agro-Henleinists." Those responsible for deciding the matter never presented President Masaryk with a directive on the problem. In early April 1935, when a decision could no longer be delayed, Prime Minister Malypetr received a piece of paper with a single typewritten sentence opposing the dissolution of the Henleinist organization, which Malypetr believed had been dictated by the younger Masaryk.[98] The ministers respected what they thought were the wishes of the president and the Henleinists participated in the elections. Writing in the early 1970s, former Czech politician and publisher Julius Firt noted that Beneš's failure to convince Masaryk, who had met and allegedly been impressed by Henlein, to abolish the SHF marked the only time Beneš did not have his way with Masaryk.[99]

Because the government had banned two German parties eighteen months earlier, Masaryk was probably reluctant to recommend the same measure for the Henleinists, who had thus far respected Czechoslovak laws. Although the German Social Democrats fulminated against the SHF they were not in a position to demand the dissolution of another German party, especially because they had already been accused of being national traitors. Only the Czechoslovak coalition parties were in a position to agitate actively for the banning of the SHF, and those who favored this step were unable to achieve it in the face of the Czechoslovak Agrarians' opposition and Masaryk's disinclination.

Sozialistische Aktion accused both the German Agrarians and Social Democrats of acting in self-interest regarding the Henleinists. Following the failure of their negotiations with the SHF, the German Agrarians sought to have the Henleinists disbanded because they would otherwise lose most of their support to them. The German Social Democrats reportedly did not demand that the SHF should be banned for reasons of equal self-interest: former Henleinists would be unlikely to vote for them and in addition, if the SHF were to draw away votes from the German bourgeois parties, the DSAP could win the election.[100] This criticism of the German Social Democratic position is harsh, given the party's condemnation of the Henleinists from the outset. In addition, the DSAP could have expected to attract some of the SHF's working-class support, had it been abolished.

The 1935 Parliamentary Elections

Torn by internal conflict and condemned by the Henleinists as traitors to the German people for participating in the government coalition, the German Social Democrats were on the defensive during the campaign of 1935. Rather than distancing themselves from the government and its unsuccessful policies, party leaders defended their participation in the coalition. The majority of the Sudeten Germans, however, many of them long-term unemployed, were unimpressed by the DSAP's government record. Arguments that social democratic efforts had prevented the political situation in Czechoslovakia from deteriorating as it had in neighboring lands fell on deaf ears.[101]

The campaign was particularly rough in 1935. Forty-six people were injured as violence erupted between German Social Democrats and Henleinists at the SdP's first two election assemblies. Similar incidents occurred, prompting the Interior Ministry to send gendarmes to many rallies.[102] Accompanied by martial music, banners, and simplistic slogans like "Volk in Dreck, Bonzen in Speck" (The people in muck, the bigwigs in luck),[103] the SdP's campaign rallies resembled those of the Nazis. The Henleinists attacked on all fronts. SdP politicians made personal attacks on DSAP candidates and took advantage of the party's internal problems.

Most Sudeten Germans were uninterested in German Social Democratic attempts to tie the Henleinists to the Nazis. German Social Democratic claims:

> The Henlein Front lies, as it has lied a hundred times in the campaign. The Henleinists lie as they have learned from their teacher Goebbels. . . .[104]

were unsuccessful. According to *Sozialistische Aktion,* the members of the bourgeoisie knew the Henleinists were fascists, and supported them precisely for that reason, while the working class already recognized the danger the SdP posed.[105] Henlein's propaganda, stressing the contrast between unemployment in Czech and in German counties and the anti-German policies of the Czechoslovak government met with far better reception. He focused on the German Social Democrats and their "betrayal" of the German worker.

The Czechoslovak Social Democrats also joined the battle against the SdP, condemning Henlein and his followers as Nazis. They asserted that those living in the border regions "have long known that SHF stands for 'Sei Hitlers Freund'" (Be Hitler's Friend).[106] For the first time since 1921, the German Social Democrats were not the major target of the Communist Party, and the KSČ thus participated in the losing campaign against the Henleinists.

The German Social Democrats realized that they would lose votes in the coming election. Although party leaders had reckoned with a "slap," what they received was a knock-out blow. *Sozialistische Aktion*'s prediction that the SdP would win 25 to 35 mandates, thus becoming the third largest party in the country, was low, but more accurate than that of the party leaders.[107] As the headlines in German Social Democratic newspapers read on the day following the election, when the extent of the Henleinists' victory became clear: "The sixth year of the [economic] crisis: in the Czech camp, democracy is victorious; in the German camp, fascism is victorious."[108]

Table 4-1

Working Class Party Votes
In the Interwar Parliamentary Elections

Chamber of Deputies

Party	1920	1925	1929	1935
German Social Democrats	689,589 11.1% 31 Mandates	411,365 5.8% 17 Mandates	506,761 6.9% 21 Mandates	299,942 3.6% 11 Mandates
Czechoslovak National Socialists	500,821 8.1% 24 Mandates	609,153 8.6% 28 Mandates	767,328 10.4% 32 Mandates	755,880 9.2% 28 Mandates
Czechoslovak Social Democrats	1,590,520 25.7% 74 Mandates	631,403 8.9% 29 Mandates	963,462 13.0% 39 Mandates	1,034,774 12.6% 38 Mandates
Czechoslovak Progressive Socialists	58,580 0.9% 3 Mandates	——	——	——
Czechoslovak Communists	——	934,223 13.2% 41 Mandates	753,220 10.2% 30 Mandates	849,509 10.3% 30 Mandates
Total for the First Three Parties	2,780,930 44.9% 129 Mandates	1,651,921 23.3% 74 Mandates	2,237,551 30.3% 92 Mandates	2,090,596 25.4% 77 Mandates
Total Vote	6,200,032 100.0% 281 Mandates	7,107,411 100.0% 300 Mandates	7,384,979 100.0% 300 Mandates	8,231,412 100.0% 300 Mandates

Senate

Party	1920	1925	1929	1935
German Social Democrats	593,344 11.4% 16 Mandates	363,310 6.0% 9 Mandates	446,940 6.9% 11 Mandates	271,097 3.7% 6 Mandates
Czechoslovak National Socialists	373,913 7.1% 10 Mandates	516,250 8.5% 14 Mandates	666,607 10.3% 16 Mandates	672,126 9.3% 14 Mandates
Czechoslovak Social Democrats	1,466,958 28.1% 41 Mandates	537,470 8.8% 14 Mandates	841,331 13.0% 20 Mandates	910,252 12.5% 20 Mandates
Czechoslovak Progressive Socialists	3,050 0.1% 0 Mandates	——	——	——
Czechoslovak Communists	——	774,454 12.7% 20 Mandates	644,896 10.0% 15 Mandates	740,696 10.2% 16 Mandates
Total for the First Three Parties	2,434,215 46.7% 67 Mandates	1,417,030 23.3% 37 Mandates	1,954,878 30.2% 47 Mandates	1,853,475 25.5% 40 Mandates
Total Vote	5,226,811 142 Mandates	6,096,717 150 Mandates	6,450,501 150 Mandates	7,277,053 150 Mandates

Source: Czechoslovak Republic. State Statistical Office (Státní úřad statistický). Official voting results published in 1922, 1926, 1930, and 1936 in Czech, French, and German-language versions.

TABLE 4 - 2
REGISTERED UNEMPLOYMENT IN CZECHOSLOVAKIA

	1930	1931	1932	1933	1934	1935
January	--	313511	583138	872775	838982	818005
February	--	343972	631736	920182	844284	833194
March	--	339505	633907	877955	789789	804794
April	--	296756	555832	795919	704388	734550
May	--	249686	487228	726629	624850	666433
June	--	220038	466948	675933	582810	605956
July	--	--	453294	640360	569450	566559
August	--	--	460952	625836	572428	557566
September	--	228357	486935	622561	576267	573362
October	115202	354201	--	629992	599464	601390
November	149164	336874	607881	691078	668937	678870
December	227058	486363	745319	778150	755149	794407

NOTE: Where unemployment numbers conflicted, the variation was less
         than one percent.

TABLE 4 - 3
REGISTERED UNEMPLOYMENT
IN NORTHWESTERN BOHEMIA

	1930	1931	1932	1933	1934	1935
January	18828	81714	150554	182681	152606	144456
February	23207	93629	161212	189943	154791	144517
March	--	96361	158997	182883	--	139272
April	--	83810	146468	169412	120478	132267
May	--	70994	127467	157713	119444	124858
June	--	--	120103	144753	115356	118005
July	--	64330	115514	136055	115752	114117
August	--	56033	114250	129649	116362	113043
September	--	93102	119009	126345	115310	115372
October	--	--	128486	--	119982	119257
November	--	--	138487	131273	128093	129009
December	--	126342	160868	144592	137110	--

NOTE: The statistics are based on 47 counties in northwestern
         Bohemia. Although they are not listed by name, due to other
         information   provided,   it is clear the counties are those
         primarily German ones between Weipert, Komotau, and Saaz in
         the west and Gablonz and Tannwald in the east.

SOURCE: The figures,   which   come   from both *Mitteilungen des
         Deutschen Hauptverbandes der Industrie* and   German-
         language newspapers citing the   former, apparently originate
         from the Czechoslovak Ministry of Social Welfare.

TABLE 4 - 4
COUNTIES WITH HIGHEST UNEMPLOYMENT

(Per 100 Residents)

County	12.1933	8.1934	9.1934	10.1934	8.1936
Graslitz	20.2	23.7	23.1	23.0	23.5
Neudek	16.5	13.1	--	12.3	--
Friedland	19.1	15.3	15.5	15.5	--
Rumburg	17.9	15.8	15.1	15.0	19.9
Starkenbach*	16.5	--	--	--	--
Sternberg	15.4	15.3	14.9	15.0	29.1
B. Leipa	14.2	--	--	--	--
Freudenthal	14.1	12.3	12.5	12.8	24.8
Neu-Titschein	14.1	--	--	--	--
Karlsbad	13.9	12.2	12.6	12.8	25.1
Pressnitz	--	12.1	12.1	12.8	27.4
Jägerndorf	--	11.2	--	--	--
Schluckenau	--	--	11.4	11.9	--
Römerstadt	--	--	11.3	--	27.0
Elbogen	--	12.4	12.3	12.4	27.0

(Per 100 Members of the Work Force)

County	7.1934	8.1934	9.1934	10.1934	3.1935
Graslitz	36.1	38.4	38.2	37.9	27.9
Sternberg	30.0	30.0	29.2	29.4	31.0
Friedland	23.4	26.3	26.6	26.6	27.4
Elbogen	21.4	26.0	25.9	25.9	26.0
Rumburg	29.1	25.5	24.3	24.2	25.2
Freudenthal	22.7	24.6	25.1	25.9	27.1
Neudek	25.4	24.2	--	22.8	30.4
Pressnitz	--	23.1	23.0	24.4	26.9
Jägerndorf	--	22.5	22.3	--	--
Karlsbad	21.3	22.3	23.0	23.5	23.5
B. Leipa	--	--	21.2	--	--
Römerstadt	--	--	--	--	26.0
Wsetin*	--	--	--	28.9	--

NOTES: Counties marked with an asterisk (*) are predominantly Czech.

SOURCE: The figures, which come from both *Mitteilungen des deutschen Hauptverbandes der Industrie* and German language newspapers citing the former, apparently originate from the Czechoslovak Ministry of Social Welfare.

CHAPTER V

IN DEFENSE OF THE CZECHOSLOVAK REPUBLIC
1935-1938

The New Coalition

The outcome of the parliamentary elections meant that a new coalition had to be formed. It would not include the largest political party in the country, the Sudeten German Party, which had received 67 percent of the German vote and 15 percent of the entire vote.[1] The DSAP with 16 percent of the German vote and 3.6 percent of the entire vote was the second largest German party. Although all of the Czechoslovak coalition parties had lost ground, their political balance remained essentially the same; the Agrarians with 14.3 percent of the vote were the largest party and the Social Democrats with 12.6 percent of the vote were the second largest.

On the Czechoslovak right, the Gajda Fascists and the National Union (a joint list of the Czechoslovak National Democrats and the Stříbrný group), together received 7.6 percent of the vote. On the left, the Czechoslovak Communists maintained their share of just over 10 percent of the vote, but had suffered major losses to the SdP in German areas. In Bohemia, German support for the Communist Party dropped by almost one-half, from 10.8 to 5.6 percent. In Moravia, where the KSČ's share of the German vote had been much smaller, losses were slightly smaller than in Bohemia.[2] Only an increase in Czech and Slovak votes prevented a decrease in that party's total share of the electorate as compared to 1929.

Following negotiations with the Slovak Clericals, whose price for participating in the coalition—amnesty for Vojtech Tuka—remained too high, Prime Minister Jan Malypetr formed a new government which was the same as the previous one, except for the addition of the Czech Small Traders. The portfolios of the German coalition parties reflected their decreasing political significance. Ludwig Czech replaced Franz Spina as Minister of Health, and the latter became Minister without Portfolio. When the German Clericals rejoined the coalition in 1936, Erwin Zajiček also served as Minister without Portfolio.

Unexpected Parliamentary Election Results in 1935?

Given the rapid spread of right-wing movements elsewhere in Central Europe, the outcome of the communal elections in 1931 and 1932, which showed increasing Sudeten German support for right-wing parties, should have alerted the German Social Democratic Party to a shift to the right among the Sudeten German electorate. Granted, the communal elections did not take place throughout the country, but where they did, they indicated what ought to have been a worrisome growth in support for the German National Socialists. Although the German Social Democrats recognized that the DNSAP was building a "reactionary collection of all of the enemies of the working class," they interpreted the results of the communal elections as reflecting support for social democratic coalition policies.[3] This conclusion was not without foundation: in some communities the German Social Democratic Party had increased its share of the vote.

The SdP was especially popular in the major German cities of Czechoslovakia, the largest of which had populations of between 30,000 and 50,000. In Bohemia, the percentage of communities in which the Henleinists gained more than fifty percent of the entire vote tended to increase with the size of the community and they had a majority in more than ninety percent of the communities with populations above 10,000. In Karlsbad, support for the SdP reached its high point, with seventy-five percent of the vote.[4] The SdP failed to win an absolute majority of the vote in only five of the largest German cities in Czechoslovakia, all of which had large Czech minorities: Bilin and Dux in Bohemia, and Neu-Titschein, Sternberg, and Zwittau in Moravia.[5]

The appeal of the Sudeten German Party varied regionally and it drew much of its support from the border areas of northwestern and western

Bohemia. The Henleinists were also popular in Troppau and Jägerndorf, Silesian communities in which the German Nationalists and the German National Socialists had previously been dominant. Support for the party was lower in Moravia, where it had yet to make major inroads among the traditionally large number of clerical voters.[6] The nationalist rhetoric of the SdP was often less attractive in the small, entirely German villages and mixed ethnic areas of southern Bohemia and Moravia, particularly the latter, where the inhabitants perceived the Czechs as less of a threat than did the Germans of northern and western Bohemia. These areas, geographically distant from Germany and historically tied to Austria, were also less immediately affected by events in the Third Reich.

The appeal of the Sudeten German Party cannot be solely explained by unemployment, although large-scale support in the Bohemian border regions was a reflection of economic conditions there. Rothau was one of the few communies in which the German Social Democrats, with 49 percent of the vote, defeated the SdP, with 33 percent. Rothau had one of the highest unemployment rates in Graslitz, the county with the highest relative unemployment in Czechoslovakia.[7] Possibly voters in this long-time social democratic stronghold remained loyal due to the social improvements made by the DSAP-dominated communal administration in the 1920s and to local DSAP leaders' great efforts on their behalf in the 1930s.

The German Social Democrats suffered great losses at the hands of the Sudeten German Party, but not on the scale of the German Agrarians and Clericals. The DSAP managed, however, to salvage its position in some of its traditional strongholds. In the Teplitz region, for example, although the DSAP failed to obtain a majority or even a plurality of the vote, it ran a close second to the Sudeten German Party in many smaller communities and support for the SdP was lower than average. Residents of Teplitz itself cast sixty percent of their votes for the Henleinists. (See Table 5-1.)[8]

The Internal Situation, 1935-1938

The German activist parties demonstratively supported the status quo when they voted for Tomáš G. Masaryk's chosen successor, Edvard Beneš, as the second president of Czechoslovakia. Their ballots proved vital in his December 1935 election when Czechoslovak Agrarian Prime Minister Milan Hodža was unable to prevent mutinous deputies from voting for another candidate. German Social Democratic support of Beneš meant endorsement of the policies of the republic rather than support of the man personally. It can be safely assumed that neither Beneš's negotiations at the Paris Peace Conference, nor his political posture toward Weimar Germany or Austria in the 1920s endeared him to German Social Democrats.

Czechoslovakia's domestic and external political problems—the dangers posed by the Henleinists and to a lesser degree by other political parties, and the growing hostility of neighboring countries—led to the expansion of internal security measures and the increase of arguably undemocratic actions in the defense of democracy. One governmental measure was the gradual nationalization of the police. Applied primarily to the border regions it meant a larger number of Czech police in German areas. When its implementation was announced for Dux, Komotau, and Teplitz, the German Social Democrats condemned it as an infringement on local autonomy, but held the bourgeois parties and their "fascist policies" responsible.[9]

Among the parties of the political left and right, the state's relations with the Czechoslovak Communists had begun to improve. The Communist Party had abandoned its slogan, "Not Masaryk, but Lenin," in the aftermath of the Czechoslovak-Soviet Bilateral Treaty and supported Beneš's candidacy for president of the republic in November 1935. The decision of the Seventh Congress of the Comintern in summer 1935 to replace its policy equating bourgeois democracy with fascism with one calling for Popular Fronts with democratic parties against the fascists, opened the door, at least in theory, for limited cooperation between the Czechoslovak Communists and other political parties. Many former members of the KSČ had been expelled between 1928 and 1933 for demanding precisely the sort of flexibility that the party was now pursuing.

The Comintern's new policy met with only limited success in Czechoslovakia for a variety of reasons, both foreign and domestic. Social democrats had not forgotten international communism's support of KPD alliances with the Nazis against the SPD, and the Czechoslovak Social Democrats remembered the anti-state rhetoric of the KSČ. German Social Democratic leadership increasingly regarded the existing government coalition as the best defense against the Henleinists. Also, the results of the plebiscite in the Saarland and the lack of success of Léon Blum's government in France provided skeptics with proof that communist-social democratic alliances did not necessarily translate into working class victories. Finally, the Stalinist purges and show trials that began in the mid-1930s hardly encouraged social democratic confidence in the communists.

The Czechoslovak Communists, National Socialists, Social Democrats, and German Social Democrats gained just over one-third of the vote in the parliamentary elections of 1935. Even if mistrust among the social democrats and the communists had not run deep, the lack of majority support would have made the formation of a Popular Front government impossible without the addition of at least one more political party. No other party even considered cooperating with the communists. Indeed, the Czechoslovak Agrarians regarded the communists as a greater danger to the country than the Sudeten German Party.

Although the socialist parties of Czechoslovakia recognized that fascism was a Central European problem in the mid-1930s, they considered fascism in the republic two separate internal problems. It appeared limited to the Sudeten Germans, whose demands were not yet openly irredentist and on whose behalf Adolf Hitler did not yet represent a major threat; and to a small minority of Czechs. The Czechoslovak Social Democrats perceived the Czech fascists as posing less of a threat to the integrity of the republic than the Slovak Clericals with their increasing demands for autonomy.

The left-wing parties disagreed on more issues than the formation of a Popular Front. They believed that action had to be taken against the SdP, but were not unanimous on the best method of combating the Henleinists. In spring 1936, *Rudé právo* expressed the Czechoslovak Communist opinion that acquiescing to the demands of the Sudeten German Party would be the worst possible defeat for Konrad Henlein. The Czechoslovak Social Democrats, however, vehemently disagreed. According to *Právo lidu,* earlier restrictions placed on the Germans in order to protect the Czech minority had become twice as important, now that Henlein had the support of two-thirds of the Sudeten Germans. The lifting of these restrictions made in "defense of democracy" would not be a defeat for Henlein, but provide him with a weapon. Their abolition would deliver the Czechoslovak minority and the German democrats of the Sudeten lands into his hands.[10] The efforts of the left-wing coalition participants to take effective measures against the Sudeten German Party were stymied by the opposition of the Czechoslovak Agrarians, whose right wing wanted to establish a *modus vivendi* with the SdP.

The Sudeten German Party was not simply a political party, but the political arm of a broad *völkisch* movement, whose leaders envisioned it as encompassing all facets of Sudeten German life. Henlein's initially nebulous demands insured their appeal to a broad section of population. Thus, the SdP was a difficult opponent for the German activist parties whose policies were designed to appeal to specific sectors of the population. In order to incorporate all aspects of Sudeten German life into the movement, German organizations, including athletic and cultural groups, were subjected to the process of *Gleichschaltung*. German Social Democratic organizations were less susceptible to this process than other groups; because their contacts had traditionally been limited to other social democratic organizations, it was difficult for the Henleinists to forge links with them.

Following the parliamentary elections, the Sudeten German Party began to challenge the legitimacy of the activist parties, claiming they represented only a fraction of the population and derisively referring to them as splinter groups. German Social Democratic deputy Wenzel Jaksch, increasingly at the forefront of his party's offensive against the Henleinists, ridiculed the Sudeten German Party claims, rightly stating that activist parties represented a larger percentage of the German electorate than the Germans did of the population of Czechoslovakia.[11]

The Sudeten German Party attempted to tighten its hold on the German population by demanding the dissolution of local administrations in the German regions. The demand had a "democratic" basis: the majority of the communal representatives were not SdP members and thus, no longer represented a majority of the Germans. This unsuccessful effort highlights one of the anomalies of the political situation in Czechoslovakia. The most recent Czechoslovak local elections had been held in 1931 and 1932, prior to the dissolution of the German National and German National Socialist parties and to the foundation of the Sudeten German Party. The dissolution of the first two parties resulted in a division of their local mandates and the division, if not to the liking of the German Social Democrats, had strengthened the German activist parties at the local level. Until the communal elections of 1938, the SdP would be represented in local administration only when communal elections had been held after 1934. Thus, despite the landslide victory of the Sudeten German Party in 1935, communal administration in many areas remained in the hands of the German activists, often the German Social Democrats. In Bodenbach, where 61 percent of the population had supported the SdP in the parliamentary elections, the German Social Democrat Fritz Kessler was mayor from 1933 through 1938. Although the SdP had gained 59 percent of the vote in Aussig in 1935, the German Social Democrats were the strongest party in the local administration, with four city council members, including Leopold Pölzl as mayor. The communal administration in Röchlitz was an example of working class party cooperation in the face of the Henleinist onslaught: from 1936 through 1938, a German Social Democrat served as mayor, with a Czechoslovak Communist first vice-mayor and a Czechoslovak Social Democrat as second vice-mayor.

The Economic Situation in the Sudeten Lands

Unemployment in Germany, which had begun to drop in late 1932 (from a high of more than six million in February 1932), was noticeably lower than in the neighboring Sudeten lands by the mid-1930s. Both the German drive for autarky in the 1930s—Germany was Czechoslovakia's largest trading partner—and trade practices in the Balkans further damaged an already weak Czechoslovak economy. In 1927, Germany purchased almost twenty-five percent of Czechoslovakia's exports, primarily agricultural products, but also timber, cheap yarns, woolens, glass, and glassware. The autarkic policies meant that German tariffs on agricultural goods had reached 136 percent by 1931, and thus brought about a partial collapse in Czechoslovak agricultural exports, as Czechoslovakia's total exports to Germany declined some sixty percent between 1927 and 1931.[12]

Germany was accused of dumping both porcelain and musical instruments in the Balkans, an area Czechoslovakia had previously considered its own commercial preserve. German-made gloves were shipped to Czechoslovakia, stamped "made in Czechoslovakia" and exported as products of that country.[13]

The Sudeten Germans living in the border areas who had lost their jobs in Germany at the onset of the economic crisis began finding reemployment there as the German economy started refueling in 1933, while those who had previously worked on the Czechoslovak side of the border remained unemployed.[14] Sudeten Germans knew that there was more work on the other side of the border, work that was, in part, better paying.

As late as 1937, when the Czechoslovak economy had shown marked improvement, there remained areas of northwestern and western Bohemia where the economy was still weak and sensitive to every change.[15] Unemployment in Czechoslovakia remained the highest along the Czechoslovak-German border through February 1938. (See Table 5-2.)[16] In Sudeten German areas, it was still more than two times higher than elsewhere in the country.[17]

Jaksch believed that the average worker did not question the source of his employment, or its relationship to rearmament (much of the improvement in both the Reich German and the Czechoslovak economy was due to greater weapons production). Employment in Germany presented social democrats with political problems, because membership in the Sudeten German Party was required. However, many German Social Democratic trade unionists and long-time party members simply put an SdP membership card in their pocket and crossed the border to find work. Jaksch asserted that these men had not changed their political allegiance and claimed that if they could have earned 120 crowns per week doing relief work in Czechoslovakia, they would gladly have done so.[18] As the economic situation in the Sudeten lands improved in the mid-1930s, an SdP membership card increasingly became a prerequisite for work: many employers were Henleinists.

Unemployment was a political issue, and the DSAP believed that the other political parties manipulated the statistics to its detriment. On the one hand, conservative newspapers claimed that government figures exaggerated the number of unemployed. When the unemployment figures for predominantly German areas dropped somewhat faster than those for Czech areas, the same newspapers assumed that emergency conditions no longer existed in the German regions. On the other hand, if unemployment in predominantly German areas failed to drop as quickly as in Czech areas, or if it rose, the Sudeten German Party used this as a welcome opportunity to attack the German activist parties and the government, although the efforts of the last two-mentioned were largely responsible for whatever drop in unemployment occurred.[19] The German Social Democrats were in the unenviable position of demanding additional aid for the German areas, while being careful not to criticize the economic policies of the coalition of which they were part, thus providing the Sudeten German Party with ammunition to use against them.

The 1935 Party Congress

Following major defeats in the parliamentary and the provincial elections, the German Social Democratic Party held its first congress in three years at Brünn in mid-June. The animosity that had been building among the party factions spilled out. Despite strict procedural rules, the minutes from the Brünn Congress reveal widespread dissatisfaction with the course of the party. Intraparty friction was apparent in reports that appeared in the *Sozialdemokrat;* the paper had hitherto attempted to maintain at least the illusion of party unity.

Chairman Czech continued to defend the course of the party leadership. In his opening remarks, Czech commented that the results of all previous elections had been more or less expected, but that their success in the 1935 elections had surprised even the Henleinists themselves. Despite catastrophic defeat of the German Social Democrats, one in six Sudeten Germans had voted for them, the same as the proportion of Czechs to support the Czechoslovak Social Democratic Party.[20] This was cold comfort, however, because four of every six Germans had voted for the Sudeten German Party. Czech held the Czechoslovak Communists responsible for the weakness of the German Social Democrats and thus, in part, for their election losses. Czech was referring both to the recently ended "social fascist" campaign, which condemned the social democrats and the fascists equally, and to the fifteen year history of enmity between the communists and the social democrats in Czechoslovakia. But, as one delegate noted, German Social Democratic losses in the 1935 elections could not be compared to previous election losses, because they were not to the Czechoslovak Communists but to the class enemy, the Henleinists.[21]

The delegates cited varied reasons for German Social Democratic electoral losses, including the state of Czech-German relations, recent domestic and foreign events, and failures of all kinds on the part of the party leadership, especially a lack of goals within the coalition. The delegates agreed on whose support had been lost and why, but disagreed on how to recoup the losses.

Both the German Social Democrats and their youth organizations were losing members. While DSAP losses primarily came from the employed, the young socialists suffered losses principally among the unemployed. The Sudeten German worker was unable to find public employment and the SdP dominated the small factories. The Henleinists used "terror" tactics against the employed to force them to join the SdP. The situation in the youth organization was different. According to its leader, Karl Kern, Henlein's radical rhetoric had a tremendous influence on the majority of German youth, precisely because they were unemployed. The Czech fascists exerted less influence on young Czechs, because there was a safety valve: government employment.[22]

Party dissidents demanded a variety of changes, many of which had been previously advocated in *Sozialistische Aktion.* They included a new party program, younger leadership, and "activism" as well as the reevaluation of the party's relationship to the Czechoslovak Communists and the expansion of the party to include farmers and the petite bourgeoisie. Complaints about centralization in Prague continued, too.[23]

Jaksch's political allies, Kessler, Richard Reitzner, and Rudolf Storch, led the call for activism and for the revitalization of the party. Kessler, particularly, strongly attacked conditions in the party and offered suggestions to turn around the DSAP's fortunes. Believing it superfluous to dwell on the past elections, Kessler concentrated rather on the source of the party's losses. He asserted that the most important result of the campaign was the appearance of the Sudeten German bourgeoisie as a mass movement, a development that called for active opposition from the German Social Democrats. He attacked the party elders for having failed to take advantage of the mass support for the party that had been exhibited in demonstrations the previous November. Kessler proposed the unification of all socialist forces. This had already happened in Bodenbach, where the German Social Democrats cooperated with the Czechoslovak National Socialists and Social Democrats, and had not categorically rejected working with the Czechoslovak Communists. Kessler ended his remarks with sharp criticism of the party leadership, particularly of Czech and Siegfried Taub.

Storch, a young delegate from Aussig, claimed that to "win back those voters we have disappointed" the party leadership needed to be younger and more active. Other delegates, including Kern, called for party activism on the local level.[24] Although "activism" was the catchword at the congress, reflecting the frustration of many of the delegates with the existing situation and their feeling that the party had to go on the offensive, few concrete proposals were made.

Jaksch, probably the major speaker for the opposition, was cautious with his comments (displaying the same cautiousness regarding his political career as he had recently displayed in his reserved attitude toward the party dissidents around *Sozialistische Aktion*). He defended the party leaders, saying that even if they had known the consequences of their politics, they would have been obliged to follow precisely the same path. After paying lip service to the social democratic tradition of Viktor Adler, Karl Kautsky, and Josef Seliger, he cited the need to overcome the party's conservatism and to "revitalize" the socialist world view. Jaksch then remarked briefly on the state of Czech-German relations and on continued cooperation with the Czechoslovak left. Criticizing party leaders, he pointed out that although Czechoslovakia was a "besieged democracy," surrounded on all sides by unfriendly dictatorships, German Social Democratic politicians were obliged to make the demands of their constituency heard. He admitted, however, that it was impossible to rectify overnight all injustices the German people suffered. Jaksch, unlike Kessler, rejected working with the Czechoslovak Communists, claiming that the Czechoslovak Agrarians had proven more trustworthy defenders of democracy than had the Czechoslovak Communists.

At the end of his speech, Jaksch discussed the need to broaden the base of the party. He asserted that it was no longer merely a question of the future of the party, but of the fate of the entire republic. This was not a battle for mandates and votes, but for leadership of the Sudeten Germans. To win the battle, the German Social Democratic Party could no longer isolate itself from the farmers and the middle class. Cooperation with these social groups would guarantee the future of socialism.[25]

His discussion of broadening the basis of the party represented the first time Jaksch used the largest party forum to discuss his idea of expanding the German Social Democratic electorate in the direction of what became known in the 1930s as *Volkssozialismus* (literally, socialism of the nation or people). Proponents advocated moderate rather than revolutionary rhetoric and a broader party basis in tacit recognition that social democratic party membership limited to the working class also limited political power.

Jaksch's comments were brief and general; they appear to have aroused little negative reaction among the other delegates. Indeed, his remarks were reported to have found a spirited echo both inside and outside the party.[26]

Jaksch's demand that the party voice more strongly the needs of its constituency underscores a problem the DSAP faced increasingly during the mid- and late-1930s. In the face of widespread Sudeten German opposition, the party defended, if reluctantly, some of Prague's undemocratic measures in defense of democracy. At the same time, conservative Czechoslovak politicians condemned the DSAP's national and social demands as endangering the republic.

In his closing remarks, Chairman Czech paid little attention to the critical remarks made by Jaksch and his colleagues. Czech was of the opinion that the 1935 elections had left the party with a series of difficult internal problems, the most urgent of which was the re-winning of lost members by making them aware of the cause of their misfortune: capitalism. Czech simplified a complex issue by coming to the formula that the next goal of the DSAP would be to win back the workers through the creation of a generous program of employment in the most severely depressed German areas.[27] His only response to the multi-faceted demands of the opposition was to comment that an alliance of all socialist forces was a "self-evident" goal, and that solidarity with the Czechoslovak Social Democrats was one of the reasons the DSAP had joined the government coalition in the first place. More than this was needed to turn the tide and to uplift the lagging morale in the party.

Czech interpreted the political situation in traditional Marxist terms: the primary goal of the German Social Democratic Party was the seizure of political power by the proletariat, and the conversion of the capitalist economic system that had been fundamentally shaken [by the economic crisis] into a socialist economic system: the realization of socialism. This meant little, however, as long as the German Social Democrats were junior partners in a Czechoslovak Agrarian-dominated coalition. Czech offered no new direction for the party.

The party executive committee, with a few dissenting votes, elected to remain in the coalition government. Most committee members believed that the reasons the party joined the coalition at its previous congress in Aussig remained valid in 1935. In fact, given external and internal political developments, even more so. The committee confirmed what Czech had announced before the parliamentary elections: the German activist parties had decided to remain in the government whatever the outcome of the vote.[28] In response to the growing pressure on Czech to resign at least one of his positions after the disastrous election results, it was also agreed that in the future, no party chairman would serve simultaneously as a government minister. As long as Czech remained minister, however, he would retain both functions.

The newly-elected party executive committee, with an average age of almost forty-five years, was nearly five years younger than the one selected in 1932. It included one member under thirty years of age, Willi Wanka, a leader of the socialist youth organization and a friend of Jaksch's, who celebrated his twenty-fifth birthday at the congress. Jaksch's ally Reitzner was also among the sixteen newly-elected members of the executive committee.

The congress ended in a compromise: Czech and his allies, the old guard, maintained control of the party, but Jaksch was elected deputy party chairman. Jaksch and like-minded colleagues had made use of the party's most important forum to express—in Jaksch's case, with caution—both their concern about the party's lack of direction, and their ideas for a new party course. Some of the problems the DSAP faced had been identified, although it appears that the issue of reversing thus-far politics and going into opposition was not discussed. The congress ended with the party no closer to solving any of its problems than when it had begun.

From this point, one can speak of two directions within the party. Johann W. Brügel has used the terms "loyalist" or "traditionalist" to designate those DSAP members who generally supported Czech, and "revisionist" to designate Jaksch and his allies.[29] Jaksch referred to himself and his followers as the "Seliger Wing" of the party, maintaining that they were the true heirs to the political tradition of Josef Seliger.[30] Jaksch's use of the term "Seliger Wing" is overstating the case; he would cite the party founder particularly after the Second World War in defense of his disputed exile politics. Brügel's use of the terms, "traditionalist" and "revisionist" is accurate, because the politics of the former group were more in keeping with traditional Marxist tenets than those of the latter.

Years later, Jaksch described, with the benefit of hindsight, this congress as a missed last chance for an opportune change of generation in party leadership. He claimed that Austrian Social Democratic émigrés Otto

Bauer and Julius Deutsch and SPD émigrés Hans Vogel and Otto Wels, all of whom attended the congress, let it be known that they would welcome such a change. Further, the Czechoslovak Social Democrats found it "impossible" that in a "life or death situation," both the chairmanship of the party and the minister's portfolio were in the hands of a seventy-year-old (Czech was actually sixty-five). The Czechoslovak Social Democrats allegedly wanted to replace Czech as government minister with someone who offered less room for criticism.[31]

The Czechoslovak Social Democrats increasingly considered Czech a burden during the 1930s, due to his Jewish origins. In the June 1935 issue of *Sozialistische Aktion,* there was speculation as to the source, alleged to have come from Hrad circles, of the reports in some Czechoslovak periodicals that Jaksch would replace Czech as minister in the new coalition, with the DSAP again holding the portfolio of the Ministry of Social Welfare. The Czechoslovak Social Democrats were rumored to have demanded that Czech resign, which he agreed to do if he were replaced by Taub (also Jewish)—who rejected the idea—or Hackenberg.[32] Eugen de Witte wrote in a similar vein of the attempt by Czechoslovak Social Democratic Party chairman Antonín Hampl and Senate President František Soukup in the Spring of 1936 to convince Hackenberg, Heller, Taub and himself to pressure Czech to resign his portfolio.[33]

Some Czechoslovak Social Democratic leaders probably wanted to see another German Social Democrat hold that party's ministerial portfolio, but the extent of their efforts to achieve this end is unknown. Certainly, some German Social Democrats would also have liked to see a change in the party government minister and in the party leadership, but again it is not certain how widespread this feeling was.

Czech was considered an able administrator and a hard worker. A self-conscious internationalist, he couched his politics in traditional Marxist terms. As government minister, Czech had concentrated on socio-economic reforms to benefit the entire working class, rather than on reforms to improve the legal and national position of the Germans. His efforts were, however, limited by agrarian domination of the coalition and by the inauspicious economic and international situation.

Beginning in the 1930s, intraparty opponents belittled Czech as a bureaucrat with little or no political ability, who had led the party up a blind alley. He was indeed a doctrinaire socialist, and it was questionable if these tenets were any longer applicable to Czechoslovakia. Both his political outlook and his personality handicapped him in dealing with the great problems of the time. Lacking aggressiveness and flexibility, Czech did not have the necessary qualities for dealing with either the economic situation or with the confrontational politics of the Sudeten German Party.

Clearly, Czech's Jewish origin was a strike against him in the 1930s. Not only Czech was Jewish; so were many of the other leading party functionaries, including Heller, senator and party treasurer; Taub, party secretary and vice president of the House of Deputies; and Wiener, party parliamentary faction secretary.[34] One of the few women in the upper echelons of the party, long-time parliamentary deputy Fanny Blatny, was also a Jew. This became an increasing sensitive issue.

Jaksch has been linked to the intraparty opposition and the intraparty left, but his connections with the opposition were tempered by his instinct for political survival. However, the left-wingers with whom Jaksch was allied, Kessler and Reitzner, appear to have been less "left," than they were opposed to Czech's political leadership. Furthermore, Jaksch favored changes in the direction of the party that can hardly be labeled "left."

Jaksch inspired mistrust, both personal and political, among many members of the party through his friendship with the former leader of the Nazi left wing, Otto Strasser. Although a tireless worker and an inspired, popular speaker, his ambition and his apparent need for absolute loyalty, caused him to be referred to in some quarters as "Ujef," (*unser junger Führer*—our young leader). Czech, Heller, and other party elders considered him a rude, pushy careerist.[35] Yet, precisely some of Jaksch's negative qualities—he was more adept than Czech at political mud-slinging—made him a more effective opponent to Henlein.

Volkssozialismus: A New Direction for the DSAP?

The enduring economic crisis and the rise of authoritarian governments throughout Central Europe led some European social democrats to look outside traditional party precepts for political solutions. On the social democratic left, Popular Fronts with the communists, on the example of Blum's government in France, were demanded. On the right, there were calls for nationally-oriented socialist solutions to replace the internationalism that formed one of the cornerstones of Marxism. In a sense, part of the social democratic right was also calling for a "Popular Front," one that would include segments of society not previously part of the social democratic palette, among them, farmers and members of the middle class. Jaksch and Franzel were the leading representatives of this direction within the German Social Democratic Party.

By the early 1930s, Franzel, one of the party's foremost intellectuals, began exploring political ideas that led him farther and farther afield from strict Marxist doctrine and would eventually lead to his estrangement from the party. A resident of Prague, in addition to writing for DSAP journals, he also contributed to non-party publications, including the liberal Czech magazine, *Přítomnost* (The Present), the most influential cultural-political periodical in the First Republic. Bilingual, he was part of an intellectual milieu that included Czech and German liberals and social democrats, and others. Among the last was Strasser, who had come to Prague in 1933.

Franzel introduced Strasser to Jaksch and both of them exerted a substantial influence over the young social democratic leader. Jaksch, searching for a means to overcome the apparent irrelevance of his party's politics, as well as to find solutions to the economic and political problems of the Sudeten Germans, began developing his ideas of *Volkssozialismus*.

In the mid-1930s, all three men published studies on socialism. In the brochure, "Der Marxismus ist Tot, der Sozialismus Lebt," Strasser outlined his ideas for a particularly German form of socialism, one that embraced a *Volksgemeinschaft* (community of the people or the nation in an ethnic sense). He sought to prove his thesis, that the goal of socialism was unshakable, but that the Marxist path was incorrect, by demonstrating the worldwide breakdown of Marxist socialism.[36]

Franzel's book, *Abendländische Revolution,* appeared in 1936. In what he later called his definitive repudiation of Marxism, Franzel advocated a "new orientation of the socialist idea." *Abendländische Revolution* drew criticism from the entire social democratic camp. Sopade rejected Franzel's critique of the working-class movement in Germany and the politics of the SPD, condemning his ideas as dangerously close to the Nazi way of thinking as well as afflicted with "counter-revolutionary romanticism."[37]

Shortly after the 1935 party congress, Jaksch had chided leading Henleinists, telling them that they might have three-quarters of the Sudeten Germans behind them, but they had led them up a deadend. He challenged the SdP's "catastrophe" policy with his party's true "Volk" policy:[38] but what was it? Jaksch had begun to stress the community of interest the worker shared with other social classes in his 1934 brochure, "Was Wird aus Österreich?," and his 1936 book, *Volk und Arbeiter*, was the most concrete formulation of his ideas to date. The book was an attempt to analyze contemporary political and social problems independently of party precepts. *Volk und Arbeiter*, which appeared at the same time as *Abendländische Revolution*, met with a mixed reception within the party[39] and a negative reaction from Sopade which rejected anything influenced by Strasser.[40] The lukewarm reaction within the party seems to have been due as much to Jaksch's connection with Franzel and Strasser as to the content of the book, although some DSAP members simply mistrusted Jaksch's ideas, because Henlein allegedly found them not so different from his own.[41]

Franzel left the DSAP under pressure in late 1937. Many developments contributed to his departure, above all his increasingly pro-Habsburg sentiments. In the interest of economic, military, and political stability in Central Europe, Franzel had begun to support the notion of a conservative, democratic Danubian federation centered around Austria and Hungary. His attendance at the funeral of Sudeten German Party "foreign policy advisor" Heinrich Rutha, however, precipitated the actual break. Rutha had committed suicide while in prison awaiting trial on sodomy charges. Though Franzel had attended the funeral as representative of the *Völkerbundliga* rather than of the German Social Democratic Party, his appearance at the funeral of a leading SdP advisor and close friend of Henlein provided adequate pretext to start expulsion proceedings. Franzel, however, resigned on his own accord.

18 February 1937

Party officials recognized that the ill effects of the economic crisis on the Sudeten Germans made them susceptible to Henlein's propaganda, but they had no means of fighting the SdP. In the coalition, their options were limited to urging, practically begging, the other government parties to help improve the economic situation in the Sudeten lands.

A German Social Democratic Party district conference held in Aussig in autumn 1935 profiles this problem. Conference speakers reiterated the party's usual litany of the five-year-long crisis of capitalism and the need to create work and to promote exports. The DSAP wanted emergency aid —especially for youth, three-quarters of whom were unemployed—to fight wha it branded the fascist "purchase of souls" through the *Volkshilfe* (Help for the People) program.[42] Emergency aid in the border areas had a political aspect: the *Sudetendeutsche Volkshilfe* and the *Freiwilliger Arbeitsdienst* had been established in the early 1930s by the *Bund der Deutschen* and the *Deutscher Turnverband*—closely allied with the Henleinists, the latter had supplied the SdP with many of its leaders, including Henlein —in response to massive unemployment in the border regions. The first provided food, clothing, and other necessities obtained through collection or donation; the second was a series of voluntary work camps for young men who mainly built playgrounds and sports facilities. In 1937, about two-thirds of the work camp participants were under twenty-one, and almost half had joined the ranks of the unemployed only that year: despite declining unemployment, many young Germans were still unable to find work. After their apprenticeship, they were let go by employers who had no work for them.[43]

One attempt to encourage the government to come to terms with the situation was an interparty offensive that marked the first time the German coalition parties had cooperated with one another.[44] *Jungaktivismus* (literally "youthful activism"), refers to the efforts beginning in spring 1936, of three German parliamentary deputies: Jaksch, Agrarian Gustav Hacker, and Clerical Hans Schütz, representing the younger generation of the activist German parties. They sought to revitalize their parties as well as to improve Czech-German relations through economic reconstruction and recognition of the Germans as a second national people—the "Czechoslovaks" were the first national people. The idea of a second national people already had a place in the Czech political vocabulary: in 1934, Czechoslovak Social Democrat Rudolf Bechyně had referred to the Germans as "becoming a second national people" and by 1936, Foreign Minister Kamil Krofta had remarked to an audience of Sudeten German educators that the Germans were not simply a minority, but a second national people.[45]

Although the efforts of the three did not bring about concrete results, they laid the groundwork for a memorandum on government minority relations in Czechoslovakia, the last independent effort by Prague and the German government parties to come to terms with one another. On 18

February 1937, the government would issue a seven-point proclamation on minority relations based on the "Activist Memorandum" that the three German government ministers had presented to Hodža the previous month.

Hacker, Jaksch, and Schütz made their demands public on 26 April 1936, when they made similar speeches before their constituencies. Jaksch spoke at a district meeting of the German Social Democratic metal workers' union in Tetschen, Hacker to hops farmers in the Saaz countryside and Schütz to Clerical trade unionists in Giesshübel in the Erzgebirge. While voicing support for the Czechoslovak state, all three called for a change in Prague's relations with the Sudeten Germans, unless the government wanted all Germans to move into the Sudeten German Party camp. Their motto was "Things can't go on any longer, the Czechs must cooperate with us more." ("So kann es nicht weitergehen! Die Tschechen müssen uns mehr entgegenkommen.")[46]

The efforts of the three did not receive an entirely warm reception in their respective political camps, although they attracted the attention both of the German and Czech public.[47] Jaksch later commented, in a slap at the party traditionalists, that he had run up against the "stubborn inertia of the die-hard social politicians."[48]

Recently elected President Beneš appeared willing to listen to the German activists, although the long-time foreign minister lacked expert knowledge of the details of the German grievances. Beneš's well-received travels through the German regions of southern Bohemia and Moravia in spring 1936 and northern Bohemia the same summer left him better acquainted with the situation.[49] However, he continued to oppose any moves toward autonomy or federalization—not least because of the problem of similar Slovak demands—calling instead for regulation of Czech-German relations on the basis of the constitution, which he considered liberal enough to solve the problems the country faced. As one of the founders of the Czechoslovak national state, it was probably difficult for him to accept that the problems of education and language could be solved to the satisfaction of the German activist parties and of the German public at large, only by amending the constitution to remove the status of the Germans as a legal minority. Despite the attention the Young Activists aroused abroad, Prague did little to meet their challenge.

In November 1936, German Social Democratic politicians and trade unionists presented Hodža with a program for economic reconstruction and impressed upon him the necessity of concrete governmental economic measures. Soon afterward, Hodža requested that the three German government ministers produce a joint program embodying the German demands. The ministers, joined by the Young Activists, spent two months preparing the program. Brügel credited Czech with writing it, but this is by no means certain; Zajiček described it as a joint effort.[50] The section on aid to youth, a passion of Czech's, is probably his work. Jaksch, in any case, rejected responsibility for the proposals, claiming to have produced his own, which were "unraveled, plucked to pieces, and watered down" by the German Social Democratic Party executive committee.[51] Jaksch implied that he called for rejection of the national state principle, which is unlikely. Given the existing political situation, Prague would have rejected this demand out of hand. Jaksch was too astute a politician not to have recognized that such a demand would have jeopardized the entire program.

On the very day the program was presented, Hodža rejected the constitutional anchoring of concessions to the German minority and was discouraging about the possibility of changing existing laws to satisfy its demands. However, according to Zajiček, who participated in both the formulation of the program and negotiations with Hodža, the prime minister agreed with the sections on creating work, public service, and youth welfare, as well as those on education and culture.[52]

After negotiations that followed the presentation of the German activist parties' program in January, the government presented a communiqué, popularly known as the Memorandum of 18 February, for the day it was announced. The memorandum was not a legal document, but a statement of intent, the strongest extra-parliamentary measure Hodža could take without amending the constitution. Avoiding the question of regulation of national relations in Czechoslovakia, the memorandum concentrated instead on practical demands to improve the German standard of living. It was divided into six sections covering investment, welfare, state employment, linguistic questions, education, and self-administration.[53]

Just as negotiations over the memorandum were ending, Jaksch went to London at Krofta's request where he was to serve as a pro-Czechoslovak Sudeten German counterweight to Henlein and Rutha, both of whom had previously been there to publicize the Sudeten German Party's political demands. While in England, Jaksch discussed the 18 February Memorandum with members of the House of Commons. He also gave a lecture on the subject, lauding Czechoslovakia as a democratic state where numerous nationalities lived free and unimpeded.[54]

Some Czechoslovak and Sudeten German newspapers embraced the memorandum as a first step on the way to satisfying Sudeten German demands. However, the Sudeten German Party decisively rejected it as old principles, repeated yet again, and still without guarantee of fulfillment, in a series of demonstrations and rallies. Further, without reparations [for past wrongs], there could be no Czech-German equality.[55]

The section of the memorandum that raised the most discussion concerned the percentage of Germans in state employment, which varied from ministry to ministry. Estimates vary, but in early 1937, when the memorandum was presented, the number of Germans in the Health, Justice, and Post ministries was between ten and twelve percent. Their level in both the Ministry of Interior and the Ministry of National Defense was significantly lower, and the number of Germans in the Foreign Office was only 1.5 percent. Germans were almost non-existent in high positions of the central government. The percentage of Germans in the Education Ministry corresponded approximately to that of the Germans in the population only when teachers were included.[56]

During his tenure as Health Minister, Czech had enlarged his staff and added Germans to it. The percentage of Germans in some areas of his ministry, physicians and lawyers, for example, was not far below that of Germans in the population as a whole (twenty-three percent), when he left office in April 1938. The two other German ministers were unable to exert the same influence on hiring practices, because both served without portfolio. The Czechoslovak Social Democratic ministers, Bechyně in Railroad, Ivan Dérer in Justice, and Jaromír Nečas in Social Welfare, also appointed more Germans to government positions. In the twelve months between 18 February 1937 and 28 February 1938, 4,270 Germans were temporarily hired by the national railroad. At the same time, 1,500 German officials and more than 5,000 German workers found positions in state service, and the percentage of Germans entering public employment rose from four to between ten and twelve percent.[57]

Business taxes for glass, textile, and porcelain producers, the majority of whom were German, were lowered and government aid for textile and porcelain exports was increased. Finally, the number of German firms receiving government contracts increased significantly.[58] These measures were also facilitated by the improvement in general economic conditions. However, in a time of industrial recovery and increased spending, strategic considerations surely played a role in the government's failure to locate more new industry in the border regions. A large portion of the budget went to defense, and defense industries were overwhelmingly located in secure (Czech) areas.

In London again, Jaksch spoke to a small gathering of the Institute of International Affairs at Chatham House on 12 November. He presented the German gains resulting from the Memorandum of 18 February in a positive light, citing the increase of the number of Germans in government service. Jaksch also referred to Switzerland, asserting that the basis for autonomy was good will between all segments of the population, something sadly lacking in his homeland. Jaksch would maintain this viewpoint —support for the principle of autonomy, when relations between the groups involved were positive—in the coming months.[59]

However, as Jaksch made clear in a speech at the parliamentary budget hearings in Prague a few days later, while he considered the memorandum a sign of governmental good faith, he believed its tenets were being enacted far too slowly. The German demand for proportionality in state employment had thus far met with success only in the school system, and not necessarily as a result of the 18 February agreement. So far as he was concerned, some issues remained unresolved: to date, there was no effective battle plan for economic relief in crisis areas, nor had proportionality in public works been attained.[60]

In a speech before parliament on 1 December 1937, DSAP deputy de Witte echoed Jaksch, calling the memorandum a "good beginning," but went on to say that Jaksch's estimate of the Germans lacking 40,000 places in government service was low. The Germans wanted the positions that were their due and this did not mean just section chiefs and judges, but also policemen and postal employees. Further, when possible, German officials and German workers should be employed in German-speaking areas, and Czech employees in Czech areas.[61]

The question of German representation in public works remained a source of friction. The joint effort of local Germans and Prague officials to construct a police station in Karlsbad ended up pleasing no one. The repair of Teplitz's main train station by a Czech construction crew met with complaint from local Germans due to the high rate of unemployment among German construction workers there.[62]

Brügel has pointed out that the problem of German governmental participation also had a reverse side: the Czechs had justified complaints that in choosing local employees, German city and district officials tended to ignore the Czech minority. On the one hand, in Brünn, the Czech majority worked with activists from the German minority. The German minority was twenty percent and had that percentage of the official positions in the commune. On the other hand, in Troppau, where the Czechs formed one-third of the population, only 10 of 200 communal employees were Czech.[63]

Although the tenets of the Memorandum of 18 February were not enacted as quickly as the German activist parties would have liked, nor were the results as positive as they would have liked, the respective party presses continued to present the memorandum in a favorable light. Sudeten German Party leaders had discouraged members from taking advantage of opportunities opened up by the memorandum, and official SdP reaction to the first anniversary of its announcement was merely to comment that the activist memorandum had brought the Sudeten German Party an increase of 75,000 in membership.[64]

Change in Party Leadership

The crisis within the party that had first made itself known in 1934 with the *Sozialistische Aktion* group, and later at the 1935 party congress, grew markedly as the political situation in Czechoslovakia worsened in the days and weeks preceding the German Social Democratic Party congress in the spring of 1938. According to Ernst Paul, the commander of the *Republikanische Wehr*, there had been increasing demands from local party officials that spring for Czech to be replaced as party chairman. Paul had received letters from leaders of that organization saying that the party needed new leadership in order to be able to "hold the front" against the Sudeten German Party. He also claimed that district secretaries from Laun,

Czech's own voting district, were demanding a change in leadership. Jaksch's name had been mentioned as a possible replacement for Czech. Following discussions with party secretary Taub, Paul brought these demands to Czech's attention, who ignored them.[65]

Recent events such as the *Anschluss* of Austria to Germany, significantly lengthening the Czechoslovak-German border; and the *Gleichschaltung* of the German Agrarians on 22 March and of the German Clericals the next day, with the Sudeten German Party; made Czechoslovakia's situation, but especially the situation of the German Social Democrats, far more difficult.

The DSAP congress originally planned for Reichenberg, was postponed until late March 1938, when a shorter congress was held in Prague rather than in the border regions, where the DSAP feared public hostility. At the *Reichskongress* (an abbreviated party congress) that preceded the party congress by a week, Jaksch made his aspirations clear: he was available for the position of party chairman. In what participant Rudolf Zischka later termed a "Brandrede," (highly critical address), Jaksch attacked the party traditionalists as not having proved worthy heirs of Seliger.[65] Jaksch threatened to resign from the party, reportedly because of the alleged attempts of Czech and Taub—the last on the grounds of the critical world situation—to delay further the congress, which by statute should have been held in 1937.[66]

The executive committee met on the morning of 25 March, the day before the party congress was to open, to create a unified proposal to present to the delegates because it was clear that the events of the congress would greatly affect the future of the party. At that point, it was uncertain if Jaksch would become party chairman or government minister or both, although it was apparent that no solution to the party's internal problems could be reached without him.[67] Recent events, above all *Anschluss,* had strengthened his position versus the Austromarxists within the party. According to participant Hans Dill, the district secretary from Pilsen, it was agreed to replace Czech with Jaksch, against Czech's wishes, and to remain in the government despite the exit of the other two activist parties.[68]

Czech's resignation was announced at the party congress. Jaksch was duly elected—unanimously, although some delegates withheld their ballots—his successor as party chairman. Czech's grounds for resignation were both personal and political; he found it impossible to work with Jaksch and he disagreed with the *volkssozialistische* direction within the party. He planned to remain in the party and to work against this trend.[69] This ended the political career of a well-meaning but not wholly effective leader.

Speaking before the congress, Jaksch described generally the political situation in Central Europe and its effect on Czechoslovakia. He then discussed both the German Social Democratic attitude toward the Czechoslovak state and the party's demands. This portion of his speech was contradictory: Jaksch confirmed his support for Beneš's pronouncement in 1936 that a solution for the country's minority problems would be found within the boundaries of the constitution, but he also renewed his demand that the Sudeten Germans be made a "second state people," which explicitly required amending the constitution. Jaksch described himself as a member of the party's middle generation, one of those who accepted the precepts of social democracy in the prewar period but had to apply them in the greatly changed world of the postwar period. He also provided the delegates with another vague description of *Volkssozialismus* as he understood it, citing the Swedish Social Democrats as an example of a party that had followed a policy of *Volkssozialismus* successfully for years. Among the moderate parties of the International, the Swedish Social Democrats like other Scandinavian social democratic parties, had scored moderate successes during the 1930s, in part because Scandinavia was less affected by the Depression than elsewhere in Europe. In an attempt to reassure the many delegates who did not trust his political ideas, Jaksch attempted to downplay the implications of this politically-loaded word, rather confusingly claiming that it was simply another name for social democracy.[70]

The delegates gave the party executive committee complete power to proceed with discussions on party policy. On the basis of the results of the discussions, the executive committee was to make any necessary decisions concerning the further tactics of the party in accordance with the ideas Jaksch had outlined in his speech.[71]

That a man disputed by many party members—he was practically isolated from his fellow German Social Democratic deputies in parliament after 1935[72]—could have been elected party chairman has since been a subject of contention among those who attended the party congress. The role of two outsiders, President Beneš and Prime Minister Hodža, in the turn of events is a matter of dispute.

In a speech on 28 March, when Hodža announced plans to codify all measures concerning minorities into a single minority statute, he indicated his lack of inclination to have the German Social Democrats remain as the only German political party in the government. And, they did not. When Czech resigned as Minister of Health, he was not replaced by another German Social Democrat, or by another German, at all. Hodža's intentions, even as the three German parties were still participating in the government are revealing. In late February, he informed the German Ambassador to Prague, Ernst Eisenlohr, that although he could not "sack" the German activist ministers, he planned to replace Health Minister Czech with Jaksch.[73] In a memorandum to Berlin just before the German Social Democratic Party congress, Eisenlohr reported that Hodža had said he planned to demand that Czech take a leave of absence and then disappear from the political scene altogether. Again, Jaksch was mentioned as a possible successor to Czech, as someone more to the liking of both Berlin and the Sudeten German Party.[74] Whether Hodža actually spoke to Czech or not, as the Eisenlohr correspondence indicates he planned to do, is unknown.

Beneš's role in Czech's resignation and Jaksch's subsequent election has been a matter of dispute among three who attended the congress: Brügel and Zischka on the one hand, and Paul on the other. The first two agree that Beneš intervened to some degree, through the person of party secretary Taub, to obtain Czech's resignation. They are less unanimous on Beneš's role in the selection of Jaksch as Czech's successor. Zischka, a member of the committee responsible for nominating the party executive committee and the chairman, claimed that during the committee's six hour meeting, in which both Czech and Jaksch participated, Taub did honor to his name, remaining deaf and dumb (*taub*). He made no attempt to lead the discussion toward the nomination of a party chairman. When Zischka commented on Taub's uncharacteristic behavior to executive committee member Heller, the latter was not surprised. Heller said that Taub's behavior was correct; he had promised Beneš to obtain Czech's resignation as party chairman, and thus, was not free to act as concerned the proceedings of the meeting.[75] Brügel has written that Beneš called on the German Social Democratic Party to put ideological and other differences aside in the name of state interests and to elect demonstratively Jaksch as party chairman.[76]

Paul's objection to the above versions of events was based on both a personal and a political sense of affront: he took umbrage at the suggestion that an outsider could dictate his party's choice of chairman and further, that he, as co-chairman of the congress, would not have been aware of such goings-on.[77] Paul's line of reasoning ignores the fact that Beneš did not have to intervene in the congress, for it was unnecessary. According to Dill's remarks at the time, the decision to replace Czech had been made previously, at the meeting of the party executive committee. It is safe to assume that Paul was left out of private discussions taking place outside the scope of the party congress.

Jaksch himself was not forthcoming in his postwar comments on the events, although he wrote that Hodža intervened for a change in party leadership.[78] Franzel, who did not attend the congress, but had good connections through Franz Rehwald and Storch, also provided his version(s) of the events. In his memoirs, Franzel wrote that when it became clear during pre-congress discussions that Czech did not intend to resign, Charles University professor Oskar Fischer contacted Beneš, whom he knew through the Freemasons, to ask him to exert pressure on Czech. Beneš then intervened to obtain Czech's resignation. Franzel did not specify if Beneš dealt directly with Czech, or if he spoke to Taub. Franzel seems to have been more interested in the Masonic link between Beneš and Fischer—he mistakenly considered the Freemasons an important political element in the First Republic—than in the specifics of Czech's resignation.[79]

It is probable that Brügel, Paul, and Zischka each described the events surrounding the congress as they remembered them. One can conclude that either Beneš or Hodža, or both, intervened prior to the party congress to obtain Czech's resignation as party chairman and minister. Even if only Beneš were involved, the outcome corresponded to Hodža's wishes. Perhaps, there was no external intervention at the party congress itself. This did not matter because the congress confirmed the previously made decision to replace Czech as party chairman.

Although Jaksch's negative character traits, especially his vanity and overwhelming ambition, had not gone unnoticed by party members, and although there was general suspicion over his friendship with Strasser, he had faced no competition to replace Czech. Jaksch had acquired a solid political reputation among many segments of both the Czech and the

German population, and in the end, this mattered more than his personal shortcomings.

Jaksch's election as party chairman also signalled a changing of the guard in the party executive committee. Many of Czech's closest colleagues, including long-time executive committee members Fanny Blatny, Theodor Hackenberg, Carl Heller, and Wilhelm Niessner, also resigned. In Heller's case, at least, anti-Semitic remarks by members of the new executive committee were the reason for his resignation.[80]

That a strain of anti-Semitism should have existed in a party that also had a strain of anti-intellectualism is hardly surprising. The majority of the party intellectuals were Jews,[81] as was the case with the Czechoslovak Social Democratic Party, and to an even greater degree the Communist Party. According to Franzel, a former member of the Independent Coalition of the Socialist Academics (*Freie Vereinigung sozialistischer Akademiker*), the organization was composed of both social democrats and communists, but above all, Jews.[82] In addition, the German Social Democrats suffered from the poisoning of the political and social atmosphere caused by Hitler's virulent anti-Semitism. So did the Czechoslovak Social Democratic Party, although to a lesser extent, because while Czechoslovak Social Democrats of Jewish origin had been active as government ministers in the early years of the First Republic, none had held a portfolio after 1935.[83]

It has been asserted that the 1938 retirement of several party executive committee members reflected a change of generation in the DSAP leadership and that many of the new members were little-known provincial officials, but neither is entirely correct.[84] Although most of those who retired were in their sixties, others who remained active were equally old. The average age of the 42-member executive committee, forty-four and three-quarters, was virtually the same as that of the executive committee elected in 1935 and older than the average age of the executive committee members of the early 1920s. The main difference was that for the first time, more than just a handful of members had been born after the turn of the century and had been schooled in the politics of the First Czechoslovak Republic, rather than the Habsburg Monarchy. The majority of the younger representatives were allied with Jaksch and many worked with him later on in the immigration.[85]

Several first-time members of the executive committee had previously served on other party committees or worked as party journalists. For example, Wiener, the long-time parliamentary faction secretary, was among the newly-elected members of the party executive committee. The majority were in their forties and fifties, members of what Jaksch had labeled the "transitional" generation. Clearly, at least some of the new members were elected less because they had the "youthful vigor" necessary to oppose the Sudeten German Party in the coming days, than because of their political allegiance to Jaksch.

TABLE 5 - 1
SELECTED PARLIAMENTARY ELECTION RESULTS, 1935

COUNTY REICHENBERG

Commune	DSAP	BdL	DCl	SdP	Other	SdP Majority	
Alt-Habendorf	74	41	76	1054	432	Yes	62.85%
Alt-Harzdorf	123	113	90	1668	477	Yes	67.50%
Dörfel	182	60	96	1342	823	Yes	53.62%
Eichsicht	42	28	61	572	966	No	
Franzendorf	167	5	45	1023	613	Yes	55.20%
Liebenau	142	39	82	646	734	No	
Maffersdorf	240	150	391	2578	1205	Yes	56.49%
Neu-Paulsdorf	90	21	53	1094	305	Yes	69.99%
Reichenberg	1254	93	1110	17497	5298	Yes	69.29%
Röchlitz	240	33	191	1915	1639	No	
Rosenthal	88	46	94	1700	867	Yes	60.82%
Ruppersdorf	134	21	109	2101	429	Yes	75.20%

COUNTY TEPLITZ

Eichwald	767	34	101	1355	447	Yes	50.11%
Graupen	759	40	168	1456	313	Yes	53.21%
Hertine	338	73	3	452	292	No	
Klein-Augezd	495	13	2	520	369	No	
Pihanken	521	34	17	551	419	No	
Probstau	449	35	15	875	991	No	
Settenz	396	46	38	1183	636	Yes	51.46%
Soborten	199	23	37	612	627	No	
Teplitz-Schönau	2180	125	743	11782	4869	Yes	59.81%
Tischau	580	38	25	559	578	No	
Turn	1489	116	30	5957	3000	Yes	54.84%
Weisskirchlitz	726	52	19	1587	594	Yes	51.56%
Wisterschan	633	98	51	144	882	No	
Wistritz	519	35	24	707	530	No	
Zuckmantel	623	21	17	841	768	No	

SOURCE: "Das Ergebnis der Wahlen für das Abgeordnetenhaus in den deutschen Gemeinden," 20 August 1935, columns 879-82.

TABLE 5 - 2
COUNTIES WITH HIGHEST UNEMPLOYMENT
(Percentage of Employable Persons)

County	9.1935	12.1935	2.1936	6.1936	8.1936	3.1938
Graslitz	36.3	39.3	39.0	34.0	33.5	18.1
Sternberg	31.0	32.0	31.0	31.0	29.1	--
Jägerndorf	29.0	27.3	--	--	--	--
Neudek	29.0	--	--	24.3	--	19.4
Pressnitz	28.0	30.0	31.0	29.0	27.3	18.0
Friedland	27.0	29.0	29.5	--	--	19.0
Römerstadt	27.0	28.0	29.0	28.0	27.1	15.4
Freudenthal	26.4	29.4	29.0	23.0	25.0	19.0
Rumburg	26.3	--	--	22.4	20.0	--
Elbogen	24.3	28.0	30.1	26.1	26.5	--
Karlsbad	--	28.0	30.0	27.0	25.1	--
Wsetin*	--	28.1	38.0	--	--	--
Starkenbach*	--	--	27.1	22.0	--	--
Falkenau	--	--	--	--	--	20.1
Tepl	--	--	--	--	--	20.0
Tachau	--	--	--	--	--	18.5
Plan	--	--	--	--	--	16.4

COUNTIES WITH LOWEST UNEMPLOYMENT

County	9.1935	12.1935	2.1936	6.1936
Jitschin*	.5	2.7	4.3	.5
Muhlhausen*	.7	--	--	--
Kralowitz*	1.1	--	--	.9
Datschitz*	1.5	--	--	1.2
Kralup*	1.5	--	--	2.5
Chotebor*	1.5	4.9	--	--
Melnik*	1.6	--	--	1.5
Neustadt*	1.7	--	--	--
Beneschau*	1.7	--	5.8	--
Jilové*	1.8	--	--	--
Ledetsch*	--	4.6	4.4	1.5
Tabor*	--	4.2	4.2	1.8
Blatna*	--	5.0	5.8	--
Prague*	--	2.6	2.5	--
Zlin*	--	3.5	--	.6
Königinhof*	--	4.1	4.3	--
Strakonitz*	--	4.2	5.3	--
Laun*	--	5.2	--	1.8
Prossnitz*	--	--	5.6	--
Schlan*	--	--	5.9	--
Neupaka*	--	--	--	1.5

NOTES: Counties with an asterisk (*) have a Czech majority.

SOURCE: *Mitteilungen des deutschen Hauptverbandes der Industrie* and
Sudeten German newspapers citing it as their source.

CHAPTER VI

THE BEGINNING OF THE END
1938

Spring 1938

In the months before the Munich Conference, the disagreements within the German Social Democratic Party moved to the background as the party leadership sought to provide a united front against the Sudeten German Party. At least publicly, the German Social Democrats were one in their positive attitude toward the First Republic, on which their survival depended, and their recognition of the importance of its defense.[1] Their slogan was "Hitler, that's war!"[2]

With the not unexpectedly disastrous communal election results at the end of May, Czechoslovakia's British and French allies increased pressure on Prague to come to an understanding with the Sudeten German Party. Diplomatic pressure eventually amounting to blackmail was used in an attempt to force President Beneš to accept Henlein's spiraling demands. The German Social Democrats' former allies, including the Czechoslovak Social Democrats, who were less and less willing to carry on what they correctly assessed as a losing battle against the Henleinists, increasingly disregarded and deserted them. Although the influence of DSAP politicians was diminishing daily and by mid-May, most internal party functions appear to have been suspended,[3] party leaders—particularly Wenzel

Jaksch and his closest colleagues—waged a desperate battle against the Sudeten German Party for international public opinion.

Following his election as party chairman, Jaksch faced two interrelated tasks: the revitalization of the party, and the proposal of reforms acceptable both to his constituency and the Czechoslovak government. Realization of these aims would give him legitimate claim to be leader of more than a handful of Germans, as well as lend him international credibility. This in turn would, with luck, lessen external pressure on Prague—and thus on his organization—to come to terms with the Sudeten German Party. Proposals that did not correspond too closely to those already put forth by the Henleinists were difficult to develop. Jaksch concentrated on administrative and linguistic reforms, avoiding discussion of territorial autonomy, now the major demand of the Sudeten German Party. He was more critical of the government's attitude toward the Sudeten German problem in articles appearing in the *Sozialdemokrat* for domestic consumption than in articles for the *Sudeten-German Newsletters,* a trilingual DSAP publication designed to influence foreign public opinion that began to appear in July 1938.

Although at this time Jaksch certainly supported the Czechoslovak state, frequent references in the Sudeten German Party press to the German Social Democrats as "Germanized Czechs" were behind Jaksch's need to explain that members of his party should not be considered representatives of the "Czechoslovak nation" among the Germans. They were, instead, representatives of the German people living in a common state with the Czechs, and a part of the German people that loved "peace, freedom, and democracy."[4]

Immediately following the party congress, Jaksch set about presenting his political program to German Social Democrats in the border regions. He spoke at a series of gatherings in northwest Bohemia, including ones in the traditional party strongholds of Aussig and Bodenbach, voicing the demand that the Germans be accepted as a second national people, on the one hand, but rejecting demands for territorial autonomy, on the other. Jaksch's efforts to improve party morale were to no avail. The number of Sudeten German Party supporters kept increasing; membership had jumped from 759,289 in March 1938 to more than one million in April, the month following the *Anschluss.*[5] Jaksch nonetheless made clear the German Social Democrats' plans for continuing as an activist party and for cooperating with the Czechoslovak Social Democrats. On 5 April, the two parties presented the House of Deputies with a joint proposal for expenditures on public works in the German areas of the country.[6]

At the same time, former party member Emil Franzel arranged an unpublicized meeting for Jaksch with his former schoolmate, the Prague professor Josef Pfitzner, a Henleinist representative who would become vice-mayor of Prague under the Protectorate. Pfitzner was the author of a 1937 book, *Sudetendeutsche Einheitsbewegung,* which identified a group of young social democrats, led by the non-Jews Franzel and Jaksch, who were interested in German nationhood (*Volkstum*), particularly its relation to the German worker, and the possible use of this relationship in the renewal and reshaping of social democracy.[7] Pfitzner felt that the views of these German Social Democrats were not so widely divergent from those of the Henleinists. The meeting—which was hardly secret, taking place as it did in a cafe on Wenzelsplatz—was of no political consequence at the time. When published after the Second World War, however, Pfitzner's record of his meeting with Jaksch caused the latter to be condemned not only by Czechoslovak and German Communists, but also by some former German Social Democrats, who considered it further evidence of his revanchist (*volkssozialistische*) tendencies.[8] Jaksch later defended his meeting with Pfitzner as an attempt to investigate the attitude of SdP leaders, particularly those of the autonomous wing—members most independent from the Nazis—toward the DSAP.[9] Pfitzner, however, apparently regarded the meeting as another opportunity to work toward his goal of a Sudeten German unity movement.[10]

Historian Martin K. Bachstein, who has done extensive work on the German Social Democratic Party, has commented on postwar communist criticism of Jaksch's failure to meet with the "autonomous wing" of the Czechoslovak Communist Party, noting that tactically the Popular Front concept would have been interesting, but would not have helped Jaksch. It would have been opposed—as it had been in the mid-1930s—by the majority of the party, whose members had been schooled since the party division in 1921 to consider the communists "traitorous brothers."[11] At least one reason for his apparent lack of interest in an "autonomous wing" of the Czechoslovak Communist Party seems clear: Jaksch recognized that the Sudeten German Party, not the Communist Party, would play a determining role in Czechoslovak politics in the near future.

On 11 April, Pfitzner met again with Franzel, whose comments on the German Social Democratic political situation in northwestern Bohemia, from which he had recently returned, are illuminating. In Karlsbad, the German Social Democratic camp had been badly shaken; everyone was waiting for someone else to come up with a solution. The workers were also afraid of being designated traitors by the Henleinists. Given the fate of the Hitler opposition in Austria—some 70,000 had been sent to Dachau—this was not surprising. According to Franzel, however, the German Social Democrats in the Aussig-Teplitz-Tetschen area still had the will to resist the Sudeten German Party. The German Social Democratic mayor of Bodenbach, Fritz Kessler, had told Franzel that he intended to travel to Scandinavia to seek help for the party.[12]

In his battle for favorable public opinion, Jaksch faced an uphill fight both in Czechoslovakia and abroad. Czechoslovak Agrarian Prime Minister Milan Hodža had been unable to prevent the continued flirtation of his party's right-wing, led by chairman Rudolf Beran, with the Sudeten German Party. Beran had followed up his New Year's article in the Agrarian mouthpiece, *Venkov* (Countryside), in which he urged the government to bring both the Henleinists and the Slovak Clericals into the coalition as well as to come to terms with Germany, with numerous meetings with German Ambassador Ernst Eisenlohr. The threat of a political compromise between Czechoslovakia's two largest political parties, the Czechoslovak Agrarians and the SdP, in which they would form a right-wing coalition government after the approaching communal elections, surely played a part in the coolness that both Beneš and Hodža displayed toward the German Social Democrats.

The German Social Democrats viewed the Czechoslovak Agrarian behavior as an attempt to weaken social democracy, something the former considered short-sighted. They maintained that Agrarian attempts to come to an understanding with the Nazis along the lines of the German-Polish Friendship Treaty of 1934, in the hope that Adolf Hitler would then lose interest in the Sudeten lands, were doomed to failure.[13]

The Sudeten German Party had early caught the ear of various English public opinion makers and had for a long time remarkable public relations in that country. Even the generally Czechophile *Slavonic Review* had initially given it a not unfriendly hearing.[14] The difficulties Jaksch thus faced in wooing international, especially British, public opinion are underscored in a report from the British Ambassador in Berlin, Nevile Henderson, to the Foreign Office. He cited claims that Jaksch—who, while in London during April again at the request of the Czechoslovak Foreign Ministry, was to apprise British Labour Party leader Clement Attlee and his colleagues of the political situation in Czechoslovakia— represented only ten percent of the Sudeten Germans.[15] From Prague, the British Ambassador Sir Basil Newton reported what he considered Henlein's well-founded assertions of former DSAP members joining the SdP,[16] as well as his claim to being the sole representative of the German minority in Czechoslovakia. The last was based, in part, on the number of worker organizations that had joined the Sudeten German Party, although in the summer of 1938, the German Social Democrats asserted that their unions had 200,000 members versus the Sudeten German Party's 80,000.[17]

During his stay in London, in addition to negotiating a construction loan from the British government and speaking to Labour Party leaders, Jaksch continued his attempt to inform the British public of the state of Czechoslovak-Sudeten German relations. One result was the publication in the London *Daily Telegraph* of his seven-point "Reconciliation" program on 23 April, which also appeared in German Social Democratic newspapers at home. While the DSAP had earlier made many of the same demands, Jaksch presented them more forcefully than previously. They were: linguistic equality, the strengthening of autonomous self-adminis-tration, self-administration in educational matters and youth welfare, expedition of administrative jurisdiction in the lower courts, the creation of German sections in the state grain monopoly, accident insurance and social security offices, the application of the concept of proportionality by nationality in cultural affairs and the constitutional "anchoring" of this concept as concerned state personnel, including state officials, state-owned industries, and state-sponsored institutions.[18]

At least two of the points, linguistic equality and proportionality by nationality in state employment, specifically required amendment of the constitution. In the case of the second, however, Jaksch was simply call-ing for legal assurances that Hodža had already promised with the creation of a minority statute. Jaksch was more straightforward in articulating his demands than he had been just one month earlier; at the party congress he had ingenuously supported both the existing Czechoslovak constitu-tion and advocated goals, the realization of which required amending the constitution.

With the exception of the numerically insignificant fascist parties, the reaction of Czechoslovak public opinion to Jaksch's proposals was positive. Henlein's Karlsbad speech, made the day after the publication of Jaksch's proposals, can be considered the former's reply to Jaksch's plan. In an eight-point program, Henlein announced new demands, chief of which was complete political autonomy in the Sudeten lands with freedom "to profess adherence to the German element and German ideology." In three and one-half years, his demands had escalated from administrative decentralization (Böhmisch Leipa, 21 October 1934), to federalization by nationality (Eger, 21 June 1936), to complete political autonomy.

The German Social Democratic parliamentary faction secretary Robert Wiener, speaking for the party, rejected Henlein's call on both economic and social grounds. He noted that the disruption of existing economic connections would do more harm than good in the Sudeten lands. Wiener further objected to the "work ordinance" proposed by the Henleinists as being modeled on that of the Third Reich.[19] Wiener pointed out that *Anschluss* had actually damaged rather than helped the Sudeten Germans economically. Those branches of the economy most adversely affected by the recession, the porcelain, glass, and textile industries, had been deprived of their traditional Austrian markets, while Austrian Alpine lumber had replaced Sudeten German timber in its former Reich German market. Finally, Wiener blamed National Socialism for continuing socio-economic problems in the border regions, where factories had closed or moved due to fear of Henleinist blackmail or boycott.[20] The idea that *Anschluss* would damage the Sudeten German economy was not new; Jaksch had already warned of the negative effect it would have on the Sudeten lands in 1934.[21]

The Communal Election Campaign

The oft-postponed communal elections in Czechoslovakia took place the last two Sundays in May and the second Sunday in June. Unrest in the Sudeten lands led Interior Minister Josef Cerny to announce measures to insure peace and quiet in nationally mixed areas. The government demanded unconditional adherence to all laws. No terror of any kind was to be tolerated.[22]

The Czechoslovak government, under the growing diplomatic pressure to come to terms with the Sudeten German Party, tolerated the Henleinist abuse, much of which was not directed at ethnic Czechs, few of whom lived in the border areas, but rather at those Germans who opposed the Sudeten German Party. The Czechoslovak Social Democratic newspaper, *Právo lidu* indicated that the attitude of the government toward the Henleinists until that time had been to allow them to do generally what they liked in the border areas, thus endangering both the Czechs and the non-Henleinist Germans resident there.[23] German Social Democrats reported that it was as if a civil war had broken out in the border regions and there was open season on them and other "democratically minded" Germans. Party secretary Siegfried Taub privately spoke of the passivity of Czechoslovak government officials throughout the campaign, commenting that those who opposed the Henleinist terror could truly be called heroes.[24]

Anti-Henleinist German politicians found themselves prevented from campaigning. In Böhmisch Leipa, they were unable, due to Sudeten German Party threats, to have posters printed, although one of the local printing houses was owned by a Jew. Participants at German Social Democratic campaign meetings in Mährisch Trübau had to make their way through jeering crowds of Henleinist supporters.[25] The German Social Democrats had difficulty finding party members willing to stand for election in the smaller communities due to SdP threats that they would be massacred following Hitler's occupation of the Sudeten lands.[26] In a thinly veiled threat to DSAP members, the lead article in the 15 May edition of the SdP newspaper, *Die Zeit,* announced that anyone not voting for the Henleinists could consider himself an émigré.[27]

The political situation was further complicated by the "May Crisis," a partial Czechoslovak troop mobilization on the eve of the elections in response to alleged troop movements on the Reich German side of the border. German troop movements between Austria and Germany had actually caused the panic. The troop mobilization, while showing the Nazis how well prepared the Czechoslovak army was for war, also further unnerved an already jittery British government and enraged Hitler.

The Socialist International met in Brussels during the Czechoslovak communal elections. Jaksch, as main speaker, discussed the European political situation. In his report on Czechoslovakia, he commented on events surrounding the recent elections. Jaksch claimed that in conjunction with the alleged German troop mobilization, the Henleinists had planned a sort of a "St. Bartholomew's Night" for the border regions,

with attacks on Czech and German democrats as well as the occupation
of worker cooperatives and worker homes.[28] Jaksch also discussed the
need to win the "propaganda battle" that would decide Czechoslovakia's
fate in the coming weeks and months. He asked that social democrats of
other lands spread the word that the Henleinists were not oppressed, that
they were themselves oppressors and terrorists, that Henlein was "a
starter of wars," and that Czechoslovakia was important in the defense
of European peace.[29] Delegates to the International passed a resolution
in support of the recent Czechoslovak troop mobilization and recognized
the DSAP loyalty to the principles of personal freedom and democracy.[30]

More than ninety percent of the votes cast for German political parties
went to the Henleinists. When German votes for the Czechoslovak Communist Party are included, the Sudeten German Party still received more
than 85 percent of the total German vote.[31] The German Social Democrats won a majority of votes in only a few of the smaller communities.
Nonetheless, the *Sozialdemokrat* called the election results "the greatest
moral victory in the party's history." The left-wing Parisian newspaper,
Le Soir, supported this interpretation, noting that Henlein had reckoned
with one hundred percent support from the Sudeten Germans, along the
lines of the earlier plebiscite in Austria.

German Social Democratic leaders continued to work closely with the
Czechoslovak government, rather than attempting to come to any sort
of understanding with with the Henleinists on the basis of nationality
following the elections. It is unclear how much support this stance had
from the party rank and file; Franzel has reported that some party members thought it senseless to fight the SdP, rather than join it.[32]

On the evening after the first day of elections, a government broadcast
thanked all citizens and political parties for their model behavior on election day. The German Social Democratic press noted, however, that in the
border regions, such behavior was the result of the presence of the Czechoslovak military, although calm in other areas of the country was due to
voter self-discipline.[33] Immediately after the vote, in a further attempt
to rally party members, Jaksch spoke at German Social Democratic meetings in Aussig, Dux, and Tetschen-Bodenbach. His arrival at the last of
these was delayed, because Henleinists were blocking all of the major roads
entering the city.

Summer 1938—Prelude to Munich

At least one argument favored Germany's claims to the Sudeten lands.
From the end of the First World War until Hitler's reoccupation of the
Rhineland in 1936, much of the European left had claimed that the tenets
of the Versailles Treaty were both unfair and unworkable and that all
peoples, even those defeated in the war, deserved the right of self-determination. Approximately at the time when the left had abandoned this
argument, it was adopted by some of the parties on the European right,
among them, the English Conservatives. By the late 1930s, these parties
were asserting that the Germans of Austria, Czechoslovakia, and Poland,
like the other peoples of Europe, were entitled to self-determination,
even if the result was an increase in the power of Nazi Germany. In their
eyes, Hitler was no worse a dictator than Josef Stalin, with whom some
left-wing parties advocated alliances.

In the eyes of left-wing politicians, however, the situation appeared different. In an analysis of Czechoslovakia's political situation written shortly
before his death in July 1938, Otto Bauer condemned Nazi attempts to
use the Sudeten German struggle for the right of self-determination at
the end of the First World War as justification for Hitler's violent campaign against Czechoslovakia. Berlin had cited German Social Democratic-
led demonstrations for self-determination in 1918, 1919, and 1923 as an
excuse for its behavior. Bauer opposed British and French government
demands that the Czechoslovak government make broad concessions to
the Sudeten German Party in return for the continued guarantee of
Czechoslovakia by the Western powers. Concessions to German cultural,
economic, and linguistic demands, if timely, might have been able to
prevent Henlein's ascendancy in the Sudeten lands, but by the summer
of 1938 they would simply have been seen as a Nazi success in Czechoslovak internal affairs, thus strengthening Hitler's hold on the Sudeten
Germans. Territorial autonomy, again if timely, could have won over
the Sudeten Germans to the Czechoslovak state, but would now mean
the surrender of ethnic Czechs in German communities to the Henleinists. Every county leader would become a little Seyss-Inquart, with the
same unfortunate result that had already been seen in Austria. In Czechoslovakia, it would also unleash a world war. The Sudeten German appeals
for self-determination in 1918 and 1919, based on the principle of free

nations, had been calls for freedom from all "imperialist forces," for the creation of an enduring peace in Europe, wrote Bauer. The present Sudeten German cry for self-determination was a demand for "imperialism." Those using the cover of struggle for national self-determination in the Sudeten lands were using the struggle as the means to a completely different goal.[34]

Relations between the German Social Democrats and the Henleinists remained at a boiling point all summer. Rumors of a Sudeten German Party inspired uprising circulated in Prague; the Henleinists proved themselves masters at disseminating rumors both at home and abroad.[35] Sudeten German Party leader Karl Hermann Frank, later State Secretary of the Protectorate of Bohemia and Moravia, accused first a Czech, then a German Social Democrat of killing an SdP member in a tavern brawl, although a later official inquiry found both men innocent.[36] There were allegations of DSAP members attacking SdP members,[37] but it was members of the SdP who stabbed a local DSAP official during a political debate.[38]

During the late 1930s, the German Social Democratic Party came to depend more and more on its paramilitary corps, the *Republikanische Wehr*. This organization, numbering some 7,000 members by 1937,[39] functioned as a party guard against possible SdP attacks on DSAP meetings and rallies. They were a ubiquitous presence at German Social Democratic demonstrations in the summer of 1938. Relatively little has been written about the *Republikanische Wehr,* which was organized along the lines of the Austrian Social Democratic *Republikanischer Schutzbund* and the Weimar German Social Democratic *Reichsbanner Schwarz-Rot-Gold.* Founded in 1926 as the *Rote Wehr,* its activities during the 1920s and early 1930s appear primarily to have been limited to appearances at festivities marking the first of May. The organization's first national parade took place in Aussig in July 1937. A number of leaders of the *Republikanische Wehr* had been members of the German Social Democratic gymnastic organization (ATUS) or the youth organizations. Ernest Paul, the commander, had been head of the latter. Especially during the 1930s, a large percentage of the organization's members came from among the ranks of the unemployed, particularly former members of the youth organization.

As the summer of 1938 progressed, the attitude of most Czechs toward the German Social Democratic Party became clear: the DSAP represented a minority within a minority and was creating as many problems as it was solving. Many Czechoslovak Social Democrats also gave up the battle to aid the DSAP. The journal of the Czechoslovak Social Democratic metal trade unionists, whose leader, Antonín Hampl, was chairman of the party, printed an article calling for the DSAP to disband. Comments that were attributed to Hodža by German Ambassador Eisenlohr, concerning the attitude of the Czechoslovak Social Democratic Party toward the Sudeten German Party, are instructive here. Although the left-wing Czechoslovak parties provided the strongest opposition to the Henleinists, Hodža believed that the Czechoslovak Social Democrats, whom he considered "social reformers," were at least willing to discuss the possibility of SdP participation in the government. Further, Hodža hoped that the Henleinists had no fundamental opposition to continued Czechoslovak Social Democratic participation in the government coalition, because he needed them to overcome the anti-Heleinist attitudes of two other coalition parties, the Czechoslovak National Socialists and Czech Clericals. Finally, Hodža claimed that in social questions, the Sudeten German Party had more in common with the Czechoslovak Social Democrats than with the otherwise more pro-German Czechoslovak Agrarains.[40] The same Czechoslovak national-state ideology that had made the Czechoslovak National Socialists such unlikely allies for the German Social Democrats made them implacable enemies of the Henleinists.

Some Czech and Slovak democrats, however, such as the Czech liberal journalist Hubert Ripka, a colleague of Beneš's, continued to support the beleaguered German Social Democrats. Speaking alongside Jaksch at one of the party's summer meetings, Ripka discussed the Czech people's will to resist fascism and the need for the alliance of all democratic Germans in this conflict. Jaksch spoke of war: it could be avoided, but the price of peace was a democratic solution to the German problem. He was convinced that Czechoslovakia could be turned into a Central European Switzerland, but noted that the nationality laws of Switzerland were based on the common belief of all Swiss in freedom.[41]

The German Social Democratic Party continued to hold meetings, but they were no longer announced for fear of disruption by the Henleinists, with whom party members had been advised to avoid political confrontations. The number of meetings and demonstrations that were held appears to have decreased as the summer progressed. Attendance at party gatherings had, in any case, became more and more dangerous. The party began to hold many of its meetings in predominantly Czech areas.[42]

Republikanische Wehr leader Paul spoke before a German Social Democratic public gathering at Dux on 11 September, the night before Hitler's Nuremberg rally speech. He stressed the party's commitment to freedom and democracy, but emphasized the German worker's willingness to defend the republic against fascism. He warned that the Sudeten German Party must recognize that there was no place for the politics of Seyss-Inquart on Czechoslovak soil. Paul made obligatory remarks on DSAP loyalty to Beneš and the Czechoslovak state and stressed the ability of the Czechoslovak army to fight as well as to preserve the peace.[43]

British Intervention

A rumored second troop mobilization in July frightened the British government into demanding that Beneš request a mediator for the situation. The wealthy British businessman, Walter Runciman, forced upon Prague as negotiator between the government and the Sudeten Germans, arrived in Czechoslovakia on 3 August. According to Jaksch, although German democrats had not been pleased when Runciman was thrust upon them, they welcomed the fact that he and his staff spent so much time with the Henleinists. Jaksch hoped that Runciman and his colleagues would be able to form an independent judgment of the situation. They would then be in a position to be important witnesses for world public opinion, if the present negotiations were to break down, as Jaksch expected.[44]

While the Henleinists staged demonstrations for the benefit of Runciman and his staff, and while Runciman was being entertained by members of the former nobility in their castles, shops belonging to non-Henleinists were being picketed in the border regions, and their customers were photographed. Jews in the border regions had been forced to hire Sudeten German Party members under threat of boycott and worse.[45]

According to Taub, Runciman appeared to be of the opinion that a solution to the problem of the Sudeten Germans could be reached by negotiations between the Sudeten German Party and the government, an opinion that German Social Democratic leaders did not share. The latter believed they could show Runciman the "well-trod path" of negotiations with the SdP would produce no results.[46] The party viewpoint remained that concessions to Henlein served no purpose, because he was Hitler's agent and Hitler would be satisfied only with the capitulation of Czechoslovakia.[47]

Although Taub, at least, awaited an invitation to participate, the German Social Democrats were not called upon to take part in the negotiations.[48] They did meet with Runciman or his aides three times, however, and Berlin made a semi-official protest as a result.[49] At a meeting on 5 August, Jaksch declared that he considered the DSAP's most important tasks to be the preservation of the peace and the achievement of an understanding between the Czechoslovak and the German people of the state.

At the beginning of August, German Social Democratic executive committee members had developed a four-point plan for equality of nationalities and the safeguarding of the Sudeten German social existence to present at the national political negotiations then taking place. The points were equality of nationality, democratic self-administration, guaranteed proportional representation, and economic reconstruction.[50] They formed the basis for a memorandum Jaksch wrote with the help of his ally Willi Wanka and party economic expert Franz Rehwald, which was signed by Jaksch, Rehwald, and Taub and presented to the Runciman mission on 12 August. The memorandum called for complete equality of nationality and the safeguarding of the Sudeten Germans' social and cultural existence through a peaceful solution of the Czechoslovak nationality problem.[51] Bachstein has pointed out that this memorandum—the last of the party's political proposals concerning linguistic matters and self-administration before Munich—was also the furthest reaching. Built both on his "Reconciliation Plan" and on the proposals he made at Brünn in May 1938 during the communal election campaign, the memorandum shows the development of Jaksch's political demands. His handling of the entire matter also underscores his awareness of the political tightrope he had to walk between the Sudeten German Party's demands, on the one hand, and the refusal in some Czech political circles to recognize equality of nationality for the Sudeten Germans, on the other.[52]

On 2 September, Beneš announced that he was ready to accede, as far as possible, to Sudeten German Party demands. Despite the worsening situation, at least some German Social Democrats, including the ever-optimistic Taub, awaited a peaceful solution to the problem. Jaksch seems to have been less confident. In an article appearing on 4 September in *Neuer Vorwärts*, Jaksch wrote that he had the impression that the Prague government was doing its best to avoid giving Berlin any excuse to make relations between the two countries worse. Despite growing Czech resentment of the Germans, due in part to attacks aired on Nazi German radio and provocations by local Henleinists, the Czechoslovak government had begun placing democratically minded Sudeten German officials in positions of responsibility in the government and appeared ready to make further concessions in the course of successful negotiations over the outline of a nationalities' statute. In short, Prague was willing to come to terms, but Berlin was not. Jaksch commented on the four main points under discussion and where they stood: personnel, public works and government contracts, the language question, and reorganization of the administrative system of the republic. He believed that the first two had already been dealt with in the 18 February agreement. It was now a question of insuring and expediting their application. As concerned the language question, the Czechoslovak political parties had recognized that the then existing laws would no longer work. The Czechoslovak National Socialist deputy and Charles University professor Jan Kozák had already called for granting linguistic equality to the country's Germans. It was only the area of administrative reform that presented problems. Jaksch believed it was not so much a question of material difference of opinion, but of ideological opposition. The government foresaw the restoration of self-administration at the county and provincial level. Through the creation of national curiae at the latter level, the Germans were to be given broad powers, which would have signified a major administrative gain for them. The Sudeten German Party opposed this major concession from Prague, because it did not fit in with party plans to erect a totalitarian National Socialist state within the Czechoslovak Republic.[53]

On 7 September, Beneš announced his "Fourth Plan," which would have granted the Germans full autonomy, the cornerstone of the Sudeten German Party demands. Jaksch later wrote that this plan would have been a good basis for a solution to the Sudeten German problem, although it did not provide a direct solution for the economic problems of the Sudeten lands. Jaksch described it as a combination of Bauer's and Renner's plans for personal and territorial autonomy in Cisleithania.[54] On that same day, however, under a flimsy pretext, the Henleinists broke off negotiations

with the government until 13 September, the day after Hitler was to speak
at the Nuremberg party rally. Henlein fled to Germany on the day Hitler
spoke, appearing in public there on 15 September to demand the "return"
of the Sudeten lands to Germany ("Wir wollen heim ins Reich."). Prague
announced the dissolution of the Sudeten German Party on grounds of
high treason immediately following Henlein's speech.

Clearly, Runciman's mission had been a failure.

Following Hitler's speech at Nuremberg on 12 September, in which he
denounced the Czechoslovak government for oppressing the Sudeten Germans, there was further unrest in the border regions of Czechoslovakia. In
Asch, some 8,000 persons assembled and tore down Czech language signs.
Telephone lines surrounding Karlsbad were cut and in Eger, the windows
of Czech and Jewish stores were smashed.[55] This is in sharp contrast with
Franzel's description of central Prague that evening: the streets of the
normally bustling Wenzelsplatz and Am Graben were completely empty.
Martial law was declared in eight predominantly German counties, all of
them except Böhmisch Krumau in western Bohemia, and all public assemblies were forbidden. Shortly thereafter, some civil rights, including
privacy of persons and letters, were temporarily suspended or curtailed
throughout the country.[56]

Sudeten German Party members, who controlled most of the border
regions, made random attacks on German Social Democratic property.
The defense of the Volkshaus and party headquarters in Eger by one
hundred members of the *Republikanische Wehr* with four revolvers has
become part of party lore. The echo of their gun fire in the building's
vaulted hallway convinced the more numerous—and allegedly better
armed—Henleinists that the social democratic defenders had a machine
gun, saving the day. *Republikanische Wehr* members defended another
Volkshaus with the effective use of fireworks.[57]

The German Social Democrats published a desperate call for struggle
against the Henleinists on 14 September. Entitled "Mitbürger! Es geht um
alles!" (Fellow citizens! It's now or never!), the manifesto spoke of an
"honorable peace" between the Sudeten Germans and their Slavic neigh-
bors.[58] The manifesto has been described as Jaksch's final attempt to
create a collective movement of Sudeten Germans loyal to the state.[59] The
prescience Jaksch displayed here as concerns the result of Sudeten German
participation in an "imperialist" war is worth noting: if Germandom

were again to take the road of imperialist power politics, rejecting equality and seeking to dominate other peoples, it would sooner or later come into conflict with the Slavs and the Balkan peoples. The world would again rise up against the Germans. The Sudeten Germans would be the first victims and their homeland would be destroyed in the clash of world powers and their future lost.[60]

Shortly after the publication of this manifesto, Jaksch was joined by some of the few remaining non-Henleinists and non-communist Sudeten German politicians in a last plea to "save the peace." They noted that although Beneš's Fourth Plan did not fulfill all of the Sudeten German Party demands, it did provide a good starting point for discussions. The appeal of long-time German Democratic parliamentarian Karl Kostka, former German Agrarian parliamentarian Anton Köhler, Roman Catholic functionary Emmanuel Reichenberger, German Democratic academic-politician Kurt Sitte, and Jaksch went unheeded.

At the same time, the Czechoslovak Ministry of Interior sent Paul an order via the police, forbidding the wearing of *Republikanische Wehr* uniforms, effective immediately.[61] Members of what Paul termed "the most reliable organization in the country" had been ready to defend the republic, but their effectiveness as a large scale fighting force was never tested.

Munich 1938

Well before Hitler's speech at Nuremberg, the option of finding a solution for the regulation of Czechoslovak-Sudeten German relations within the confines of the Czechoslovak state had been closed. The problem had developed into an international power play in which Hitler used German grievances as a pretext for meddling in Czechoslovak internal affairs. Although he apparently wanted to annex the German-inhabited areas of the republic, thus saving the Sudeten Germans from the alleged excesses of the Czechs, what Hitler really sought was an excuse to wage war against Czechoslovakia and occupy it as a gateway to Eastern Europe and the Balkans.

Pressure on Prague increased as Britain and France—the latter bound by treaty to aid Czechoslovakia in case of an attack by Germany—attempted to force Beneš to come to terms with Hitler. Following a 15 September

meeting between Hitler and Conservative British Prime Minister Neville
Chamberlain at Berchtesgaden, the British and French governments demanded that Prague accede to Germany's most recent demands. The
German-populated areas of Czechoslovakia must be ceded to the Reich as
soon as possible, on the basis of the right of self-determination and new
frontiers determined afterward by an international commission. Britain
would then join in an international guarantee of the new borders. When
Beneš refused to accept these demands, calling instead for arbitration with
Germany, London and Paris presented Prague with an ultimatum: accept
the proposals or lose British and French aid if war ensued. Possible reasons
for Beneš's capitulation included: lack of regard for the military might of
his Soviet ally, fear of facing the German army alone, and possible Fifth
Columnist actions by the Henleinists, should there be a war.

Prague residents took to the streets on 21 September, the day the
Czechoslovak capitulation to the British and French was announced, protesting through the night and into the next day that they wanted to fight.
The government of Prime Minister Hodža, which resigned on 21 September, would be replaced immediately after Munich with a government less
tied to Beneš's policies and presumably more to Berlin's liking.

The situation was not resolved, however, because Hitler again raised the
stakes. By 23 September, his ever-increasing demands had created such an
international crisis that Czech troops were mobilized and French troops
were sent to the Maginot Line. No concrete plans were made, however, to
wage a war that neither Czechoslovakia nor its allies wanted.[62]

Some citizens of Czechoslovakia were ready to fight to defend the
country. According to one source, the Czechs, Slovaks and Germans (if
less enthusiastically) complied with the mobilization order.[63] Franzel
has written of the difficulties that followed the military call-up, quoting
friends who were mobilized as remarking on the mutual mistrust between
the Legionaries and younger Czech officers as well as the fear of a German
mutiny.[64]

Karl Kern's reminiscences of the 23 September troop mobilization and
expected Reich German attack are perhaps romanticized, but interesting.
He and fellow German Social Democrats drinking at their favorite Prague
bar cheered news of the Czechoslovak troop mobilization when it came
over the radio. In contrast, the Czech bartender claimed that Beneš had been
badly advised and should have submitted to Hitler's demands. Kern and a

colleague made their way through the darkened back streets of Prague to the headquarters of the official German language newspaper, *Prager Presse*. There, they and other colleagues swore not to surrender in the battle against the Nazis. Late that night, Kern returned home to await the expected Reich German air raid.[65]

Chamberlain's negotiations with Hitler during that month led to the Munich Conference. Chamberlain and Hitler, joined by the French Premier Edouard Daladier and Italian dictator Benito Mussolini, signed the Munich Agreement on 30 September, forcing Czechoslovakia to cede Sudeten German areas immediately to Germany. New boundaries were to be drawn up and plebiscites held where necessary, both under the auspices of an international commission. The new boundaries were then to be internationally guaranteed. Beginning on 1 October, Hitler occupied the Sudeten lands and more.

Afterward

Even before the Munich Accord, ethnic Czechs, Jews, and Sudeten Germans began to make their way into the interior of Bohemia and Moravia. When it was learned that the lands ceded at Munich were to be occupied almost immediately, the stream of refugees, which included some 30,000 Sudeten German Social Democrats, grew to a flood. Not all of those attempting to enter the Czechoslovak rump state were successful; about 20,000 Sudeten Germans were returned as they tried to cross the border.[66]

Indeed, many Czechs seemed to desire a state free of the Sudeten Germans, even at the price of a loss of territory ("Malá ale naše!"—"small, but ours!"). The Prague government feared that the mass of Jews and Sudeten Germans would create additional problems with Berlin.[67] The hostile reaction of the Czechs came as a surprise to some refugees, one of whom explained:

> We shouted and worked for local autonomy, [but] we did not expect this . . . . Last night we went to sleep in Czechoslovakia; today we wake up to find ourselves in Germany.[68]

Kern sought to describe the reaction of the German refugees and the Czechs to one another. He commented that in most cases, rather than a flight to one's compatriots, who were fellow citizens of the Czech tongue, the situation appeared to be a flight abroad, to rejection based on nationality or open animosity. That German Social Democrats had risked life and limb in the struggle against National Socialism was overlooked. Sudeten German refugees were seen by many Czechs (though certainly not by all) as intruders, unwelcome foreigners, even Nazis.[69]

According to Kern, this situation was due, in part, to the often separate lives led by the two peoples throughout the First Republic. He pointed out that the Czech press began reporting on events and developments in the Sudeten lands only when the influence of Hitler had begun to threaten the existence of the entire state. The converse, Kern said, was also true: the German press did not discuss events and developments in Czech or Slovak areas, but limited its comments to Prague policies toward the national minorities. Thus, the Sudeten Germans were as foreign to the Czechs as were the Czechs to most Sudeten Germans.[70]

German Social Democrats managed to evacuate many members of the *Republikanische Wehr,* who had not been returned to the annexed areas due to the successful intervention of the Czechoslovak Social Democratic Party, as well as most of their party's endangered functionaries.[71] The political situation was, however, growing increasingly dangerous for the DSAP. Shortly before Munich, German Social Democratic leaders had decided to cease operation of the provincial press in order not to endanger subscribers. On 10 October, the party executive committee actually expelled members living in the annexed regions en masse, in a further attempt to insure their safety. On the same day, Hitler demanded that all Sudeten Germans, including social democrats and communists, be returned to the annexed areas.[72] Three days later, he demanded the extradition of all German Social Democratic deputies and senators. In early November, the Nazi occupiers forced the dissolution of both the German Social Democratic hiking organization, *Die Naturfreunde* (Friends of Nature) and ATUS. All of the property of these organizations was seized, including camping, gymnastics, and sports facilities.

Under these difficult conditions, German Social Democratic officials, many themselves threatened, worked to find the means—both legal and financial—to enable their most endangered members to leave the country. Because *Anschluss* had lengthened Czechoslovakia's border with Germany, the best possibilities for overland flight were Poland and Rumania. Poland, with closer connections to Scandinavia and Western Europe, was the more popular option.

Initially, it seemed as if the party would be unable to find either the funds, or more importantly, the visas and other permits necessary for emigration abroad. Then, an emissary of the Swedish working class movement appeared in the Prague party headquarters with twenty visas and a promise of funds and more visas. The British government, its conscience perhaps pricked by the Munich events, and to a lesser extent, the French government, where the French Socialists, influenced by pacifist ideas, had supported the *Diktat* in parliament, also provided funds and visas to needy Austrians, Jews, and Reich and Sudeten Germans. The German Social Democrats actually proved very competent at obtaining funds from many segments of the British public. In addition to the trade unions, the Lord Mayor of London Fund and the Czech Refugee Trust Fund provided aid to refugees from Czechoslovakia.[73]

Some 3,000 Sudeten German Social Democrats were thus able to escape in the months after Munich, primarily to Great Britain and Sweden, but also to Canada. Younger exiles to both Canada and Great Britain enlisted in those countries' armies during the Second World War.

On 22 February 1939, after a majority of its members had found relative safety abroad, the party executive committee held its last meeting on Czechoslovak soil. In order not to endanger further party members who remained in Nazi-occupied areas, the executive disbanded the party altogether and formed an exile organization, the Association of Loyal Sudeten German Social Democrats (*Treuegemeinschaft Sudentendeutscher Sozialdemokraten*). The term, "Sudeten," stressing the *Volksgruppe* aspect of the newly formed organization, indicates the influence of Jaksch. Later, in another slap at Ludwig Czech, Jaksch claimed that the decision to transfer the party headquarters abroad had been opposed by the "unwavering social-politicians, who no longer understood the world." Czech would pay with his life for his belief that the party could continue to lead a legal existence in the rump Czechoslovak state.[74]

According to Jaksch, there were still Austrian, Jewish, Reich and Sudeten German refugees in camps in rump Czechoslovakia as late as mid-March 1939. Most of them, however, were women and children.[75] The last group of refugees left Czechoslovakia for Poland on 14 March. Nazi troops were on duty on the Czechoslovak side of the border at the Oderburg crossing as dawn broke on the morning of 15 March.[76]

The sudden Nazi occupation of rump Czechoslovakia that day had left many German Social Democratic officials still in Prague. The British government negotiated the release of Franz Krejci, Rehwald, and Taub, who along with Jaksch had taken refuge in the British Embassy. The Nazis were apparently not interested in negotiating free passage for Jaksch. He was to be arrested and interned. Disguised as a worker, however, Jaksch sneaked out of the Embassy almost a week later. The following day, this time in winter sports attire, he and several similarly dressed colleagues left for the northern Moravian border, where they skied over the mountains into Poland. They were met just across the border, as planned, by a British aid worker. With the cooperation of Polish Socialists, who were able to slash through governmental red tape, Jaksch and his colleagues obtained visas from the British Consul in Katowice in record time.

Although the majority of the high party officials managed to escape from Czechoslovakia, some 7,900 German Social Democrats were imprisoned or placed in concentration camps. Some party members of course were of Jewish origin and thus imprisoned on racial grounds. In addition to party leaders and trade unionists, officials of ATUS and *Republikanische Wehr,* and others who had incurred the wrath of Nazi officials, were incarcerated. Some party members, like former Chairman Czech, stayed behind because they considered themselves too old and too ill to attempt an illegal border crossing.[77] Among those who lost their lives in Theresienstadt were Ludwig Czech, Bohemian provincial diet member Franz Illner, and former party senator Johann Polach. Party journalist Emil Strauss died in Auschwitz. Some, including Leopold Pölzl, long-time editor of *Die freie Gemeinde,* died following Gestapo torture. Others survived police detention and concentration camps, including ATUS general secretary Alois Ullmann, who spent the years after 1939 in Dachau. Still others chose suicide rather than face imprisonment, torture, and possible slow death.

CONCLUSION

In the twenty years between 1918 and 1938, the German Social Democratic Party declined from the largest German political movement in Czechoslovakia to a numerically and politically insignificant grouping. Given the completeness of the party's eclipse, one must ask to what degree its decline was due to internal problems and to what extent the party was a victim of larger European developments. An attempt to evaluate the meaning of German Social Democratic interwar history must consider the party in three different, but interrelated contexts: the party's internal situation, the political milieu of the First Czechoslovak Republic, and the larger European situation.

The large-scale German Social Democratic victories in the 1919 communal elections and the 1920 parliamentary elections were part of the European-wide postwar move toward left-wing parties. Local circumstances in Czechoslovakia, however, also played a role. At the time of the foundation of the Czechoslovak state, the Sudeten Germans had a well-developed political and social structure, which included parties representing a broad spectrum of political opinion. Only the German Social Democrats, however, were well-organized throughout Bohemia, Moravia, and Silesia at the provincial level. Thus, many non-socialists voted for the German Social Democrats, who were apparently most able to represent their interests.

By mid-1919, the German Social Democratic Workers' Party in Czecholovakia had accepted the existence of the republic, as indicated by its choice of name. The party program, which was not revised during the interwar period, demanded the restructuring of the state on national lines, creating a sort of Central European Switzerland. While the German Social Democrats never removed these demands for national autonomy from their program, they did drop them from their political vocabulary after 1929, because of their participation in the coalition. When calls for national autonomy resurfaced in the DSAP in 1935, party leaders carefully distinguished their proposals for a democratic solution t this issue from those of the SdP. That the DSAP had no means, domestic or foreign, to force the acceptance of their demands, caused the Czechs to view them with somewhat more tolerance and certainly less fear, than similar demands of the SdP.

Beginning in 1920, the German Social Democrats suffered from the intraparty strife common to European social democratic parties at the time. Party moderates solved the conflict of opinion at their own expense in early 1921, expelling the entire membership of one of the party's largest, wealthiest and most influential organizations, Reichenberg, for breach of party discipline. One point of contention had been that leading Reichenberg German Social Democrats advocated immediate "revolutionary" change on the example of Soviet Russia, rather than focusing on the national claims of the German workers. Many former German Social Democrats from Reichenberg later joined the Czechoslovak Communist Party.

Because all German political parties were in opposition until 1926, Czech politicians often failed to distinguish between the German Social Democratic national demands, which were based on Marxist precepts, and those of the other German parties. To be sure, in some cases, particularly as regards national equality, the demands were similar, differing only in their theoretical basis. During the 1920s, the German Social Democratic Party maintained its oppositional position, alternately on national and on socio-economic grounds. Across the entire Czech political spectrum, the German Social Democrats were condemned for their national politics. Further, in the eyes of the Czech right, the DSAP was suspect as an "international revolutionary" party.

When the German Agrarians and Clericals entered the Gentlemen's Coalition in 1926, the German Social Democrats joined with the German nationalists in condemning this betrayal of Sudeten German national interests.

The exclusion of the Czechoslovak Social Democrats from the coalition might have been expected to result in a prompt rapprochement between the Czechoslovak and German Social Democrats on the basis of some common class and economic interests, but nothing of the kind occurred. German Social Democratic calls for national autonomy had alienated the Czechoslovak Social Democrats, whose commitment to Czech national politics had proved stronger than their commitment to the international working-class movement. In addition, Czechoslovak Social Democratic leadership recognized that it could obtain more advantages for its constituency through cooperation with the governing parties, than through opposition to them. Finally, during the interwar period, unwavering Czechoslovak Social Democratic support for the First Republic insured that its relations with the Czechoslovak National Socialists were warmer than with the German Social Democrats, for the former two parties shared more common interests.

A slow thaw in relations had led to a rapprochement between Czechoslovakia's two major social democratic parties in 1928. With the relative improvement of the positions of both parties in the 1929 parliamentary elections, the Czechoslovak Social Democrats sponsored the German Social Democratic entry into the government coalition. The Czechoslovak Social Democratic negotiation of German Social Democratic participation in the coalition, rather than independent negotiations by the latter, is but one example of the German party's relative political weakness. The relationship between the two parties remained unequal throughout the rest of the interwar period. The German Social Democrats proved loyal allies to the Czechoslovak Social Democrats, partly out of necessity, while the larger Czechoslovak party neglected German interests when political expediency demanded it. Inequalities between respective Czechoslovak and German parties was not limited to the social democrats. Coalition participation by both the German Agrarians and Clericals was contingent on each party's ties with the respective Czech (or Czechoslovak) party. Proportional representation gave the national minorities a representative voice in parliament. Ideological divisions guaranteed, however, that their parliamentary politics would remain reactive unless the minority political parties allied themselves with ideologically similar Czechoslovak parties or overcame their differences with one another and formed national blocs.

International communism's "social-fascist" campaign against European social democracy between the wars cannot be said to have had any direct effect on Konrad Henlein's political ascendancy in the Sudeten lands.

Through its attempts to destroy the SPD, however, this policy helped ease Hitler's road to rule in Germany. Hitler's subsequent consolidation of power in 1933 was followed by an increasingly aggressive foreign policy that by the late 1930s included fomenting unrest and encouraging "Fifth Columnists" among ethnic Germans outside the Reich. This policy was particularly successful in Czechoslovakia.

Following the Comintern's about-face in 1935, calling for Popular Front governments against the fascists, Czechoslovak Communist relations with the social democratic parties improved somewhat. The formation of a Popular Front government was not feasible for several reasons. Earlier Communist Party attacks on the Czechoslovak and Geman Social Democrats had alienated them and they interpreted the new proposals as merely another attempt to destroy them. Furthermore, the proposals for a Popular Front came at a time when a part of the DSAP's constituency was responding favorably to nationalist, rather than internationalist rhetoric. In any case, those parties that may have been willing to participate in such a coalition represented less than one third of the electorate.

The attraction Henlein exercised over the entire Sudeten German population is apparent from the results of the vote in Czechoslovak elections of 1935 and 1938. Both the German Social Democrats and the Czechoslovak Communist Party (in German areas) suffered great losses at the hands of the Sudeten German Party. In May 1938, a majority of both parties' former constituency voted for another movement that transcended international borders: German nationalism. Only the diehard Sudeten German internationalists continued to support either the communists or the social democrats.

It seems clear that the majority of Sudeten German workers perceived a decline in their position from that in the Habsburg Monarchy and they considered themselves disadvantaged when compared with the Czechs of the First Republic or the Germans of the Third Reich. This perception, rather than the degree to which it was justified, is the important point. Sudeten German worker support for the Henleinists is not surprising. The SDAPÖ had had to contend with Czech-German nationality conflict during the nineteenth century. The German Workers' Party had been founded in Bohemia just after the turn of the century partially in response to the failure of orthodox social democracy to solve what German workers there had perceived as a threat to their livelihood: the influx of Czech workers into previously German areas. Worker support for the SdP in the late 1930s was a desperate response to the policies of the Czechoslovak state, which were seen to threaten the German economic and national existence. Many workers were no longer willing to wait for the improvement of their lot envisioned by either the communists or the social democrats.

The German Social Democratic Party has been criticized as an excessively bureaucratic institution whose leaders meager political abilities were overshadowed by their bureaucratic tendencies. Party chairman Ludwig Czech, secretary Siegfried Taub, and their closest allies have been criticized for the inability to adopt their Austromarxist world view to the political realities of the interwar period, especially in the 1930s. Certainly, Czech lacked demagogic talent; his natural speaking ability was limited. Nor was his a commanding or innovative political personality. Party secretary Taub has been criticized for a similar lack of political acuity. Taub's passion for organization, his contacts throughout the government, and his linguistic ability were useful nonetheless for administering a political party and for dealing with the formidable Czechoslovak bureaucracy.

During the early and mid-1920s the application of Austromarxist tenets in Czechoslovakia was reasonable, given the apparent success, at least at the local level, of the Austrian Social Democrats at the time. Austromarxist theory had been developed in response to the peculiar needs of social democracy in a multinational state. The crisis in German Social Democratic leadership during the 1930s was part of a Central-European-wide political problem; party elders adhered to an outmoded political ideology that was largely inapplicable to contemporary events. The German Social Democratic Party thus proved incapable of defending either its ideals or its members against the politics of the radical right.

Critics of the traditional leadership have offered the younger, more vital Wenzel Jaksch as an alternative to Czech's moribund leadership. Clearly, Jaksch brought new direction to the party when he took its reins in March 1938. But, given the international situation, Jaksch did not have enough time to institute his political ideas, so comparison of anything other than his and Czech's differing styles of leadership is almost impossible. It also remains an open question if the direction Jaksch had in mind for the party could, indeed, be called "Social Democratic."

The party accomplished little as a coalition member. The reasoning of the German Social Democratic leadership, that more could be gained by participation in the government than by opposition had merit, however, particularly given the dominance of the parliament by the coalition. Political decisions in Czechoslovakia tended to be made by the informal group around President Tomáš G. Masaryk, the Hrad, and then rubber-stamped by the parliament. This was due in part to fragile, short-lived government coalitions resulting from the large number of parties represented in parliament, which made political compromise a necessity. The arrangement continued after Edvard Beneš succeeded Masaryk as president. Because of the plethora of political parties in the First Republic, most of which divided along both ideological and national lines, no single political party was able to impose its world view on the country. Coalitions, which were dominated by the Czechoslovak Agrarians and their allies during most of the interwar period, were unlikely to give either the national minorities or the organized working class any concessions without strong pressure from other parties. Such pressure was more effectively applied from within the coalition, than from without, although often without positive results.

The economic policies—both domestic and foreign—of the First Republic, while not deliberately anti-Sudeten German, tended to favor the Czech and Slovak citizens of the country as the expense of the national minorities. With the widespread unemployment of the 1930s, which affected the Sudeten Germans twice as severely as their Czech counterparts, the economic advantages that accrued to the national people were even more apparent and all the more resented.

As coalition members, the German Social Democrats focused on economic rather than national issues, correctly assuming that socio-economic improvements benefiting citizens of all nationalities were easier to achieve than improvements in the position of the national minorities. The economic gains made by the working class during the 1930s were, however, minimal and only grudgingly obtained from the Czechoslovak Agrarian-dominated coalition. They were also clearly insufficient to counter the devastating effects of the Depression.

The growth of Czech national consciousness during the nineteeth century, in conscious opposition to the dominant German culture of the Cisleithanian portion of the Habsburg Monarchy, had by the end of the century resulted in a struggle between the Czechs and the Germans for political dominance in the Bohemian Crownlands. Austria-Hungary's defeat at the hands of the Allies in the First World War clearly improved the political position of the Czechs vis-à-vis the Germans. At the Paris Peace Conference, Czech leaders were able to negotiate the formation of a Czechoslovak national state. The inclusion in the state of an equally nationally self-conscious minority of some three-and-a-quarter million Germans—the largest German ethnic minority in Europe—not only made the First Republic in reality a multinational state but guaranteed problems. Problems stemmed, in part, from the nation-state policy of the Prague government, which at times allowed it to discriminate against the national minorities, creating a situation in some ways analogous to the situation among the minorities in Cisleithania during the last years of the Monarchy.

Both presidents of the First Republic, Masaryk and Beneš, were committed to the idea of the Czechoslovak national state. Recognition of Masaryk's Czechoslovak national views often has been obscured by his international reputation as a humanist intellectual. His characterization of the Sudeten Germans as "immigrants and colonists" accurately reflected his feelings about the First Republic: it was a Czechoslovak state. Beneš, negotiating at the Paris Peace Conference, made his "Czechoslovak" attitudes clear when he attempted to dismiss Sudeten German claims, concealing the truth about their numbers and the possible validity of their demands.

In retrospect, it is clear that the commitment of the Czechs to the idea of the nation state compounded internal problems with the national minorities: the Germans, Hungarians, Poles, and Ruthenians, who comprised almost one-third of the population. The grievances of the Slovaks, the decidedly junior partner within the "Czechoslovak" nation, crystallized in the establishment of a German puppet state of Slovakia in March 1939.

The national claims of the Czechs were not the same as their political claims, although the two did overlap; too often, friendly observers have made the same mistake as the Czechs, assuming that they were identical. Beginning in the interwar period, both Czech and Czechophile observers, including the dean of Anglo-American historians of Czechoslovakia, R. W. Seton-Watson, have too often excused overtly nationalist behavior on the part of individual Czechs or the Czechoslovak government as the normal, and somehow acceptable result of several hundred years of Habsburg misrule. Abuses have been dismissed because Czechoslovakia was seen as a bastion of democracy in Central Europe, which in fact it was, especially in contrast to the other Central European states. Hungary, Rumania, and Yugoslavia, as well as Austria, Germany, and Poland, all moved toward varying forms of dictatorship in the interwar period. The Munich *Diktat*, the subsequent Nazi German occupation of the former Crownlands and the formation of the Nazi-dominated Protectorate of Bohemia and Moravia only served to strengthen the democratic reputation and blur the imperfections of the First Republic.

Ultimately, neither the correctness of the German Social Democratic Party's politics nor the sincerity of President Beneš's negotiations with the Sudeten Germans mattered, once Hitler had decided to destroy Czechoslovakia. The national complaints of the Sudeten Germans were merely a convenient pretext for his planned aggression. Britain's and France's less than honorable diplomatic maneuvering during the summer and autumn of 1938, although based on an understandable desire to avoid a world war, simply eased Hitler's task.

The most effective defense against Henlein's anti-Czech nationalist rhetoric would have been the granting of some measure of national autonomy to Czechoslovakia's minorities. This did not occur, however, due to the prevailing Czechoslovak political conception of the First Republic as a national state. The chances for success such measures would have had remain, of course, a matter of speculation, given the attraction Hitler held for most ethnic Germans outside the Reich.

Perhaps, a timely change of German Social Democratic leadership would have damped the flow of Germans into Henlein's Sudeten German Party. It would not, however, have stopped the rise of the latter party, which was part of a European wide phenomenon of the growth of mass, non-democratic radical nationalist parties. Neither would it have prevented Hitler's occupation of the Sudeten lands, nor the onset of the Second World War. The inadequacies of the German Social Democratic Party were tragically magnified by historic circumstances.

NOTES

Notes to Chapter I

1. The term, "bourgeois," as used in this study signifies members of the class that owns property or engages in trade, members of the middle-class. German Social Democratic rhetoric tended to include under the rubric, "bourgeois political party," all parties except those self-described as "working class" and those, especially during the 1930s, which they designated as "fascist."

For the difficulties of precisely defining the term "bourgeois," see Peter Gay's introductory comments in "The Strain of Definition" in *The Bourgeois Experience: Victoria to Freud*, vol. 1: *Education of the Senses* (New York: Oxford University Press, 1984; paperback edition by the same publisher, 1985), pp. 17-44.

2. *Protokoll der Verhandlung des Parteitages der Deutschen sozialdemokratischen Arbeiterpartei in der Tschechoslowakischen Republik* (hereafter *Protokoll des Parteitages* with location and year), Karlsbad, 1920, 146-66.

3. "Czech Social Democrat," refers to the members of the Czech-Slav Social Democratic Party in Cisleithania and in the Czechoslovak Republic until December 1918. "Czechoslovak Social Democrat" refers to the members of the party formed in December 1918.

4. Paul Reimann, *Geschichte der Kommunistischen Partei der Tschechoslowakei*. Beiträge zur Geschichte der Arbeiterbewegung 4 (Hamburg: Verlag Carl Hoym Nachfolger, 1931; reprint ed., Munich, 1975). Written

some sixty years ago, this book remains a classic in Czechoslovak Communist Party historiography.

5. Rudolf Jaworski, *Vorposten oder Minderheit? Der sudetendeutsche Volkstumskampf in den Beziehungen zwischen der Weimarer Republik und der ČSR.* (Stuttgart: Deutsche Verlags-Anstalt, 1977), p. 20.

6. Heinz O. Ziegler, *Die berufliche und soziale Gliederung der Bevölkerung in der Tschechoslowakei.* (Brünn: Verlag Rudolf M. Rohrer, 1936), pp. 64, 70.

7. Ernst Paul, "Das sudetendeutsche Dorf," *Arbeiter-Jahrbuch* (1936): 25-30.

8. Jaworski, *Vorposten*, p. 21.

9. Ibid., p. 17.

10. Paul, "Das Dorf," p. 26.

11. Alfred Bohmann, *Menschen und Grenzen* (Cologne: Verlag Wissenschaft und Politik, 1975), p. 120.

12. Hans Mommsen, *Die Sozialdemokratie und die Nationalitätenfrage im habsburgischen Vielvölkerstaat* (Vienna: Europa-Verlag, 1963); Emil Strauss, "Die nationale Frage in der Frühzeit der tschechischen Arbeiterbewegung," *Der Kampf* 14 (1921): 253-58.

13. Otto Bauer, *Die Nationalitätenfrage und die Sozialdemokratie* (Vienna: Wiener Volksbuchhandlung, 1907); Karl Renner [Rudolf Springer] *Der Kampf der österreichischen Nationen um den Staat* (Vienna: Deuticke, 1902).

14. On Bohumír Šmeral, see Bernard Wheaton, *Radical Socialism in Czechoslovakia: Bohumír Šmeral, the Czech Road to Socialism and the Origins of the Czechoslovak Communist Party* (Boulder: East European Monographs, 1986). The most important recent scholarly work on Šmeral in the Czech language is Jan Galandauer, *Bohumír Šmeral, 1880-1914* (Prague: Nakladatelství Svoboda, 1981).

15. On the question of Czechoslovak Social Democratic-Czechoslovak National Socialist unification, see Vladimíir Kašík, "Snahy o jednotnou reformistickou stranu v letech 1917-1918 a jejich porážka" (Příspěvek k otázce formování marxistické levice v českém dělnickém hnutí) *Rozpravy Československé akademie věd* 71 (1961). For a brief study of the Czechoslovak National Socialist Party, see: Detlef Brandes, "Die Tschechoslowakischen National-Sozialisten," *Die Erste Tschechoslowakische Republik als multinationaler Parteienstaat* (Munich: R. Oldenbourg Verlag, 1979).

16. The Czech National Socialists, like the Czech Social Democrats, changed their party name in the interwar period to accommodate Slovak members. The term, "Czechoslovak National Socialist," is used here to refer to members of the party known as *Československá strana socialistická* until 1926, when the party's name was changed to *Československá strana národně-socialistická*.

17. The first major strike in the Czech lands took place on 26 April 1917 at Prossnitz and there was also a strike at the Pilsen Škoda plant in the summer of 1917. A strike that occurred at the Daimler plant in Wiener Neustadt in Lower Austria on 14 January 1918 had its origin in a reduction in flour rations, and was followed by strikes in Brünn, Mährisch Ostrau and in Germany. Although the strike spread rapidly, it lasted only a week.

18. Reimann, *Kommunistische Partei*, pp. 40-42; Zdeněk Šolle, *Dělnické hnutí v českých zemích za imperialistické svetové valky* (Prague: Nakladatelství Rovnost, 1952).

19. Joseph Rothschild, *East Central Europe Between the Two World Wars* (Seattle: University of Washington Press, 1974), p. 76; Zdeněk Kárník, *Socialisté na rozcesti. Habsburk, Masaryk či Šmeral?* (Prague: Nakladatelství Svoboda, 1968).

20. For a recent analysis of the development of Tomáš Masaryk's political ideas, see Eva Schmidt-Hartmann, *Thomas G. Masaryk's Realism: Origins of a Czech Political Concept* (Munich: R. Oldenbourg Verlag, 1984). See also Hanus Hajek, *T. G. Masaryk Revisited: A Critical Assessment* (Boulder: East European Monographs, 1983) and Roman Szporluk, *The Political Thought of Thomas G. Masaryk* (Boulder: East European Monographs, 1981). A comprehensive biography of Edvard Beneš or Tomáš Masaryk has yet to be written.

21. For an overview of the political situation during the formative years of the First Republic, see the relevant chapters in Victor Mamatey and Radomír Luža, eds. *A History of the Czechoslovak Republic, 1918-1948* (Princeton: Princeton University Press, 1973).

22. Czechoslovak Social Democratic deputy Jan Prokeš, quoted in *Bohemia* (Prague), 17 October 1918.

23. Approximately 106,000 Czech and Slovak soldiers (primarily the former) were recruited from among prisoners of war and deserters on three fronts to fight on the side of the Entente during the First World War.

Legionaries returning from France and Italy occupied the Sudeten lands in late 1918. Some 60,000 fought in Siberia and they are the best known. Although they came from a wide variety of occupations and included few professional soldiers, Legionaries were given preferential treatment in the army of the First Republic and were influential in the officer corps until 1938. See Jackson Shaw, "Massenorganisationen und parlamentarische Demokratie," *Die demokratisch-parlamentarische Struktur der Ersten Tschechoslowakischen Republik* (Munich: R. Oldenbourg Verlag, 1975) and Jonathan Zorach, "The Czechoslovak Army, 1918-1938" (unpublished Ph.D. dissertation, Columbia University, 1975).

24.   For discussion of the conflicting attitudes of the Bohemian Germans toward inclusion in German Austria versus inclusion in Czechoslovakia, see F. L. Carsten, *Revolution in Central Europe, 1918-1919* (Berkeley: University of California Press, 1972), pp. 287-94.

25.   Although the 44-day government in German Bohemia was headed by nationalist politician Rudolf von Lodgman, it was interpreted by the DSAP as "a proud chapter in the political history of the German people of Bohemia and in particular the German working class movement of the land . . . ." Emil Strauss, "Die deutschböhmische Landesregierung," *Tribüne* 7 (1928): 230.

26.   Die Anklagerede des Dr. Czech gegen die tschechoslowakische Sozialdemokratie," *Právo lidu* (Prague), reprinted and translated in *Der Neue Weg* 5 (1925): 9.

27.   *Freiheit* (Teplitz), 30, 31 October 1918, 6, 7, 11, 12 November 1918; Manfred Alexander, ed., *Deutsche Gesandschaftsberichte aus Prag, Staatsgrundung bis zum ersten Kabinett Beneš 1918-1921* 1 (Munich: R. Oldenbourg Verlag, 1983), pp. 72, 156. Like Bauer and Renner, the majority of Austrian Social Democrats initially supported the idea of a greater German settlement area and sought to incorporate the German-speaking remnants of the Habsburg Monarchy into the new democratic German state. See John Francis Patrick Wynn, *The Socialist International and the Politics of European Reconstruction 1919-1930* (Lanham, MD: University Press of America, 1976), p. 7.

28.   For a balanced interpretation of the situation from the Sudeten German point of view, see the relevant chapters in: Johann Wolfgang Brügel, *Tschechen und Deutsche 1918-1938* (Munich: Nymphenburger, 1967).

29.   The authenticity of this comment has been the subject of some

debate: the Czechoslovak Social Democratic newspaper *Svoboda* (Kladno), reported on 28 August 1919 that Czechoslovak Finance Minister Alois Rašín did, indeed, make the comment, although he later denied it. See also Klaus Zessner, "Die Haltung der deutschböhmischen Sozialdemokratie zum neuen tschechoslowakischen Staat 1918/1919," *Die 'Berg,'* vol. 1 (Munich: R. Oldenbourg Verlag, 1973).

30.   *Právo lidu,* 11 February 1919; for the German text, see: *Freiheit,* 2 March 1919. Signatories were Czechoslovak Social Democrats Rudolf Bechyně, Antonín Hampl and Rudolf Tayerle as well as Czech National Socialist Emil Franke. Czech Social Democratic Worker Party leader Edmund Burian, also attended the International, but did not sign the proclamation.

31.   *Právo lidu,* 6 March 1919.

32.   Othmar Feyl, "Die böhmendeutsche Linke um den Reichenberger 'Vorwärts' und ihre Vorarbeit für die Entstehung der Kommunistischen Partei in der ČSR," *Wissenschaftliche Zeitschrift der Friedrich-Schiller-Universität Jena* 7 (1957-1958): 149-53.

33.   For the text of Josef Strasser's speech, see *Protokoll über die Verhandlungen des Parteitages der deutschen sozialdemokratischen Arbeiterpartei in Österreich,* Innsbruck, 1911, pp. 217-19.

34.   For a recent biographical sketch of Karl Kreibich, see Otto Novák, "Karl Kreibich," *Společenské vědy ve škole* 5 (1983-1984): 149-53.

35.   Reimann, *Kommunistische Partei,* p. 34.

36.   *Vorwärts* (Reichenberg), 24 July 1923, 20, 24, 25 July 1924; *Sozialdemokrat* (Prague), 26 July 1924; Agitpropabteilung der KPČ, Referentenmaterial für die Wahlen, "Die deutschen Sozialdemokraten in der Tschechoslowakei" (Reichenberg: Von Runge u. Co., n.d. [ca. 1924], p. 7.

37.   Bruno Köhler, "Úloha německé levice v boji o založení KSČ," *Společenské vědy ve škole* 3 (1971): 68-72.

38.   Joseph Belina, "Die tschechische Linke," *Der Kampf* 14 (1921): 233; Karl Kreibich, "Die tschechische Linke und ihr Manifest," ibid., 13 (1920), p. 85; *Vorwärts,* 5 January 1921.

39.   *Vorwärts,* 13 May 1919. The German Social Democrats formed a joint list with other German parties, including the German National Socialists in Dux, a city on the Czech-German language barrier, and were thus able to maintain a German majority in the communal administration. *Freiheit,* 17 June 1919.

40. *Právo lidu*, 3 July 1919.

41. *Protokoll des Parteitages* (DSAP), Teplitz, 1919.

42. Mommsen, *Die Nationalitätenfrage*, pp. 332-37.

43. See, for example, *Vorwärts*, 2 September 1919.

44. Ibid., 6 September 1919.

45. *Právo lidu*, 2 September 1919. The use of Switzerland as a political model for Czechoslovakia appears to have first been made by Beneš in a memorandum to the Paris Peace Conference. The memorandum was cited during the interwar period by Sudeten Germans of various political views as evidence of his duplicity regarding minority policy in the First Republic. See discussion in Brügel, "The Germans in Pre-war Czechoslovakia," in *A History of the Czechoslovak Republic*, p. 172. In addition to Josef Seliger, Wenzel Jaksch, the last interwar chairman of the German Social Democrats, used the concept during 1937 and 1938.

46. *Právo lidu*, 2 September 1919.

47. Zessner, *Josef Seliger und die nationale Frage in Böhmen* (Stuttgart: Seliger-Gemeinde, 1976), p. 116.

48. "Může byti 'Právo lidu' listem vládném," *Sociální demokrat*, 8 August 1919.

49. Friedrich Austerlitz, "Politik und Sozialismus in der Tschechoslowakei," *Der Kampf* 14 (1921): 97-106. See also German Social Democratic newspapers from this period.

50. *Právo lidu*, 20 August 1919.

51. Ibid., 30 January 1920; German text, *Vorwärts*, 31 January 1920.

52. *Freiheit*, 25 January 1920.

53. Emil Strauss, "Die Umschichtung der tschechischen Parteien," *Der Kampf* 13 (1920): 84.

54. Karl Kreibich, "Die tschechische Linke und Ihr Manifest," ibid., p. 89.

55. *Sociální demokrat*, 29 April 1920.

56. *Rádného sjezdu československé sociálně demokratické strany dělnické*, November 1920, p. 80. Some historians have argued that a serious effort was made to include the German Social Democrats in Vlastimil Tusar's government. Brügel, *Teschen und Deutsche*, p. 147, has written that Tusar's attempts to form a Red-Green coalition government were torpedoed by DSAP insistence on the prior granting of national autonomy.

57. *Vorwärts*, 12 May 1920.

58. *Trautenauer Echo*, 23 July 1920.

59. *Sociální demokrat*, 27 May 1920.

60. *Řádného sjezdu*, pp. 126-29.

61. *Právo lidu*, 18 August 1920.

62. *Böhmerwald Volksbote*, 22 August 1920.

63. See applicable reports from the German Embassy in Prague, June-August, Alexander, *Gesandschaftsberichte*, pp. 112-28; 286-319.

64. *Právo lidu*, 15 September 1920.

65. Harry Klepetař, *Seit 1918. . . . Eine Geschichte der tschechoslowakischen Republik* (Ostrau: Verlag Julius Kittls Nachfolger, 1937), p. 141.

66. Ibid., p. 143.

67. *Staré právo lidu*, 19 September 1920; *Volksrecht* (Aussig), 20 September 1920. The Marxist Left had added the word, *staré*, [old] to the masthead to signify the supposed return of the Czechoslovak Social Democratic Party to its original, "revolutionary" politics as well as to differentiate it from the *Právo lidu* of the party leadership.

68. Leopold Grünwald, *Wandlung. Ein Altkommunist gibt zu Protokoll*. Foreword by Wolfgang Leonhard. (Vienna: Verlag der Wiener Volksbuchhandlung, n.d. [1979 or 1980]), p. 24. Grünwald was writing more than fifty years after the fact. The incident, however, appears to have captured the spirit of the debate.

69. *Vorwärts*, 2 September 1920.

70. Ibid.

71. *Protokoll des Parteitages* (DSAP), Karlsbad, 1920, pp. 287-391.

72. Ibid., pp. 377-78.

73. *Protokoll des Parteitages* (DSAP), Tetschen, 1921, p. 175.

74. In his article, "Jews in Political Life," *The Jews of Czechoslovakia* 2, pp. 243-52, ed. Guido Kisch, et al. (Philadelphia: JPS, 1971), Brügel has described most of the First Republic's non-Roman Catholic Czech political parties as receptive to Jewish membership. While this assertion is not incorrect, Brügel's failure to address the anti-Semitism of some of the Czech parties' prewar predecessors causes him to underestimate similar attitudes during the interwar period. Cf. Christoph Stölzl, "Die 'Burg' and die Juden," *Die Burg'* 2. Stölzl has written that Czechs, in general, held anti-Semitic attitudes both prior to the First World War and during the interwar period. (He has further claimed that anti-Semitism

of varying degrees of intensity existed in some of the Czech political parties of the First Republic.)

In their articles on the development of Czech-German-Jewish relations in the Bohemian Crownlands, Gary Cohen and Ruth Kestenberg-Gladstein have provide information on inter-ethnic political relations. They agree that most Jews initially identified with German, rather than Czech, language and society, but that toward the end of the nineteenth century, there was increasing Jewish identification with the numerically and politically ascendant Czechs. See Cohen, "Jews in German Society: Prague, 1860-1914," *Central European History* 10 (1977): 28-54 and Kestenberg-Gladstein, "The Jews Between Czechs and German in the Historic Lands, 1848-1918," *The Jews of Czechoslovakia*, pp. 21-71. For a brief survey of the Jews of Czechoslovakia during the interwar period, see Ezra Mendelsohn, "Czechoslovakia," in *The Jews of East Central Europe Between the World Wars* First Midland Book Edition (Bloomington: Indiana University Press, 1987), pp. 130-69.

The contention that anti-Jewish attitudes among the more nationalist Czechs stemmed in part from the perception of Jews as Germans finds support in an anonymous comment in *Přítomnost* 19 (1933): (for the Czech nationalist) "There are three levels of evil: to be German is bad, to be Jewish is worse, and to be a German Jew is the worst of all."

For Czech Zionist perception of Czech and German political attitudes in the First Republic, see the Zionist weekly, *Selbstwehr*.

75. *Právo lidu,* 26 October 1920; *Böhmerwald Volksbote,* 17, 21 November, 15 December 1920.

76. *Bohemia,* 20 November 1920. See also Alexander, *Gesandschaftsberichte,* pp. 350-54 and Karl Čermak, *Těsnopisecké zprávy o schůzích Národního shromáždění republiky Československé* (hereafter *Těsnopisecké zprávy* with date and page number), 24 November 1920, pp. 502-11 and Bruno Kafka, ibid., pp. 514-19.

77. *Právo lidu* quoted in *Vorwärts,* 18 November 1920.

78. *Rudé právo* (Prague), 10 December 1920.

79. See Ludwig Czech, *Těsnopisecké zprávy,* 14 December 1920, p. 1318.

80. *Trautenauer Echo,* 24, 28, 31 December 1920; 4 January 1921.

81. *Právo lidu,* 10, 11 December 1920.

82. *Rudé právo,* 10 December 1920; *Sociální demokrat,* 24 December 1920.

83. *Rudé právo* quoted in *Vorwärts,* 18 November 1920.

84. *Böhmerwald Volksbote,* 26 January 1921.

85. *Vorwärts,* 19 January 1921.

86. *Protokoll des Parteitages* (DSAP), Karlsbad, 1920, p. 89.

87. Karl Kern, "Reichenberg," *Tribüne* 2 (1930): 38.

88. See, for example, *Trautenauer Echo,* 17 December 1920, 21 January 1921 on the behavior of Kreibich and other German Social Democratic left-wing leaders from Reichenberg.

89. *Vorwärts,* 2 September 1919.

90. Kreibich, "Die tschechische Linke," pp. 84-89.

91. *Rudé právo,* 4 January 1921.

92. *Vorwärts,* 5 January 1921.

93. See ibid., March through May 1921.

94. Ibid., 27 April 1921.

95. Ibid., 17 May 1921; *Rudé právo,* 18 May 1921.

96. *Rudé právo,* 17 July 1921.

97. Estimates of the percentage of the German Social Democratic constituency that the Czechoslovak Communist Party attracted vary greatly depending on the source.

98. Mitteilungen des statistischen Staatsamtes der Čechoslovakischen Republik, *Die Wahlen in das Abgeordnetenhaus im Jahre 1925* (Prague: Statisches Staatsamt, 1926). See also Wolf Oschlies, "Die Kommunistiche Partei der Tschechoslowakie in der Ersten Tschechoslowakischen Republik (1918-1938)," *Die demokratisch-parlamentarische Struktur.*

Bohemia had the highest percentage of Czechoslovak Communist Party members, followed by Ruthenia, Moravia-Silesia, and Slovakia, according to Czechoslovak Communist Party statistics for 1924.

99. *Protokoll des Parteitages* (DSAP), Tetschen, 1921, p. 235.

100. According to Reimann, *Kommunistiche Partei,* p. 168, Czech Social Democratic trade union membership sank to about 43,000 during the First World War. The extraordinary increase in membership through 1920 was partially due to the postwar unification of the Czech Social Democratic trade union centralists and separatists. German Social Democratic trade union membership increased by some 100,000 in 1920 alone, with trade union membership reaching its high point in that year.

German Social Democratic trade union membership: 1919: 262,077; 1920: 393,852; 1921: 372,027; 1922: 291,269 and Czechoslovak Social

Democratic trade union membership: 1918: 122,160; 1919: 643,276; 1920: 856,305; 1921: 675,625; 1922: 404,984. Státní úřad statistická, *Statistická přiručka republiky Československé* 2 (Prague: Nakladem Vlastim, 1925), p. 463.

101. International Federation of Trade Unions, *Report on Activities During the Years 1924, 1925 and 1926.* Submitted to the Fourth Ordinary Congress Paris, August, 1927 (Amersterdam: 1927), p. 121.

102. International Labour Office Studies and Reports, series A, No. 30 *Freedom of Association* (Geneva, 1928; London: P. S. King & Son).

103. Reimann, *Kommunistische Partei,* p. 171.

104. *Trautenauer Echo,* 15 April 1921.

105. Reimann, *Kommunistische Partei,* p. 179.

106. Heinrich Kuhn, *Zeittafel zur Geschichte der Kommunistische Partei der Tschechoslowakei* (Munich: Fides-Verlagsgesellschaft, 1973), p. 36.

107. Bericht über die Tätigkeit des Präsidiums und der Exekutive der Kommunistischen Internationale für die Zeit vom 6 März bis 11 Juni 1922, "Die KPČ–Bericht der tschechischen Kommission," (Hamburg: Hoym, 1922), pp. 86, 119.

Notes to Chapter II

1. For German Social Democratic comments on the Locarno Treaty, see *Tätigkeitsbericht* (DSAP), 15 November 1925–1 July 1926 (Teplitz-Schönau: Selbstverlag, n.d.), p. 29.

2. *Protokoll des Parteitages* (DSAP), Tetschen, 1921, p. 36.

3. Ibid., pp. 37, 215.

4. For example the Arnau county organization, *Protokoll des Parteitages* (DSAP), Aussig, 1923, p. 147.

5. For descriptions of the racist attitudes of the German National Socialist Party, see Norbert Linz, "Die Binnenstruktur der deutschen Parteien im ersten Jahrzehnt der ČSR," *Die demokratisch-parlamentarische Struktur,* pp. 209-10 and Andrew Whiteside, "Nationaler Sozialismus in Österreich vor 1918," *Vierteljahrshelfte für Zeitgeschichte* 9 (1961): 333-59.

6. See Harold Bachmann, "Sozialstruktur und Parteientwicklung im nordwestböhmischen Kohlenrevier vor dem Zusammenbruch der

Monarchie," *Bohemia* (1969): 270-89; Andre [Andrew] G. Whiteside, "Industrial Transformation, Population Movement and German Nationalism in Bohemia," *Zeitschrift für Ostforschung* 2 (1961): 261-71; Whiteside, "Nationaler Sozialismus."

7. *Freiheit*, 25 January 1921.

8. Zdeněk Filip, "Die Zeitschrift 'Volkswacht' in den Jahren 1899-1921," Ein Beitrag zur Geschichte der deutschen Arbeiterbewegung in Mähren (typewritten).

9. *Die freie Gemeinde*, 16 October 1924.

10. *Protokoll des Parteitages*, 1921, p. 92.

11. Ibid., 1923, p. 124.

12. Compare voting results for 1919 and 1923; 1920 and 1925.

13. Compare voting results, 1925 voting statistics, Mitteilungen des Statistischen Staatsamtes, *Die Wahlen in das Abgeordnetenhaus*, vol. 2 (Prague, 1926), pp. 18-19.

14. See *Die freie Gemeinde*, 16 June 1924; *Protokoll des Parteitages*, 1921, p. 98.

15. *Trautenauer Echo*, 18 September 1923.

16. *Sozialdemokrat*, 13 December 1921.

For statistics on German Social Democratic Party membership, see Linz, "Die Binnenstruktur," pp. 205-9.

17. Robert Danneberg, "Die Organization der Österreichischen Sozialdemokratie," *Die Gesellschaft* 9 (1924): 264-68; *Protokoll des Parteitages* (DSAP), Tetschen, 1921, pp. 189-90.

18. *Bohemia*, 18 September 1923.

19. Ibid.

20. *Trautenauer Echo*, 18 September 1923.

21. Paul Zinner, *Communist Strategy and Tactics in Czechoslovakia, 1918-1948* (London: Pall Mall Press, 1963), p. 60. See his discussion of KSČ membership figures, based on party sources.

22. Rothschild, *East Central Europe*, p. 110.

23. Zinner, *Communist Strategy*, p. 64. Figures are for those districts over ninety percent Czech or German, respectively.

24. Rothschild, *East Central Europe*, pp. 102, 110.

25. Using the autobiographies of women workers, Friedrich G. Kürbisch has concluded that some 87 percent of the women in the organized worker movement in the German-speaking areas of the Habsburg Monarchy

came from proletarian backgrounds, particularly small artisanal and *Heimarbeiter,* and only rarely from the middle classes. Little research has, however, been done specifically dealing with their role in the German Social Democratic Party of Czechoslovakia. See Richard Kluscarits and Kürbisch, *Arbeiterinnen kämpfen um ihr Recht* (Wuppertal, F.R.G.: Peter Hammer Verlag, [1975]) and Kürbisch, "Wie früher Frauen Sozialdemokratinnen wurden," *Arbeiterbewegung und Arbeiterdichtung. Beiträge zur Geschichte der Sozialdemokratischen Arbeiterbewegung im Sudeten-, Karpathen- und Donauraum* 5 (1982): 84-99.

26. Members of the Executive Committee, 1919: Ludwig Czech, Theodor Hackenberg, Brünn; Hans Jokl, Troppau; Hieronymus Schlossnickel, Sternberg. 1920: Czech, Hackenberg, Jokl, Ludwig Morgenstern, Schönberg; Eduard Zorn, Freiwaldau. 1921: Czech, Jokl, Wilhelm Niessner, Brünn, Schlossnickel. 1923: Hackenberg, Jokl, Niessner, Schlossnickel.

27. *Protokoll des Parteitages,* 1921, p. 212.

28. *Die freie Gemeinde,* 2 August 1919.

29. *Sozialdemokrat,* 14 March 1926. German Social Democratic complaints about land reform in parliament began almost immediately after the 1920 elections. See Deputy Adolf Pohl's speech condemning the 1919 land reform law that had been passed by the constituent National Assembly. *Těsnopisecké zprávy,* 11 June 1920, pp. 321-28.

30. Harry Klepetař, *Die Sprachenkampf in den Sudetenländern* (Prague: Strache Verlag, 1930), p. 138.

31. *Sozialdemokrat,* 19 February 1926.

32. Ibid.

33. Ibid., 17 February 1926.

34. Ibid., 19 February 1926.

35. Ibid., 27 May 1926.

36. Rothschild, *East Central Europe,* p. 113.

37. Brügel, "The Germans in Czechoslovakia," p. 183.

38. *Trautenauer Echo,* 25 September 1925.

39. Brügel, "The Germans in Czechoslovakia," p. 184.

40. "Die Anklagerede des Dr. Czech," p. 8.

41. *Sozialdemokrat,* 5 November 1925, citing Josef Stivín in *Právo lidu* (evening edition), 20 December 1924.

42. Ibid.

43. Ibid., 13 December 1924.

44. Ibid., 19 November 1924.

45. *Trautenauer Echo,* 23 May 1923.

46. Ibid.

47. Ibid., 25 May 1923.

48. "Antwort," p. 3. International Institute of Social History (hereafter IISH), Amsterdam, Archives of the Socialist International (hereafter SAI), 844-848, 844/4, Kommission für die Tschechoslowakei, 1923.

49. *Volkswille* (Brünn), 8 June 1923.

50. Ibid.

51. *Právo lidu,* 31 May 1923; *Stráž socialismu,* 16, 31, June 1923.

52. *Resolutions of the International,* 1923, p. 6; *Congress of the Labour and Socialist International,* 1925, p. 86.

53. *Trautenauer Echo,* 4 September 1925.

Notes to Chapter III

1. *Sozialdemokrat,* 11, 12 June 1926.

2. Ibid., 7 May 1926.

3. Rothschild, *East Central Europe,* p. 112; see also Hans Schütz's comment that German participation in government coalitions slowed, but did not stop, the process of removing Germans from public office, "Der 18. Februar 1937," *Sudetendeutsche Arbeit* (1938): 4-8, reprinted in *Hans Schütz—Helfer und Wegwisser in schwerer Zeit* (Munich, 1982), p. 144.

4. Mamatey, "The Development of Czechoslovak Democracy, 1920-1938" in *A History of the Czechoslovak Republic,* p. 134, fn. 94, citing Karel Sidor, *Slovenská politika na pôde pražského snemu, 1918-1938,* vol. 1, p. 309.

5. Brügel, *Tschechen und Deutsche,* p. 178.

6. *Tätigkeitsbericht* (DSAP), p. 47.

7. Klepetař, *Seit 1918,* p. 250.

8. Ibid., p. 257.

9. *Protokoll des Parteitages* (DSAP), Teplitz-Schönau, 1930, p. 203.

10. Ibid., pp. 35-36; *Sozialdemokrat,* 31 March; 4, 6 April 1928.

11. Ibid., 6 October 1927; *Bohemia,* 28 January 1928.

12. Ibid.

13. Klepetař, *Seit 1918,* p. 258.

14. *Sozialdemokrat,* 15 June 1927; Leopold Pölzl, "Wie kann eine gesunde Grundlage der Gemeindegeldwirtschaft geschaffen werden?"

Tribüne (February 1929): 32-37; Bruno Schwab, "Zur Frage der Regelung der Gemeindefinanzen," ibid. (December 1928): 257-62; Robert Wiener, "Gemeindefinanzen und Parteitaktik," ibid. (April 1929): 381-84.

15. "Democratic Administration and National Autonomy" (DSAP publication), Prague: 1921, p. 21.

16. Brügel, *Tschechen und Deutsche*, p. 180.

17. Klepetař, *Seit 1918*, p. 259.

18. *Deutsche Landespost*, 3 July 1927.

19. Franz [František] Soukup, Special Article: "Ein grosser sozialdemokratischer Sieg in der Tschechoslowakei." IISH, SAI 2797/11, Tschechoslowakei.

20. Ladislav Lipscher, *Verfassung und politische Verwaltung in der Tschechoslowakei 1918-1939* (Munich: R. Oldenbourg Verlag, 1979), p. 97.

21. Klepetař, *Seit 1918*, p. 252.

22. *Central European Observer*, 21 October 1927, p. 683.

23. *Sozialdemokrat*, 5 December 1928. The German Labor and Economic Association (*Deutsche Arbeits- und Wirtschaftsgemeinschaft*, DAWG), campagning for the first time in a national election, was technically an opposition party, although it had been formed with the intent to cooperate with the government. Governmental statistics for the 1928 elections list votes for DAWG as coalition votes. Opposition sources, including the German Social Democratic Party, do not.

24. Brügel, *Tschechen und Deutsche*, p. 181.

25. *Sozialdemokrat*, 4 December 1928.

26. Statistisches Handbuch der Čechoslovakischen Republik, *Die Wahlen in den Landesvertretungen im Jahre 1928* 3 (Prague: Statistisches Staatsamt, 1929), p. 9.

The percentages listed in the text are based on the following figures:

Votes cast in the former Crownlands:

German Social Democrats	403,359
German Agrarians	263,332
German Clericals	252,791

Votes cast in Bohemia:

German Social Democrats	308,791
German Agrarians	197,009
German Clericals	152,456

Votes cast in Moravia-Silesia
    German Social Democrats   94,568
    German Agrarians   66,323
    German Clericals   100,335
27. *Bohemia,* 4 December 1928.
28. *Sozialdemokrat,* 5 December 1928.
29. Ibid.
30. Josef Hofbauer, "Vor den Wahlen," *Tribüne* (November 1928): 223-25.
31. Wenzel Jaksch, "Übergangswahlen," ibid. (December 928): 249.
32. Ibid., p. 250.
33. "Erläuterungen zum Programm der nationalen Autonomie" [German Social Democrats], pp. 806-7. IISH, SAI 806/7-23, Tschechoslowakei, 1926.
34. "Protokoll der Sitzung der Minoritätenkommission," 13 April 1926, p. 3. SAI 804; "Vollzugausschuss" [Czechoslovak Social Democrats] of 11 May 1926, dated 19 May 1926. SAI 805, ibid.
35. *Vorwärts,* 17 February 1927.
36. The administrative report of the German Social Democratic railroad union is a good example. The union showed a more than fourfold increase in membership, from 6,000 to 28,000, in the immediate postwar period. Many members left the union, however, beginning in 1921. Trade union officials believed that the sudden, massive increase meant that the trade union did not have time to educate the new members in social democratic tenets. This is consistent with earlier remarks by party leaders. "Verwaltungsbericht, 1923-1927."
37. *Sozialdemokrat,* 29 January 1928.
38. Brügel, *Ludwig Czech, Arbeiterführer und Staatsman* (Vienna: Verlag der Wiener Volksbuchhandlung, 1960), p. 99.
39. *Sozialdemokrat,* 29 January 1928.
40. Ernst Paul, *Was nicht in der Geschichtsbüchern steht* 2 (Munich: Verlag "Die Brücke," 1966), p. 65.
41. Ibid.

Notes to Chapter IV

1. Figures are from *Die Wahlen in das Abgeordnetenhaus im Oktober 1929*, p. 9.

2. Emil Franzel, "Der neue Kurs der Kommunisten," *Tribüne* (November 1928): 229.

3. Reimann, *Kommunistische Partei*, p. 305.

4. *Vorwärts*, 30 October 1929.

5. Ibid.

6. Brügel, *Ludwig Czech*, pp. 102-3; Klepetař, *Seit 1918*, p. 285.

7. Ibid., p. 287.

8. Ibid., p. 289-90.

9. Ibid., p. 293.

10. *Vorwärts*, 26 January 1929.

11. Senator Carl Heller and provincial diet representative Bruno Grund at campaign rallies in Abertham and Niemes, respectively, on 13 October 1929. Ibid., 15 October 1929.

12. *Protokoll des Parteitages* (DSAP), Tetschen, 1930, p. 89.

13. Ibid., pp. 90-91.

14. Ibid., p. 264.

15. *Aufbauarbeit im Krisesturm* (DSAP Publication prior to the 1935 election, n.d.), p. 9.

16. *Protokoll des Parteitages*, 1930, p. 97.

17. *Sozialdemokrat*, 10 June 1930.

18. Brügel, *Ludwig Czech*, p. 102.

19. For contemporary social democratic attitudes, see Emil Sobota, "Socialism a Národnostní Autonomie," *Nová Svoboda* 14 (1930): 209-11 and *Sozialdemokrat*, 9 April 1930 for comments on both Sobota's article and one on the same topic by Alois Hajn in *Právo lidu*. For discussion of the Czechoslovak Social Democrats' 1930 program and of the party's attitude toward the republic, see Jiri Horak, "The Czechoslovak Social Democratic Party, 1938-1945." Ph.D. dissertation, Columbia University, 1960, pp. 63-69.

20. *Sozialdemokrat*, 3 March 1931.

21. Ibid., 24 February 1931.

22. Ludwig Czech speech of 17 October 1930, "Im Dienste der Arbeiterklasse," at Teplitz Party Congress (Prague, 1930), p. 10.

23. Jaksch, "Das Drama von Rothau," in *Sucher und Künder* ed. by Karl Kern (Munich: Verlag die Brücke, 1967), pp. 103-10.

24.   Czech speech, "Exposé des Ministers für soziale Fürsorge," at the senate budget debate, 12 December 1931. (Privately published, n.d.), p. 4. Soligor Archiv c. V., Stuttgart.

25.   *Sozialdemokrat,* 16 March 1930.

26.   Ibid., 18 May 1930.

27.   Adolf Pohl speech, "Die Wirtschaftskrise und die Sudetendeutsche Arbeiterschaft," in *Protokoll der gemeinsamen Reichskonferenz der Deutschen sozialdemokratischen Arbeiterpartei in der tschechoslowakischen Republik und des Deutschen Gewerkschaftsbundes* (Prague, 1930), p. 13.

28.   Ibid., pp. 21-22.

29.   "Seznam soudních okresů v nichz jsou podle z sčítání lidu z roku 1930 kvalifikované (alespoň 20%) národní a jazykové menšiny," Státní ústřední archív (hereafter SÚA). Prague. Ministerstvo sociální péče, J. zn. P 3166-30/11.

30.   *Sozialdemokrat,* 16 March 1930; 16, 24 February 1931.

31.   Ibid., 16 February 1935.

32.   *Volkswille* (Brünn), 24 November 1934.

33.   F. Moscheles, "Le caractère des villes tchécoslovaques et les trois habitats humains: habitat rural, habitat urbain, habitat industriel," *Revue statistique* (1932): 12.

34.   Ibid., p. 13.

35.   Ibid., pp. 12, 23-24.

36.   Brügel, *Ludwig Czech,* p. 117.

37.   *Arbeiter-Jahrbuch,* 1933, p. 34.

38.   Letter to Siegfried Taub, 17 November 1934, Okresní archív Cheb (hereafter OACh). Německa sociálně demokratická strana dělnická Cheb (hereafter DSAP/Ch), Carton 45/1.

39.   Brügel, *Ludwig Czech,* p. 130.

40.   *Bohemia,* 21 November 1934.

41.   *Protokoll des Parteitages* (DSAP), Prague, 1932, p. 87.

42.   Ibid., 1930, pp. 121-22.

43.   Kern, "Reichenberg," *Tribüne* (June 1930): 39-40.

44.   *Freiheit,* 2 October 1935.

45.   Author's conversation with Sopade member Fritz Heine in Bonn, 22 March 1984.

46.   Archiv der sozialen Demokratie (hereafter AdsD), Bonn. Letter to the Czechoslovak Social Democratic Executive Committee, 25 October 1937, Sopade file 26 and letter to Wenzel Horn, 26 March 1938, Sopade file 55; conversation with Fritz Heine.

47. Martin Bachstein, "Die Hilfe der sudetendeutschen Sozialdemokratie für reichsdeutsche Flüchtlinge," *Bohemia* 2 (1987): 371. For discussion of DSAP aid to both the Austrian and the Reich German émigrés, see Paul, *Was nicht* 3, pp. 19-28.

48. Brügel, *Ludwig Czech*, p. 122.

49. Bachstein, "Programmdiskussion und Krise in der Deutschen Sozialdemokratischen Arbeiterpartei (DSAP) in der Tschechoslowakischen Republik," *Bohemia* 2 (1970): 316.

50. Robert Wiener, "Die Sozialdemokratie in der Koalition," *Tribüne* (September-October 1932): 134-35.

51. Franzel, "Eine Aufgabe des Parteitages," *Tribüne* (September-October 1932): 129-34.

52. Bachstein, "Programmdiskussion," p. 312, fn. 14.

53. See *Sozialistische Aktion* 19, 15 March 1935 comment that when the committee met, members discussed their inability to meet their task, and *Protokoll des Parteitages* (DSAP), Brünn, 1935, p. 142.

54. *Sozialistische Aktion*, 1, 1 June 1934.

55. Ibid.

56. Announcement signed by leaders of the socialist youth group, *Freiheit*, 31 March 1935.

57. Letter to DSAP Eger district secretary Wilhelm Novy, 11 December 1934, OACh, DSAP/Ch; *Sozialistische Aktion* 9, 1 October 1934.

58. Bachstein, "Die Jugend- und Bildungspolitik der DSAP als Beispiel deutscher Aktivistischer Bemühungen," in *Kultur und Gesellschaft in der Ersten Tschechoslowakischen Republik* (Munich: R. Oldenbourg Verlag, 1982), p. 185.

59. Josef Hofbauer, "Die Gemeindewahlen," *Tribüne* (October-November 1931): 159; on the attraction the Czechoslovak Communists and German National Socialists held for Sudeten German youth, see Karla Schwelb, "Die Partei der Jugend," *Tribüne* (May-June 1931): 39-42.

60. Franzel, *Gegen den Wind der Zeit. Erinnerungen eines Unbequemen.* (Munich: Aufstieg Verlag, 1983), p. 70.

61. Bachstein, *Wenzel Jaksch und die Sudetendeutsche Sozialdemokratie* (Munich: R. Oldenbourg Verlag, 1974), p. 73.

62. Bachstein, "Programmdiskussion," p. 317.

63. Franzel, *Gegen den Wind*, pp. 272-73; Karl Richard Kern, *Heimat und Exil—von Böhmen nach Schweden* (Nuremberg: Helmut Preussler Verlag), p. 57.

64.   See June and July issues of *Sozialistische Aktion*.

65.   Ibid.

66.   According to *Lexikon zur Geschichte der Parteien in Europa*, Frank Wende, ed. (Stuttgart: Kröner Verlag, 1981), p. 684, the three were expelled in November 1934, but their expulsion, along with other opposition members had already been mentioned in *Sozialistische Aktion* 9, 1 October 1934.

67.   *Volkswille* (Karlsbad), 19 June 1934.

68.   *Sozialdemokrat*, 21 June 1934; *Sozialistische Aktion* 3, 1 July 1934.

69.   Paul has claimed that the opposition was limited to some two dozen persons, none of them in Brünn, *Was nicht* 3, p. 45, but this is incorrect. When Rybnicky left Czechoslovakia, he took with him records of more than 1000 subscriptions to *Sozialistische Aktion*, Bachstein, *Wenzel Jaksch*, p. 73, fn. 26. Franzel, *Gegen den Wind*, p. 272, estimated that some 2000 copies were printed and 1200 sold.

70.   See letter to Taub, 7 November 1934, OACh, DSAP/Ch.

71.   Compare Franzel, "Eine Aufgabe," and "Antifaschistische Aktion ohne Programm?," *Tribüne* (October 1933): 289-92. Although the author of the program appears to have drawn from many sources, including Franzel, see the latter's claim that although he read the program, he did not influence it, in Bachstein, "Programmdiskussion," p. 319.

72.   *Sozialistische Aktion* 3, 1 July 1934.

73.   Ibid.

74.   Franzel, *Gegen den Wind*, p. 127.

75.   *Sozialistische Aktion* 19, 15 March 1935.

76.   Ibid. See also Franzel's comments, *Gegen den Wind*, pp. 161-63.

77.   *Sozialistische Aktion*, ibid.

78.   *Sozialistische Aktion* 4, 15 July 1934.

79.   Jiri Vojtessky, "Zum Generationsproblem in der Arbeiterbewegung," *Sozialdemokrat* 12, 16 October 1941, pp. 205-6.

80.   Information on the age, occupation, and number of terms of service of the parliamentarians is available from numerous sources. Here, a handbook on the deputies from the fourth parliamentary period has been used. Ústavu pro dějiny university karlovy, 83 C 4, Prague.

81.   *Sozialdemokrat*, 24 May 1935.

82.   Mimeographed letter, "An die Lesern der sozialistischen Aktion," signed by Karl Ribnicky, July 1935.

83. Bayerisches Hauptstaatsarchiv (hereafter BayHStA), Munich. F1S1g 443, "Arbeiterführer?," "Bonzokratie," "Schützet die Heimat."

84. British Ambassador Sir Joseph Addison's remarks in a report dated 6 December 1934 on the issue of press censorship in Czechoslovakia during the 1930s are useful:

. . . You may reply that the press is allowed a certain latitude, even that of attacking the government, but this means nothing. It is merely allowed by the authorities who could, in fact, put it down if they wanted to. Beneš himself explained to the Austrian Minister that he allowed the press to talk, for after all it did no harm, but, of course, if he wanted to he could at once tell them what to say . . . .

PRO-FO 371/18390, p. 22. Materials designated FO are British Foreign Office documents housed at the Public Record Office (hereafter PRO) Richmond, Surrey.

See the later comments of the German Social Democratic deputy Eugen de Witte on governmental censorship of the German activist parties, *Těsnopisecké zprávy,* 1 December 1937, 70-72.

85. Letter "An das Sekretariat der DSAP," 22 March 1934, OACh, DSAP/Ch, 391/N.

86. *Volkswille* (Brünn), 13 October 1934.

87. *Freiheit,* 3 May 1935.

88. See exchange of letters between Taub and party officials in Eger in February and March 1934, including 352/N (2 March 1934) and 65/N (10 March 1934), OACh, DSAP/Ch.

89. Deputy Franz Katz to Novy, 26 February 1934, OACh, DSAP/Ch, 276/N.

90. Henlein's specific political goals and his ties to Nazi Germany have been the subject of discussion among historians and political scientists in the postwar period. In recent western literature, the view that Henlein, coming from the tradition of the *Kameradschaftsbund* (an elite organization that followed the teachings of Viennese sociologist Othmar Spann and which was preoccupied with the unity of the Germans in Czechoslovakia, rather than with the idea of *Anschluss*) was not initially a Nazi, prevails. Ronald M. Smelser, *The Sudeten Problem 1933-1938. Volkstumpolitiak and the Formulation of Nazi Germany* (Middletown, CN: Wesleyan University Press, 1975) is the most authorative English language study, See also: Andreas Luh, *Der deutsche Turnverband in der Ersten Tschechoslowakischen Republik: Vom völkischen Vereinsbetrieb zur volkspolitischen Bewegung* (Munich: R. Oldenbourg Verlag, 1988).

91. *Volkswille* (Brünn), 3 November 1934.
92. *Sozialdemokrat,* 4 November 1934.
93. *Sozialistische Aktion* 15, 15 January 1935.
94. *Sozialistische Aktion* 20, 1 April 1935; see *Sozialdemokrat,* 22 February 1935, for comments in the left-wing press on Henlein.
95. *Sozialistische Aktion* 20, 1 April 1935. See also the comments of former DSAP deputy Rudolf Zischka that the attitude of the conservative wing of the Czechoslovak Agrarians was based on fear of Soviet occupation of the republic in case of war, due to the Czechoslovak-Soviet bilateral treaty. "Wie wurde Wenzel Jaksch zum Parteivorsitzenden gewählt? Hat Benesch auf die Wahl Einfluss genommen?" (Printed for the Arbeitsgemeinschaft der ehemaliger deutscher Sozialdemokraten aus der Tschechoslowakei by Rudolf Zischka, Tann, Niederbayern, n.d.), p. 3.
96. PRO-FO 371/19492 (11 April 1935).
97. *Lidové Listy* article reprinted in *Freiheit,* 13 January 1938.
98. Ibid.
99. Julius Firt, "'Die Burg' aus der Sicht eines Zeitgenossen," in *Die 'Burg,'* vol. 1, pp. 99-100.
100. *Sozialistische Aktion* 20, 1 April 1935.
101. *Volkswille* (Brünn), 27 April 1935.
102. Klepetař, *Seit 1918,* p. 377.
103. BayHStA F1S1g 441.
104. *Freiheit,* 16 May 1935.
105. *Sozialistische Aktion* 10, 15 October 1934.
106. *Právo lidu* quoted in *Sozialdemokrat,* 22 February 1935.
107. *Sozialistische Aktion* 21-22, mid-May 1935.
108. *Sozialdemokrat,* 21 May 1935.

Notes to Chapter V

1. "Das Ergebnis der Wahlen für das Abgeordnetenhaus in den deutschen Gemeinden," *Zeitschrift für Kommunalwirtschaft* 16/35 (20 August 1935): columns 873-74, lists results for 3,104 of 3,440 German communities. Collegium Carolinum/Sudetendeutsches Archiv, Munich, Document 01585.
2. The communist losses at the hands of the Sudeten German Party can be established on the basis of the communist share of the vote in the

overwhelmingly German (more than ninety percent of the population) counties. Karel Kaplan and Jiří Sláma, *Die Parlamentswahlen in der Tschechoslowakei 1935-1946-1948* (Munich: R. Oldenbourg Verlag, 1986), p. 18.

3.   Jaksch, "Probleme des Überganges," *Tribüne* 4 (1931): 231.

4.   In "At the Limits of a Mass Movement: The Case of the Sudeten German Party, 1933-1938," *Bohemia* 17 (1976): 252-55, Ronald M. Smelser has detailed a series of factors affecting Sudeten German Party membership, but noted that there is no perfect correlation. They include: geographic proximity to Nazi Germany, historic ties to Germany, the relative ferocity of the ethnic conflict, and the disastrous economic situation. Smelser considers the last factor critical.

5.   "Das Ergebnis," columns 875-84. Clearly, the size of the Czech minority in these cities affected the percentage of the vote for the SdP.

6.   The figures in "Das Ergebnis," although incomplete, illustrate the varying strength of the German political parties in Moravia and Silesia. The Sudeten German Party won a majority of the vote in 38.64 percent of the Moravian German communes. Votes for the three German activist parties equaled more than 50 percent in 27 percent of the communes. In Silesia, where the Sudeten German Party drew support from such traditional German National and German National Socialist Party strongholds as Troppau, the SdP won a majority of the vote in 74 percent of the German communes.

As late as March 1938, Sudeten German Party membership remained noticeably lower in parts of southern Moravia than in northwest Bohemia. Smelser, "At the Limits," p. 253.

7.   In Rothau, the German Social Democrats received 1,038 and the Henleinists 698, out of 2,137 valid votes. "Das Ergebnis," columns 877-78.

8.   "Das Ergebnis," column 885.

9.   *Die freie Gemeinde,* 2 November 1935.

10.   *Die Zeit,* 25 April 1936.

11.   *Těsnopisecké zprávy,* 29 April 1936, p. 112.

12.   H. Liepmann, *Tariff Levels and the Economic Unity of Europe* (London: George Unwin & Allen, 1938), p. 289.

13.   *Volkswille* (Karlsbad), 7 April, 21 June 1936.

14.   Conversation with German Social Democrat Rudolf Hesse, formerly from Georgenswald, Bohemia in Stuttgart, FRG, on 2 February 1983.

15. *Zukunft*, 13 March 1937.

16. *Těsnopisecké zprávy*, 5 April 1938, p. 36. See also "Boj proti neznaměstnanosti v Československu," l. oddil. SÚA, Ministerstvo sociální péče, P.3168, k. 312.

17. In areas with a German population of more than 50 percent, unemployment was 8.58 percent of all residents at the end of April 1936. In Czech areas, unemployment was 3.89 percent of all residents at the same time. *Zukunft*, 19 May 1936. Unemployment at the end of April 1937 was 6.09 percent in German areas and 2.72 percent in Czech areas. Ibid., 25 May 1937.

18. *Těsnopisecké zprávy*, pp. 36-37. By 1935, German Social Democrats were complaining that the rehired workers were all Henleinists, while DSAP members remained out of work. *Protokoll des Parteitages*, 1935, p. 40.

19. *Zukunft*, 17 September 1937.

20. *Sozialdemokrat*, 22 June 1935.

21. Ibid.

22. Ibid.

23. See *Protokoll des Parteitages*, 1935, pp. 37 ff.

24. Ibid., Kern, pp. 77-81; Storch, pp. 43-46.

25. Ibid., pp. 101-7.

26. Klepetař, *Seit 1918*, p. 388.

27. Brügel, *Ludwig Czech*, p. 135.

28. *Sozialdemokrat*, 25 May 1935.

29. Brügel, "Zur Geschichte der Zinner Gruppe (Eine Dokumentation uber die Vorgänge innerhalb der 1938/1939 nach England emigrierten deutschen Sozialdemokraten aus der Tschechoslowakei)." (Printed for the Arbeitsgemeinschaft ehemaliger deutscher Sozialdemokraten aus der Tschechoslowakei by Rudolf Zischka, Tann, Niederbayern, n.d.), p. 1.

30. Jaksch, "Um Seligers Erbe," *Sudeten-Jahrbuch der Seliger-Gemeinde* (1961): 23.

31. Ibid., p. 22.

32. *Sozialistische Aktion* 24, June 1935.

33. Eugen de Witte to Jaksch, 8 September 1942, Sudetendeutsches Archiv (hereafter SdA), Munich, CIIIB 1/156b. Nachlass Wenzel Jaksch (hereafter NWJ). See also Franzel's version, *Gegen den Wind*, p. 175.

34. Zischka interview, 26 July 1973, p. 2, SdA, Sammlung Norbert Linz (hereafter SNL).

35.　For comments on and evaluation of Jaksch, both personal and political see: Zischka, ibid.; Kern, *Heimat*, pp. 57-58; Franz Krejčí, Interview no. 1, p. 2, 23 July 1973, SdA, SNL.

36.　Otto Strasser, "Der Marxismus ist Tot, der Sozialismus Lebt" (Prague, [1934]), pp. 7-9.

37.　Review by Max Klinger (pseudonym for Curt Geyer), *Neuer Vorwärts*, 5 July 1936.

38.　Klepetař, *Seit 1918*, p. 389.

39.　For a detailed discussion of reaction to *Volk und Arbeiter*, see Bachstein, *Wenzel Jaksch*, pp. 86-92.

40.　Party executive committee letter, 29 September 1936, AdsD, Sopade file 9.

41.　Zischka, "Wie wurde," p. 5.

42.　*Volkswille* (Brünn), 26 October 1935.

43.　Rudolf Jahn, "Der Deutsche Turnverband," in *Sudetendeutsches Turnertum*, 1 ed. Rudolf Jahn (Frankfurt a.M.: Heimreiter Verlag, 1958), pp. 195 ff.

44.　Jaksch, "Um Seligers Erbe," p. 19.

45.　Brügel, Ludwig Czech, pp. 142-43.

46.　Erwin Zajiček, "Erfolge und Misserfolge des sudetendeutschen Aktivismus," *Beiträge zum deutsch-tschechischen Verhältnis im 19. und 20. Jahrhundert* (Munich: Verlag Robert Lerche, 1967), p. 136. See also "Der Aktivismus," and "Mahnungen des Jungaktivisten Hans Schütz 1936," *Hans Schütz – Helfer und Wegweiser in schwerer Zeit* (Munich: Ackermann-Gemeinde, 1982), pp. 107-8; 148-49.

47.　Paul, *Was nicht 3*, p. 54.

48.　Jaksch, "Um Seligers Erbe," p. 22.

49.　"Der Präsident in Nordböhmen. Kundgebung des Präsidenten der Republik in Reichenberg am 19 August 1936," *Das deutsche Problem in der Tschechoslowakei* (Prague: Orbis, 1937), pp. 50-51; Elizabeth Wiskemann, *Czechs and Germans* (London: Oxford University Press, 1938), p. 262.

50.　Brügel, *Tschechen und Deutsche*, p. 308; Brügel, *Ludwig Czech*, p. 144; Paul, *Was nicht 3*, p. 54.

51.　Jaksch, "Um Seligers Erbe," p. 22: "Die Lage hätte aber eine offene Abkehr vom Nationalstaatsprinzip erfordet."

52.　Zajiček, "Erfolge und Misserfolge," p. 137.

53. *Die Zeit,* 21 February 1937.

54. Ibid., 19 February 1937.

55. Ibid. and *Bohemia,* 23 February 1937, quoting Henleinist leader Rudolf Kasper.

56. Compare estimates in *Central European Observer,* 26 November 1937; Bohemicus, "Czechoslovakia and the Sudeten Germans," *Czechoslovak Sources and Documents* (Prague: Orbis, 1938), p. 24; Wiskemann, *Czechs and Germans,* p. 269 and Zajiček, "Erfolge und Misserfolge," p. 139.

57. PRO-FO 371/21131, 16 November 1937, p. 1; Paul, *Was nicht 3,* p. 56; Wiskermann, *Czechs and Germans,* p. 263.

58. Ibid.; Zajiček, "Erfolge und Misserfolge," p. 138.

59. PRO-FO 371/21131, p. 1.

60. *Zukunft,* 19 November 1937.

61. *Těsnopisecké zprávy,* 1 December 1937, pp. 73-74.

62. Ibid., 25 August 1936. For similar comments, see *Protokoll des Parteitages,* 1935, p. 43 and Wiskemann, *Czechs and Germans,* p. 264.

63. Brügel, *Tschechen und Deutsche,* p. 312.

64. *Rundschau,* 19 February 1938.

65. Paul, *Was nicht 3,* pp. 63-64.

66. *Sozialdemokrat,* 19 March 1938; *Bohemia,* 20 March 1938, citing *Deutsche Nachrichtendienst.*

67. Erich Ollenhauer to Hans Vogel, 23 March 1938, AdsD, Sopade file 79.

68. Ibid., dated 25 and 29 March 1938.

69. *Freiheit,* 27 March 1938.

70. Ibid., 29 March 1938; *Sozialdemokrat,* 29 March 1938.

71. *Freiheit,* 29 March 1938.

72. Zischka, "Wie wurde," p. 5.

73. Akten zur deutschen Auswärtigen Politik, 1918-1945, Series D, vol. 2, *Deutschland und die Tschechoslowakei,* 1937-1938, Ernst Eisenlohr letter of 25 February 1938, No. 61. Baden-Baden: Imprimerie Nationale, 1954, pp. 108-10.

74. Ibid., 24 March 1938, No. 103, p. 150.

75. Zischka, "Wie wurde," p. 6.

76. Brügel, *Tschechen und Deutsche,* p. 343.

77. Paul, *Was nicht 3,* pp. 65-68. See also Bachstein, *Wenzel Jaksch,* pp. 140-43.

78. Jaksch, "Um Seligers Erb," p. 23.

79. Franzel, *Gegen den Wind*, pp. 338-40. Bachstein contradicted Franzel's assumption concerning the dominant role of the Freemasons in the First Republic in "Die soziologische Struktur der 'Burg'—Versuch einer Strukturanalyse," *Die 'Burg,'* 1, p. 64. He found only eight Freemasons among ninety-seven leading Hrad personalities.

80. Ollenhauer to Vogel, 23 March 1938 and to Hugo Renner, 13 May 1938, AdsD, Sopade file 79.

81. In addition to Ludwig Czech, intellectuals of Jewish origin in the party included: Otto Hahn, who served in the Bohemian provincial diet from 1935 to 1938; party treasurer Carl Heller was a lawyer; Victor Haas, another lawyer elected parliamentary deputy in 1920; Arnold Holitscher, a physican who served in both houses of parliament; Johann Polach, a teacher who was a member of the senate from 1920 to 1935; and Emil Strauss, educated in both economics and history, who was an influential party journalist as well as *de facto* party historian. Brügel, "Jews in Political Life," pp. 250-51. See Jaksch's bitter postwar comments on the domination of party leadership by academics in "Um Seligers Erb," p. 22.

82. Franzel, *Gegen den Wind*, p. 74.

83. Lawyer Alfréd Meissner served as Minister of Justice for a short time in 1920 and again from 1929 to 1934. He was Minister of Social Welfare from 1934 until the 1935 parliamentary elections. Lawyer Lev Winter was Minister of Social Welfare from 1918 to 1920, and again for a brief period during 1925 and 1926. Brügel, "Jews in Political Life," p. 246.

84. Bachstein, *Wenzel Jaksch*, p. 147; Paul, *Was nicht 3*, p. 69.

85. They included: Karl Kern (1902), Fritz Kessler (1891), Ernst Paul (1897), Franz Rehwald (1903), Richard Reitzner (1893), and Willi Wanka (1910).

Notes to Chapter VI

1. Brügel, "Zur Geschichte," p. 1.

2. Kern, *Heimat*, p. 86.

3. Ollenhauer to "Lieber Freund," 16 March 1938, Sopade file 79, AdsD.

4. Jaksch article in *Přítomnost* reprinted in *Freiheit*, 2 April 1938.

5. Sudeten German Party membership:

October	1933	9,500	—
January	1934	12,976	—
October	1934	71,431	—
January	1935	107,785	—
April	1935	204,401	—
October	1935	384,982	—
December	1936	459,833	—
November	1937	—	533,260
December	1937	548,338	537,520
January	1938	541,681	530,699
February	1938	548,633	548,633
March	1938	759,289	759,384
April	1938	1,047,178	1,047,178
May	1938	1,309,389	1,309,389
June	1938	1,347,903	1,337,020
July	1938	1,338,394	1,347,903

Column A figures: Václav Král, *Die Deutschen in der Tschechoslowakei 1933-1947: Dokumentensammlung* (Prague: Nakladatelství Československé akademie věd, 1964), p. 151.
Column B figures: Smelser, "At the Limits," p. 264. For interpretation of membership increases, pp. 244-48.

Here, the discrepancies between the two columns of figures are less important than the tremendous increase in Sudeten Geman Party membership that both show.

6. PRO-FO 371/21714. For text of Jaksch's speech in parliament, see *Těsnopisecké zprávy*, 5 April 1938, pp. 35-39. Concerning Jaksch's 5 April proposal of credit allotments for the immediate economic revival of needy areas, see *Tisky k těsnopiseckým zprávám o schůzích Národního shromáždění republiky Československé*, Prague, 1938, XI, 1290-1350, p.z. 1325. The two social democratic parties continued to bring joint proposals before parliament during spring 1938.

7. Brügel, "Zur Geschichte," p. 2.

8. Ibid.; Edmund Jauernig, *Sozialdemocratie und Revanchismus* (Berlin: Deutscher Verlag der Wissenschaften, 1968), pp. 60-61. He places Wenzel Jaksch, Emil Franzel, Josef Hofbauer, Franz Katz, Karl Kern, Ernst Paul, and Eugen de Witte in the nationalist wing of the party, p. 25.

9.　Jaksch, "Ein Kampf bis zum Letzten," *Sudeten-Jahrbuch der Seliger-Gemeinde* (1958): 7.

10.　Copy of Pfitzner memorandum in possession of the author; see also Franzel, *Gegen den Wind,* pp. 340-43.

11.　Bachstein, *Wenzel Jaksch,* p. 151.

12.　Pfitzner memorandum (Kessler was mayor of Bodenbach, not Tetschen).

13.　Jaksch, "Der Kampf um die Tschechoslowakei," in *Internationale Information. Bulletin der Sozialistischen Arbeiter-Internatinale* (May 1938): 184.

14.　See A German Bohemian Deputy, "The German Minority in Czechoslovakia," *Slavonic Review* 14 (January 1936): 295-300, balanced by Emil Sobota, "Czechs and Germans: A Czech View," ibid., 301-20. Lawyer Sobota, a young leading official in President Beneš's chancellery, had joined the Czechoslovak Social Democratic Party in 1925. See also Robert W. Seton-Watson, "Czechoslovakia in its European Setting," ibid., 15 (July 1936). Here, a sixteen-page reprint, SA 6199, from NWJ, SdA was used.

15.　PRO-FO 371/21715, 10 April 1938. In his book, *London und Prag 1919-1938* (Munich: R. Oldenbourg Verlag, 1982), Reiner Franke cites numerous British governmental and newspaper sources.

16.　PRO-FO 371/21715, 11 April 1938.

17.　*Sudetenberichte/Informations des Sudetes/Sudeten-German Newsletters* no. 7, 20 August 1938. See Taub's comments on the continued growth of the German Social Democratic movement in some areas in his letter to Ollenhauer, 17 August 1938, Sopade file 134, AdsD.

18.　*Freiheit,* 23 April 1938.

19.　*Sudetenberichte,* no. 4, 30 July 1938.

20.　Ibid.

21.　Jaksch, "Donauföderation oder Europäische Union?" *Der Kampf* (1934): 216.

22.　*Freiheit,* 14 May 1938.

23.　*Právo lidu* (evening edition), cited in ibid.

24.　Taub to Otto Wels, 21 June 1938, Sopade file 134, AdsD.

25.　*Freiheit,* 24 May 1938.

26.　Jaksch, "Der Kampf," p. 185.

27.　PRO-FO 371/21721, 21 May 1938.

28. Jaksch, "Der Kampf," p. 184.

29. Ibid., pp. 185-86.

30. Jaksch, "Wer besser gekämpft hat, möge richten! Zur Frage meines sogenannten Strasser-Vorwortes," (24 April 1955): 1, NWJ, SdA.

31. Rothschild, *East Central Europe*, p. 129.

32. Franzel, *Gegen den Wind*, p. 350, has written that party friends with whom he was in contact could not understand why Jaksch delayed in joining the Sudeten German Party.

33. *Freiheit*, 24 May 1938.

34. Bauer, "Selbstbestimmungsrecht der Sudetendeutschen?" *Sozialistischer Kampf* (16 June 1938); reprinted in *Sozialdemokrat* (March 1941): 296-98.

35. Taub to "Lieber Freund," 16 July 1938, Sopade file 134, AdsD.

36. *Manchester Guardian*, 14 August 1938.

37. Ibid., 16 August 1938.

38. *Sudetenberichte*, no. 9, 30 August 1938.

39. Kürbich, *Chronik*, p. 78.

40. ADAP, Eisenlohr dispatch, no. 103, pp. 150-51.

41. *Sudetendeutscher Zeitspiegel*, 21 July 1938.

42. Brügel, *Tschechen und Deutsche*, p. 450.

43. Reprint of the speech in Paul, *Was nicht 3*, pp. 85-87.

44. Jaksch, "Vor der Entscheidung in der Tschechoslowakei," *Neuer Vorwärts*, 4 September 1938. See also *Sozialdemokrat*, 31 July, 3 August 1938.

45. *Sudetenberichte* no. 9.

46. Taub to Ollenhauer, 17 August 1938, Sopade file 134, AdsD.

47. Jaksch, "Der Kampf," p. 184.

48. Taub to Ollenhauer, 17 August 1938, Sopade file 134, AdsD.

49. *Manchester Guardian*, 13 August 1938; see also Jaksch's comments in *Europas Weg nach Potsdam. Schuld und Schicksal im Donauraum* (Stuttgart: Deutsche Verlags-Anstalt, 1958), p. 308.

50. *Soziakdemokrat*, 4 August 1938.

51. See *Sozialdemokrat*, 8 September 1938 for excerpts from the memorandum.

52. Bachstein, *Wenzel Jaksch*, p. 165, has noted Jaksch's stress on the economic aspect of the 12 August memorandum in his 20 August 1938 article, "The Economic Side of the Sudeten German Problem," *Sudeten-*

berichte, no. 7, despite his awareness that both the Czechoslovak citizens and the governments involved knew the issue was mainly a national-political one. When excerpts from the memorandum were published in *Sozialdemokrat* on 8 September, the economic aspect was again stressed and point three, guaranteed democratic self-administration, seems to have been omitted altogether.

53.   Jaksch, *Neuer Vorwärts;* see No. 159, Minister Krofta an die tschechoslowakische Gesandschaft in Paris–3. 9. 1938, Dispatch No. 916/38 in Václav Král, ed., *Das Abkommen von München 1938* (Prague: Academia–Verlag der Tschechoslowakischer Akademie der Wissenschaften, 1968), p. 212-13 and Ollenhauer to Wels, 29 August 1923, Sopade file 79, AdsD, concerning new government proposals.

54.   Jaksch, *Europas Weg,* p. 309.

55.   *Sudetenberichte,* no. 11, 17 September 1938. Jaksch, however, rejected later reports of "civil war" in the Sudeten lands, *Europas Weg,* pp. 309-10.

56.   *Sozialdemokrat,* 14 September 1938. Böhmisch Krumau, the only one of the districts not located on the western Bohemian border with Reich Germany, was one of the districts Smelser listed as having higher than average Sudeten German Party membership, "At the Limits," pp. 252, 264.

57.   Jaksch, *Europas Weg,* p. 310; Paul, *Was nicht 3,* pp. 89-91.

58.   *Sozialdemokrat,* 14 September 1938.

59.   Bachstein, *Wenzel Jaksch,* p. 169, has correctly noted that Jaksch's previous efforts in this direction, expressed in *Jungaktivismus* and *Volkssozialismus,* had been rejected by the party leadership.

60.   *Sozialdemokrat,* 14 September 1938.

61.   Reproduction of the order in Paul, *Was nicht 3,* p. 95.

62.   For Beneš's version of the Munich events, see *Eduard Beneš: From Munich to New War and New Victory* (London: Allen and Unwin, 1954). The most comprehensive volume among the vast English-language literature on Munich is Telford Taylor, *Munich: The Price of Peace* (London: Hodder and Stoughton, 1979).

63.   Grünwald, *Wandlung,* p. 61.

64.   Franzel, *Gegen den Wind,* pp. 362-63.

65.   Kern, *Heimat,* p. 86.

66.   *Daily Telegraph,* 12 October 1938.

67. *Manchester Guardian*, 14 October 1938.

68. *Times* (London), 3 October 1938.

69. Kern, *Heimat*, p. 87.

70. Ibid.

71. Jaksch and Walter Kolarz, *England and the Last Free Germans* (London: Lincolns-Prager, 1940), pp. 18-19. This does not mean that all party functionaries and *Republikanische Wehr* members were able to emigrate prior to the Nazi occupation of Bohemia and Moravia on 15 March 1939. The post-Munich government of Emil Hácha put a number of the latter in work camps, and following the formation of the Protectorate, some members of both groups were sent to concentration camps or prison. See: *Weg Leistung Schicksal* (Stuttgart: Seliger-Gemeinde, 1972), p. 399.

72. Jaksch and Kolarz, *The Last Germans*, pp. 32-33.

74. On the English funds for refugees from Czechoslovakia, see Eva Schmidt-Hartmann, "Die deutschsprachige jüdische Emigration aus der Tschechoslowakei nach Grossbritannien 1938-1945," *Die Juden in den böhmischen Ländern* (Munich: R. Oldenbourg Verlag, 1983).

74. Jaksch, "Um Seligers Erbe," p. 24.

75. Bachstein, *Wenzel Jaksch*, p. 184, fn. 23.

76. Jaksch and Kolarz, *The Last Germans*, pp. 52-53.

77. Brügel, *Ludwig Czech*, p. 156.

SELECTED BIBLIOGRAPHY

Archival Sources

Archiv der sozialen Demokratie, Bonn.
    Sopade, Exil-Korrespondenz, 1933-1938:
        Files 26, 55, 79, 134.
Bayerisches Hauptstaatsarchiv, Munich.
    F1S1g 390, 441, 443.
International Institute of Social History, Amsterdam.
    Archives of the Socialist International:
        Tschechoslowakei, 1926 (804-807).
    Kommission für die Tschechoslowakei, 1923 (844-848).
    Tschechoslowakei (2776-2805).
Okresní archív Cheb, Cheb.
    Německá sociálně demokratická strana dělnická Cheb:
        Carton 45/1.
Public Record Office, London.
    FO 371.
        File 1941: 2288-2712.
        File 1941: 2721-3069.
        File 1941: 4717-4931.
    The following single pieces have been cited:
        Sir Joseph Addison, 6 December 1934, 371/18390.
        Sir Joseph Addison, 11 April 1935, 371/19492.
        "Activist Policy in Czechoslovakia, Jaksch Lecture: Chatham House,"
            16 November 1937, 371/21131.

Státní ústřední archív, Prague.

Ministerstvo zahraničních věcí-výstřižkový archiv:

Němci v ČSR-poměr k vládě 1924-1938, MZV-VA 1140.
(3 cartons)

Němci v ČSR-hospodářské věci, 1922-1940,

Němci v ČSR-sociální záležitosh, 1924-1944, MZV-VA 1146.
(2 cartons)

Německá sociálně demokratická strana dělnická, 1920-1938,
MZV-VA 1166. (4 cartons)

Ministerstvo sociální péče.

The following single pieces have been cited:

"Boj proti nezaměstnanosti v Československu," I. oddíl

Pokles nezaměstnanosti v krajích obydlených německým
obyvaltelstvem, MSP, 1934-1942, sign. P 3168, k. 312.

Seznam soudních okresů, v nichž jsou podle sčítání lidu
z roku 1930 kvalifikovane (alespoň 20%) národní jazykové
menšiny, z roku 1936. MSP, 1934-1942, sign. P 3166
−30/11. k. 312.

Sudetendeutsches Archiv, Munich.

Sammlung Norbert Linz.

Nachlass Wenzel Jaksch.

Printed Primary Sources

Akten zur deutschen Auswärtigen Politik 1918-1945. Series D. Vol. 2.
Deutschland und die Tschechoslowakei, 1937-1938. Baden-Baden:
Imprimerie Nationale, 1954.

Alexander, Manfred, ed. *Deutsche Gesandtschaftsberichte aus Prag. Von
der Staatsgründung bis zum ersten Kabinett Beneš 1918-1921.* 1. Munich: R. Oldenbourg Verlag, 1983.

Czechoslovak Republic. State Statistical Office (Státní úřad statistický).
Prague.

Bulletin statistique de la république tchècoslovaque, vol. 1-19, 1920-
1938.

Mitteilungen des statistischen Staatsamtes der čechoslovakischen Republik. vol. 2, 1926; vol. 10, 1929.

Revue statistique, vols. 12, 1931; 13, 1932.

Statistická příručka republiky Československé, vol. 2, 1925.

Statistisches Handbuch der Čechoslovakischen Republik, vol. 1, 1920; vol. 3, 1928.

Král, Václav, ed. *Die Deutschen in der Tschechoslowakei 1933-1947. Dokumentensammlung.* Prague: Nakladatelství Československé akademie věd, 1964.

————. *Das Abkommen von München 1938.* Prague: Academia—Tschechoslowakische Akademie der Wissenschaften, 1968.

Labour and Socialist International. *Resolutions of the International Labour Congress of the Socialist Parties* (1923).

————. *Report of the Secretariat* (1925).

————. *Second Congress of the Labour and Socialist International* (1925).

Ludwig Czech Reden. Privately printed, n.d. Seliger Archiv e. V., Stuttgart.

Prameny k ohlasu Velké říjnové socialistické revoluce a vzniku ČSR. *Boj o směr vývoje československého státu 2 (July 1919-May* 1921). Kocman, A.; Pletka, V.; Radimský, J.; Trantírek, M.; Urbánková, L., eds. Prague: Nakladatelství Československé akademie věd, 1969.

————. *Souhrnná hlášení presidia pražského místodržitelství o protistání, protirakouské e protiválečné činnosti v Čechách 1915-1918,* Otáhalová, Libuše, ed. Prague: Nakladetelství Ceskoslovenské akademie věd, 1957.

Protokoll des ersten Kongresses aller Sozialdemokratischen Parteien der Tschechoslowakei. Prague, 1928.

Protokoll der gemeinsamen Reichskonferenz der Deutschen sozialdemokratischen Arbeiterpartei in der tschechoslowakischen Republik und des Deutschen Gewerkschaftsbundes. "Die Wirtschaftskrise und die Sudetendeutsche Arbeiterschaft." Prague, 1930.

Protokolle der Verhandlungen der Parteitage der Deutschen sozialdemokratischen Arbeiterpartei in der Tschechoslowakischen Republik. 1919-1935.

Protokoll über die Verhandlungen des Parteitages der deutschen sozialdemokratischen Arbeiterpartei in Österreich. Innsbruck, 1911.

Těsnopisecké zprávy o schůzích Národního shromáždění republiky Československé, 1920-1938. Prague, 1921-1939.

Tisky k těsnopiseckým zprávám o schůzích Národního shromáždění republiky Československé. 1920-1938. Prague, 1921-1939.

Verhandlungen des Gesammtparteitages der Sozialdemokratie in Österreich. Brünn, 1899.

Memoirs

Franzel, Emil. *Gegen den Wind der Zeit. Erinnerungen eines Unbequemen.* Munich: Aufstieg-Verlag, 1983.

Grünwald, Leopold. *Wandlung. Ein Altkommunist gibt zu Protokoll.* Foreword by Wolfgang Leonhard. Vienna: Verlag der Wiener Volksbuchhandlung, [1979 or 1980].

Kern, Karl Richard. *Heimat und Exil-von Böhmen nach Schweden. Erinnerungen und Bekenntnisse eines sudetendeutschen Sozialdemokraten.* Nuremberg: Helmut Preussler Verlag, [1980].

Contemporary Books and Pamphlets

Bauer, Otto. *Die Nationalitätenfrage und die Sozialdemokratie.* Vienna: Wiener Volksbuchhandlung Ignaz Brand, 1907.

————. *Werkausgabe.* 9 vol. Vienna: Europa-Verlag, 1975-1980.

Borkenau, Franz. *World Communism.* New York: Norton,1938; reprint ed., Ann Arbor, Michigan: University of Michigan Press, 1971.

Franzel, Emil. "Klassen und Parteien in der Tschechoslowakischen Republik." Prague: Druck- und Verlaganstalt Teplitz-Schönau, 1924.

Jaksch, Wenzel and Kolarz, Walter. *England and the Last Free Germans.* London: Lincolns–Prager (Publishers), 1941.

Klepetař, Harry. *Seit 1918. . . Eine Geschichte der tschechoslowakischen Republik.* Ostrau: Verlag Julius Kittls Nachfolger, 1937.

————. *Der Sprachenkampf in den Sudetenländern.* Prague: Strache Verlag, 1930.

Reimann, Paul. *Geschichte der Kommunistischen Partei der Tschechoslowakei.* Hamburg: Verlag Carl Hoym Nachfolger, 1931.

Renner, Karl [Rudolf Springer]. *Der Kampf der österreichischen Nationen um den Staat.* Vienna: Deuticke, 1902.

————. "Das nationale und das ökonomische Problem der Tschechoslowakei." Prague: Verlag der Deutschen sozialdemokratischen Arbeiterpartei in der Tschechoslowakischen Republik, 1926.

Books, Dissertations, Pamphlets

Bachstein, Martin K. *Wenzel Jaksch und die Sudetendeutsche Sozialdemokratie.* Publication of the Collegium Carolinum, no. 29. Munich: R. Oldenbourg Verlag, 1974.

Bosl, Karl, ed. *Die 'Burg.' Einflussreiche politische Kräfte um Masaryk und Beneš.* 2 vols. Munich: R. Oldenbourg Verlag, 1973, 1974.

————. *Die demokratisch-parlamentarische Struktur der Ersten Tschechoslowakischen Republik.* Munich: R. Oldenbourg Verlag, 1975.

————. *Die Erste Tschechoslowakische Republik als multinationaler Parteienstaat.* Munich: R. Oldenbourg Verlag, 1979.

Brügel, Johann Wolfgang. *Czechoslovakia Before Munich. The German Minority Problem and British Appeasement Policy.* Cambridge: Cambridge University Press, 1973.

————. *Ludwig Czech. Arbeiterführer und Staatsmann.* Vienna: Verlag der Wiener Volksbuchhandlung, 1960.

————. *Tschechen und Deutsche 1918-1938.* Munich: Nymphenburger, 1967.

Carsten, F. L. *Revolution in Central Europe 1918-1919.* Berkeley: University of California Press, 1972.

Cohen, Gary. *The Politics of Ethnic Survival: Germans in Prague, 1861-1914.* Princeton: Princeton University Press, 1981.

Cole, G. D. H. *A History of Socialist Thought.* Vol. 4, pt. 2: *Communism and Social Democracy 1914-1931.* Vol. 5: *Socialism and Fascism 1931-1939.* London: Macmillan & Co., 1958, 1961.

Galandauer, Jan. *Bohumír Šmeral 1880-1914.* Prague: Nakladatelství Svoboda, 1981.

Gellner, Ernest. *Nations and Nationalism.* New Perspectives on the Past. R. I. More, gen. ed. Oxford: Basil Blackwell, Publisher, 1983.

Hans Schütz—Helfer und Wegweiser in schwerer Zeit. Publication of the Ackermann-Gemeinde, no. 32. Munich, 1982.

Horak, Jiri. "The Czechoslovak Social Democratic Party, 1938-1945." Ph. D. dissertation, Columbia University, 1960.

Jaksch, Wenzel. *Europas Weg nach Potsdam. Schuld und Schicksal im Donauraum.* Stuttgart: Deutsche Verlags-Anstalt, 1958. Published in English as: *Europe's Road to Potsdam.* New York: Praeger, 1963.

Jaworski, Rudolf. *Vorposten oder Minderheit? Der sudetendeutsche Volkstumskampf in den Beziehungen zwischen der Weimarer Republik und der ČSR.* Stuttgart: Deutsche Verlags-Anstalt, 1977.

Kann, Robert. *The Multinational Empire.* 2 vols. New York: Columbia University Press, 1950.

Kaplan, Karel and Sláma, Jiří. *Die Parlamentswahlen in der Tschechoslo-*

wakei, 1935-1946-1948. Publication of the Collegium Carolinum, no. 53. Munich: R. Oldenbourg Verlag, 1986.

Kárník, Zdeněk. *Socialisté na rozcesti. Habsburk, Masaryk či Šmeral?* Prague: Nakladství Svoboda, 1968.

Kern, Karl, ed. *Wenzel Jaksch.* Vol. 2: *Sucher und Künder.* Munich: Seliger-Gemeinde, 1967.

Kisch, Guido; Kohn, H.; Rabinowitz, O.; and Wehle, K., eds. *The Jews of Czechoslovakia.* 2 vols. Philadelphia: J. P. S., 1968, 1971.

Knapp, Vincent J. *Austrian Social Democracy, 1889-1914.* Lanham, Maryland: University Press of America, 1980.

Lipscher, Ladislav. *Verfassung und politische Verwaltung in der Tschechoslowakei 1918-1939.* Publication of the Collegium Carolinum, no. 34. Munich: R. Oldenbourg Verlag, 1979.

Löw, Raimund. *Otto Bauer und die russische Revolution.* Foreword by Eduard März. Publication of the Ludwig Boltzmann Institut für Geschichte der Arbeiterbewegung. Materialien zur Arbeiterbewegung, no. 15. Vienna: Europaverlag, 1980.

Luh, Andreas. *Der Deutsche Turnverband in der Ersten Tschechoslowakischen Republik: Vom völkischen Vereinsbetrieb zum volkspolitischen Bewegung.* Publication of the Collegium Carolinum, no. 62. Munich: R. Oldenbourg Verlag, 1988.

Luža, Radomír. *The Transfer of the Sudeten Germans: A Study of Czech-German Relations, 1933-1962.* New York: New York University Press, 1964.

Mamatey, Victor S. and Luža, Radomír, eds. *A History of the Czechoslovak Republic, 1918-1948.* Princeton: Princeton University Press, 1973.

Mommsen, Hans. *Die Sozialdemokratie und die Nationalitätenfrage im habsburgischen Vielvölkerstaat.* Vienna: Europa-Verlag, 1963.

Paul, Ernst. *Was nicht in den Geschichtsbüchern steht. Ruhm und Tragik der sudetendeutschen Arbeiterbewegung.* Vol. 2: *Schicksalhafte Jahre 1914-1938.* Vol. 3. *Das tragische Jahr 1938–Ein Beitrag zur Vorgeschichte. Erlebnis und Rückblick.* Munich: Verlag "Die Brücke," 1966, 1972.

Pauley, Bruce F. *Hitler and the Forgotten Nazis. A History of Austrian National Socialism.* Chapel Hill: University of North Carolina Press, 1981.

Rabinbach, Anson. *The Crisis of Austrian Socialism. From Red Vienna to Civil War, 1927-1934.* Chicago: University of Chicago Press, 1983.

Rothschild, Joseph. *East Central Europe between the Two World Wars.* A History of East Central Europe, no. 9. Seattle: University of Washington Press, 1974.

Schmidt-Hartmann, Eva. *Thomas G. Masaryk's Realism: Origins of a Czech Political Concept.* Publication of the Collegium Carolinum, no. 52. Munich: R. Oldenbourg Verlag, 1984.

Smelser, Ronald. *The Sudeten Problem 1933-1938. Volkstumspolitik and the Formulation of Nazi Foreign Policy.* Middletown: Wesleyan University Press, 1975.

Strauss, Emil. *Die Entstehung der Tschechoslowakischen Republik.* Prague: Orbis Verlag, 1934.

Whiteside, Andrew Gladding. *Austrian National Socialism before 1918.* The Hague: Martinus Nijhoff, 1962.

Wiskemann, Elizabeth. *Czechs and Germans. A Study of the Struggle in the Historic Provinces of Bohemia and Moravia.* London: Oxford University Press, 1938.

Zessner, Klaus. *Josef Seliger und die nationale Frage in Böhmen.* Stuttgart: Seliger-Gemeinde, 1976.

Ziegler, Heinz O. *Die berufliche und soziale Gliederung der Bevölkerung in der Tschechoslowakei.* Brünn: Verlag Rudolf M. Rohrer, 1936.

Zinner, Paul. *Communist Strategy and Tactics in Czechoslovakia, 1918-1948.* London: Pall Mall Press, 1963.

Contemporary Articles

Franzel, Emil. "Eine Aufgabe des Parteitags." *Tribüne* 5 (1932): 129-34.

————. "Der neue Kurs der Kommunisten." *Tribüne* 1 (1928): 226-30.

Hofbauer, Josef. "Politische Aufgaben der nächsten Zeit." *Tribüne* 1 (1928): 46-52.

Jaksch, Wenzel. "Arbeiter und Bauern." *Arbeiter-Jahrbuch* (1936): 17-23.

————. "Der Kampf um die Tschechoslowakei." *Internationale Information. Bulletin der Sozialistischen Arbeiter-Internationale.* (May 1938): 184-87.

————. "Probleme des Überganges." *Tribüne* 4 (1931): 231-49.

————. "Übergangswahlen." *Tribüne* 1 (1928): 249-53.

Kern, Karl. "Reichenberg." *Tribüne* 2 (1930): 37-41.

Kreibich, Karl. "Die tschechische Linke und ihr Manifest." *Der Kampf* 13 (1920): 84-89.

Polach, Johann. "Das Manifest der Reichenberger Linken." *Der Kampf* 13 (1920): 275-80.

Strauss, Emil. "Die deutschböhmische Landesregierung." *Tribüne* 1 (1928): 230-35.

————. "Die nationale Frage in der Frühzeit der tschechischen Arbeiterbewegung. *Der Kampf* 14 (1921): 253-58.

————. "Die Umschichtung der tschechischen Parteien." *Der Kampf* 13 (1920): 76-84.

Articles

Bachstein, Martin K. "Die Hilfe der sudetendeutschen Sozialdemokratie für reichsdeutsche Flüchtlinge." *Bohemia* 28 (1987): 369-76.

————. "Die Jugend- und Bildungspolitik der DSAP als Beispiel deutscher Aktivistischer Bemühungen." In *Kultur und Gesellschaft in der Ersten Tschechoslowakischen Republik,* pp. 179-89. Munich: R. Oldenbourg, 1982.

————. "Programmdiskussion und Krise in der Deutschen sozialdemokratischen Arbeiterpartei (DSAP) in der Tschechoslowakischen Republik." *Bohemia* 11 (1970): 308-23.

Brügel, Johann Wolfgang. Zur Geschichte der Zinnergruppe (Eine Dokumentation über die Vorgänge innerhalb der 1938/1939 nach England emigrierten deutschen Sozialdemokraten aus der Tschechoslowakei)." Printed for the Arbeitsgemeinschaft ehemaliger deutscher Sozialdemokraten aus der Tschechoslowakei by Rudolf Zischka, Tann, Niederbayern. n.d. (Mimeographed.)

Čerešňák, Bedřich. "Anteil der Linken der deutschen Sozialdemokratie an der Durchdringung des Leninismus in der Arbeiterbewegung in der tschechoslowakischen Republik in den Jahren 1918-1921. *Sborník prací Filozofické fakulty Brněnské Univerzity* 28 (1981): 41-52.

Feyl, Othmar. "Die böhmendeutsche Linke um den Reichenberger 'Vorwärts' und ihre Vorarbeit für die Entstehung der Kommunistischen Partei der ČSR." *Wissenschaftliche Zeitschrift der Friedrich-Schiller-Universität Jena* 7 (1957-1958): 533-52.

Filip, Zdeněk. "Die Zeitschrift 'Volkswacht' in den Jahren 1899-1921." Ein Beitrag zur Geschichte der deutschen Arbeiterbewegung in Mähren. (Typewritten.)

Haas, Hanns. "Die deutschböhmische Frage 1918-1919 und das österreich-isch-tschechoslowakische Verhältnis." Part 1 *Bohemia* 13 (1972): 336-83.

Jaksch, Wenzel. "Um Seligers Erbe." *Sudeten-Jahrbuch der Seliger-Gemeinde* (1961): 17-26.

Kern, Karl. "Erinnerung an die Jugendbewegung." *Sudeten-Jahrbuch der Seliger-Gemeinde* (1953): 65-71.

Kašík, Vladimír. "Snahy o jednotnou reformistickou stranu v letech 1917-1918 a jejich porážka." *Příspěvek k otázce formování marxistické levice v českém dělnickém hnutí. Rozpravy Československé akademie věd* 71 (1961).

Köhler, Bruno. "Úloha německé levice v boji o založení KSČ," *Společenské vědy ve škole* 3 (1971): 68-72.

Novák, Otto. "Karl Kreibich." *Společenské vědy ve škole* 5 (1983-1984): 149-53.

Smelser, Ronald M. "At the Limits of a Mass Movement: The Case of the Sudeten German Party, 1933-1938." *Bohemia* 17 (1976): 240-66.

Whiteside, Andre [Andrew]. "Industrial Transformation, Population Movement and German Nationalism in Bohemia." *Zeitschrift für Ostforschung* 2 (1961): 261-71.

Whiteside, Andrew G. "Nationaler Sozialismus in Österreich vor 1918." *Vierteljahreshefte für Zeitgeschichte* 9 (1961): 333-59.

Zajiček, Erwin. "Erfolge und Misserfolge des sudetendeutschen Aktivismus." In *Beiträge zum deutsch-tschechischen Verhältnis im 19. und 20. Jahrhundert*, pp. 127-42. Publication of the Collegium Carolinum, no. 19. Munich: Verlag Robert Lerche, 1967.

Zischka, Rudolf. "Wie wurde Wenzel Jaksch zum Parteivorsitzenden gewählt? Hat Benesch auf die Wahl Einfluss genommen?" Printed for the Arbeitsgemeinschaft ehemaliger deutscher Sozialdemokraten aus der Tschechoslowakei by Rudolf Zischka, Tann, Niederbayern, n.d. (Mimeographed.)

Periodical and Newspapers
Periodicals

Arbeiter-Jahrbuch. 1933-1938.

Arbeiterbewegung und Arbeiterdichtung. Beiträge zur Geschichte der Sozialdemokratischen Arbeiterbewegung im Sudeten-, Karpathen-, und Donauraum. 1979, 1982.

Bohemia. 1960-1979: *Jahrbuch des Collegium Carolinum.* 1980-present: *Zeitschrift für Geschichte der böhmischen Länder.* 1965-1988.

Die freie Gemeinde. 1919-1935.

Der Kampf. 1917-1937.

Der Neue Weg. 1925.

Tribüne. 1928-1933.

Newspapers

Bohemia. 1918-1938. Prague. National German.

Central European Observer. 1925-1926; 1935-1938. Prague.

Freigeist (original title: *Sozialdemokrat*). 1921-1922; 1935-1936. Reichenberg. German Social Democrat.

Freiheit. 1918-1938. Teplitz. German Social Democrat.

Neuer Vorwärts. 1936-1938. Karlsbad. Sopade.

Pravo lidu. 1918-1921. Prague. Czechoslovak Social Democrat.

Rudé právo. 1920-1921. Prague. Czechoslovak Social Democrat (Marxist Left); Czechoslovak Communist.

Rundschau. 1934-1937. Henleinist.

Sozialdemokrat. 1921-1938. Prague. German Social Democrat.

Sozialistische Aktion. 1934-1935. Brünn. German Social Democratic intraparty opposition.

Sudetenberichte/Informations des Sudetes/Sudeten-German Newsletters. 1938. Prague. German Social Democratic for foreign observers.

Trautenauer Echo. 1920-1926. Trautenau. German Social Democrat.

Volkswille. 1931, 1934-1936. Karlsbad. German Social Democrat.

Volkswille. 1920-1924, 1934-1935. Brünn. German Social Democrat. District newspaper for Brünn, Iglau, Lundenberg, Mährisch Trübau, Znaim and Zwittau.

Vorwärts. 1918-1920; 1929-1930. Reichenberg. German Social Democratic until 1920; Czechoslovak Communist beginning 1921.

Die Zeit. 1935-1938. Prague. Henleinist.

Zukunft. 1935-1937. Prague. German Social Democrat. Paper for southern and western Bohemia.

INDEX